Praise

"Earthy and magical, *A Smoke and a Song* is a woman's anthem. With the heart of a mother and the soul of a warrior, Sherry Sidoti takes us on her unwavering quest toward self-agency, braiding music, poetry, art, culture, and mysticism with grounded spirituality and a wry New York City 'edge.' This story is steeped in healing tools from the author's decades of study and teaching, without being pushy or prescriptive. Sidoti trusts her readers to mine the raw ore from her story and polish it into gold for their own."

—ANITA KOPACZ,
author of *Shallow Waters*

"I discovered the poet Stanley Kunitz while I was a college student at NYU and his words saved my life; still do. All these years later, his granddaughter's words are saving my life, and if that isn't magic I dare you to tell me what is. By sharing her story, Sherry Sidoti invites us to remember what it is to love deeply and then to go out into the world with that knowing so that we can live big, beautiful, and messy lives."

—JENNIFER PASTILOFF,
author of *On Being Human*

"Sherry Sidoti beautifully weaves together a deeply moving memoir that captures the many complexities of love and our relationship with the ones we care about the most. I came away moved and inspired by her willingness to be so transparent and authentic."

—PAUL SAMUEL DOLMAN,
author of *Hitchhiking with Larry David*
and host of the *What Matters Most* podcast

"A seeker's story of healing intergenerational trauma. In her unwavering commitment to heal, with body-informed awareness, the author alchemizes inherited history to rewrite her own narrative breath by breath, beat by beat. Every broken family system has a healer. Sherry Sidoti is one."

—SHALOM HARLOW,
model, actress, and yoga teacher

"*A Smoke and a Song* makes me feel like I've stumbled upon a beautiful explorer's locked diary and picked the lock. The narrative is both delicious and filled with disaster, careening at breakneck pace through a life fully engaged in raw, sensual, and inspiringly elevated consciousness. You'll be completely riveted by Sidoti's story—this book will help you see and digest the deepest questions and twists of your own life and relationships. It's a book you will thrill to read and one you'll keep close for a long time to come."

—SUSAN MADDEN-COX, host of *3 Crones* podcast
and owner of the Ocean Earth Wind Fire yoga studio

A SMOKE
AND
A SONG

A SMOKE AND A SONG

A Memoir

SHERRY SIDOTI

SHE WRITES PRESS

Published 2023

Printed in the United States of America

Print ISBN: 978-1-64742-509-8
E-ISBN: 978-1-64742-510-4
Library of Congress Control Number: 2023902789

For information, address:
She Writes Press
1569 Solano Ave #546
Berkeley, CA 94707

Interior design by Katherine Lloyd, The DESK

She Writes Press is a division of SparkPoint Studio, LLC.

For Miles, your future children,
and all those who came before who made us.

And for my mother, Babette,
and all the mothers of time, who have done
the best they could, with what they
were working with.

"You either walk inside your story and own it or you stand outside your story and hustle for your worthiness."

—Brené Brown

Contents

THREE

Kitchen Window

"Coffee," she says, her voice cracking, still in a post-anesthesia daze.

"Of course, coffee," I say.

I take off her shoes and help her into bed. I can practically lift her with one arm. She's so tiny, swallowed by her oversized sweater. This normal force of a woman, with the drive of a tiger and the determination of a mountain goat, now beaten. She looks like a toddler in her California King bed.

"I'll be right back with a cup."

I walk from Mom's room toward the front of the loft, down the long hallway with the stinky kitty-litter nook and the wall of family photos, past the row of plants, and into the kitchen.

The kitchen feels smaller, darker. Out the window I see the skeleton—drapes of black netting over metal beams, sheets of plaster, and two large cranes. The new high-rise going up on Sixth Avenue is directly in front of our kitchen window, with an illuminated billboard practically screaming:

10,000 SQUARE FEET OF MODERN DUPLEXES!
THE BEST VIEWS OF DOWNTOWN NYC!
FOR ONLY $12,000 A MONTH!

As if New York City, in the middle of a pandemic, needs another high-rise.

Hasn't everyone already left the city? Didn't anyone with

this kind of money flee last spring to purchase a quaint country home, sight-unseen, in the Hamptons, or the Berkshires, or Martha's Vineyard?

Now a construction site is blocking our beloved kitchen-window view. The windowsill where our cat, Bri, slept sideways in the splashes of sunlight—two paws on the street side and two paws on the kitchen side, threatening to fall the eight stories down but thank God never did—is covered in construction dust.

I used to stare out of this window every morning. Minutes before leaving for school, waiting for my bagel to brown, I'd watch the street vendors raise the shaky metal gates of their hole-in-the-wall storefronts on Fourteenth Street. The empty street would quickly transform into a cheap-goods marketplace. Bins of small electronics that went *beep* and *bonk* and *clank*, scrunchies, and knockoff Gucci purses, taking the sidewalk hostage before I even finished cream-cheesing my bagel.

Back in the day, if you stepped over Bri's food bowl and ducked under the rack of dusty pans above our tiled kitchen island, you could stick your head way out, look to the left, *just far enough*, as I did about ten times a day, and get a view down Sixth Avenue to the red-bricked Jefferson Market Library. You'd see a Venetian Gothic landmark with an enormous clock on its steeple.

That library clock served as a compass for those of us who lived in the West Village. That clock was the neighborhood watch. Especially in our loft, where our digital clocks blinked different times of the day, depending on what room you were in. It told me when I was on time for school or late for my curfew. It told me when Mom would get off work—especially in our loft, when I waited and waited for Mom to come home.

On Christmas, Mom had a "7:00 a.m. rule." She'd say, "Girls, please, not a minute before." We'd grab our stockings from under the tree and set them down on the island while we made her coffee, because nothing happened in our loft before Mom had her coffee, not even Christmas. I'd stand on my tippy toes and lean out the window to the clock, doing my math in the air, going backward from the twelve to the big hand. Then, I'd shout out the count-down—"Twelve more minutes!"—while my oldest sister, Lisa, poured the beans into the grinder, and my middle sister, Maddy, watched water heat in the same pot we used to hard-boil eggs.

The last time the four of us were together at the window was four years ago, on Mom's eightieth. In the afternoon before the big birthday bash, complete with caterers, a bar, a band, all her people, and our own kids and friends, I led the four of us through a circle blessing.

We went around the candlelit circle, sharing our wishes for our mother. We wished that she would slow down, enjoy her grandkids, stop doing so much, and start being. We wished she'd be more vulnerable with us, call us when she wasn't feeling great, let us help her now that she was getting "up there." Mom listened but shrugged us off, waving her bangle-adorned arm, her gray ringlets bouncing with animation.

"I'm fine, girls! Don't put me underground yet! I still have plans!"

Afterward, I gave each of us sisters a little piece of rice paper, and we wrote down resentments that we had toward our mother, the ones we were ready to release. One by one, my sisters and I went to the kitchen, set the papers on fire, and let them go out the kitchen window.

Lisa went first.

"I let go of you not lovin' me in the way *I* needed to be loved," she shouted out loud to the street in her thick Brooklyn accent.

Maddy went second. Her long legs stretched higher than the windowsill, she looked back at Mom, laughed awkwardly, and spoke into her paper.

"I let go of all the fighting, and, I guess, um, the babying too."

I went last. There were so many things I wanted to say. I could have stood at that window for hours. Instead, I said the only words I could think of that summed up what mattered the most.

"I forgive you."

The rice paper looked like little lanterns floating above the open city sky.

Last spring, during the early months of COVID-19 stay-at-home orders, Mom called me nightly from the yellow phone with the extra-long, curly cord, which lives on the wall next to the kitchen window. She would stick the phone out, so I could hear the cheering, pot banging, bell ringing, and clapping from my front porch back home.

"I miss New York!" I'd say.

"I miss hugs!" she'd say.

I'd ask, "How is your heart and spirit today, Mother?"

She would tell me about her schedule. Even during lock-down, that woman found places to be. And I'd listen. I'd suck it up and be right there with open ears, as I always do when Mom talks at me.

I'd say to myself, *Be patient, just breathe. Listening helps her feel less alone.*

I suppose it helped me too.

Now, I look at an eyesore, an ugly steel twenty-five-storied skel-etal structure—positioned like a giant middle finger flipping me the bird, right through our kitchen window.

The sun sets through the netting that covers the beams and scaffolding. It is one of those sunsets you only get downtown, the kind when the sun lowers into the Hudson River, right between Hoboken and the West Side Highway, and mixes with New Jersey pollution just perfectly enough to streak fire reds and magenta across the sky.

I imagine all the humans, behind all those windows, in all those buildings living life. Ten months inside cramped New York

City apartments. Ten months missing their people, working from home, mourning life lost, but alive.

Is anyone out there standing at their window looking at me? What do they see? Do they see the self-assured, middle-aged, loving daughter who dutifully came to care for her mother? Or are they able to see the impatience that still festers in expectation and obligation, despite decades of therapy, spiritual seeking, and self-study?

It all started a month ago. As the elevator shook, Mom spun. She lost her balance and fell. She called me from the metal floor.

"I'm dizzy," she said into the phone. "I can't breathe."

"Hang up and call an ambulance," I said.

They admitted her. Every symptom pointed to COVID, but every test came back negative. They ran more tests. Neurologists and cardiologists took blood work and ordered scans. None of us were allowed to go to the hospital—pandemic rules.

I stood watch from home and worried. The thought of her going out like that was unbearable. I always imagined my mother dropping dead in the middle of a concert, or during a headstand in yoga class. Not sick, and certainly not alone in a hospital bed.

"It was just a blip."

"Just a blip," she kept insisting, after the CAT scan revealed cloudy masses in her lungs and a blood clot that caused a mild stroke in the back of her occipital, near the reptilian brain—the region of the brain that controls the autonomic nervous system. It's the part that is responsible for blinking, and swallowing, and heart rate, the sympathetic part of the brain that governs our fight-or-flight response.

They kept her there for a week. Unable to figure out the cause of the clouds or the clot, they sent her home with new blood thinners. They scheduled her to return later in the month for a biopsy, which she had today.

A Smoke and a Song

The doctor said they are optimistic that they got enough from the two masses in her lungs for staging. If they need more samples, they will go in again through her ribs, just below the left side of her heart, a dangerous procedure for someone her age. They will call within five days with the results.

So, for now, we wait.

I came to distract her. We will get in a couple of walks around the block if it's not too cold, watch some stand-up comedy. Tiffany Haddish just released season two of *They Ready*. Mom will love it. I brought my clay face mask and manicure set so we can have an at-home spa day this week.

When she's not looking, I'll put things in order: Make a list of her accounts and passwords if I can find them. Call her attorney. Take down the dishes and give them a rinse.

But mostly, I came to be next to her when the doctor calls with the results.

There is no way I'll let her get that call alone.

The teakettle sings. I pour the boiling water over the grounds that sit in the recycled filter. I open the fridge to get the milk. The fridge light flickers. I take a mental note.

Add to the list of things to do while I'm here: change out the refrigerator bulb.

There is no milk in the refrigerator. Just a half head of endive and a ziplock baggie of goat cheese curds on the third shelf. I can't find any honey in the cupboard. *Where is the honey?*

Mom usually gobbles a spoonful straight from the jar. It is her one nighttime sweet treat, the only "goodie," as she calls it, that she allows herself. Still to this day, at nearly eighty-four and rail thin, she watches her weight.

Task number two: do a big grocery shop for Mom.

I take the coffee to her room and set the mug next to her L'Occitane hand cream and a stack of *New Yorker*s on her bedside table.

Her eyes are closed; her mouth is wide open. Dry lips. Pale, green-ish skin. Her face is so wrinkled. For a second, I think, *Oh my God, did Mom just die?*

I put my face close. She's not dead. She's breathing.

I go back to the kitchen. I take a sip of my coffee. I stick my hand into my bag, which is still hanging on my shoulder, and reach for my phone.

I text Miles: "Arrived! Grandma is sleeping."

Then Jevon: "Ugh, this is hard, my love. Call you later."

And finally, a group text to Maddy and Lisa: "Sisters, not good. We should Zoom later."

At the window, I see my reflection staring back at me. I look old, like my mother looked when I was a kid, only fuller. My once-toned body has recently become someone else's, so I feel. No matter how hard I exercise these days, my body keeps getting bigger. My jawline has been hijacked. It's triple-chin city over here. My bras no longer fit. My breasts are so engorged, you can see them from behind. Even my old period jeans are too tight on me now.

I think, *Maybe we gain weight in menopause because we need a bigger suitcase to carry all the lives we have lived?* How else could we carry the stories? Careers. Homes. Lovers. Losses. Friends. Secrets. Children. Empty nesting. Success. Failures. Forgetting. Remembering again. And the cellular imprints, codes gestated from eggs and planted by sperm that lived in my mother and father and their parents before them, and the great-grand ones too.

A carry-on just wouldn't suffice!

All this living, in the folds of my skin.

Why, despite all the years of letting go, does my body hold on?

I shrug it off. I should make peace with my fifty-year-old body! It's a small price to pay for the wisdom that comes along with crone-hood. So what if the crows have nested by my eyes? These eyes are privileged to see into the souls of so many beautiful humans. I see how they look back at me with hope, approval, and affection. So what if my lips crinkle when I speak? These lips have shared words of advice, comfort, and inspiration. They have kissed the back of many necks. So what if my hands look like a 3D map of veins? These hands have held babies, tended plants, and hugged hard.

I sift through the blue-and-white folder they gave me when I picked up Mom from Mount Sinai, taking mental notes of the medical terms. I'll have to google them later. Just like I've been holding my bag, I realize I have been holding my breath since I got here. I sigh. It is burning hot in the loft. I'm sweating. The radiator beneath the window is steaming like an old-fashioned locomotive. Plus, the hot flashes. Plus, the cat hair. And the discharge papers.

I breathe.

Task number three: vacuum the loft.

I breathe again.

On page twenty-two are pictures of the nodules, the only thing in color in the entire Mount Sinai discharge packet—three thumbnail images of red soft tissue with little brown spots on them, taken from the camera they put down her throat. Under the images, the words you can never quite prepare for, even if you think you have been preparing for them for weeks.

Maybe if I get back in the elevator portal and into my time capsule of a car and drive back on I-95, through Connecticut and Rhode Island to Massachusetts, and jump on the ferry and return to Martha's Vineyard and into my bed with Jevon, time will reverse and none of this will be real?

But who am I kidding? I do not contain that type of witchy force. No matter how many times I meditate, or how many ceremonies I've been to, or how many years I've practiced and taught yoga, I do not hold any mystical powers to turn back time.

I look at the paper again, hoping that maybe the words have since rearranged themselves into a more cheerful diagnosis.

But no. It still says on page twenty-two, "Highly suspicious for malignancy."

ONE

Worn Soles

I can always hear the *rattle, rattle, thump* of the elevator long before the door opens. It lasts a good five seconds at least. Five seconds of steel cables spinning and pulleys pausing, while the elevator does its very best to land level with doorjamb number eight, where we live, on Fifteenth Street.

Those five seconds are just enough time for my body to prepare.

Take a big breath in, sit up, squeeze muscle toward bone.

It is what I do when my insides are flooded with that zingy mixture of relief and anxiety. Relieved that she is finally home, anxious to find out what mood she'll be in—like some odd cocktail of sweet with a splash of spicy flooded into the marrow of my ten-year-old bones.

Rattle, rattle, thump!

It is as if the elevator is on my side, sending me a warning signal, a friend tapping me on my shoulder from behind the kitchen island where I sit doing my homework.

Attention! Be alert! Mom's home!

The elevator opens. Mom bursts in, her long, graying ringlets covering half of her sculpted, makeup-less cheek, black leather purse draped diagonally across her jean jacket, like a pageant winner. Her other bags—the crochet tote she takes with her daily, although she has little time to crochet, and the messenger bag she uses to carry her books—are hanging on her narrow hips.

She throws her keys down on the dining table. They make a loud *clank* before sliding across the wood tabletop and bumping into the clump of dirty laundry one of us daughters had placed there earlier but forgot to put into the washer.

In her exasperated, raspy growl, skipping over a hello, Mom greets us. "God dammit, girls!"

It is as if that dining table, which is placed directly in front of the elevator door, is some reminder of all that has gone wrong in her world. Just seeing it triggers whatever she has bottled up today, shoved deep into her tiny five-foot-two body, swallowed into the bit of her bloated belly, to erupt on us like verbal vomit.

"Could you girls clean up this goddamn fucking table for once?"

Who can blame her? The dining table is a mess. It is forever cluttered with undone homework, unsigned permission slips, underwear, and a bowl of water for Bri, our enormously over-weight cat, who only drinks water from the bowl if it's on the table, never from the one on the floor, as cats are supposed to do. The table has wheels that never lock quite right, so whenever Bri musters the *umph* to jump up on it, it slides sideways. More often than not, it stays that way, crooked on the floor for weeks at a time.

It's late, after eight. Mom works from seven in the morning to noon at a nursing home in Queens. Afternoons she runs errands for some rich guy named Richard who lives on the Upper West Side. On Tuesday and Wednesday evenings, she gives sessions at the therapy clinic down on Greenwich Avenue. And some nights, like tonight, she is in school getting her master of social work.

The second she's home, she's on edge—high-strung, agi-tated, dodgy like a chihuahua, small and nonintimidating but with a loud bark. I can't understand why Mom instigates argu-ments, especially as soon as she walks in the door. And even more so, because she always loses them. Who in their right mind would choose to start their nights like this, every night? A simple

"How was your day?" first could go a long way. But not Mom. Nope. Always "God dammit, girls."

My sisters are quick to fight back, words waiting on the tip of their tongue, already formed into spiteful sentences. Lisa, the oldest, speaks up first.

"Well, if you had one motherly bone in your body to actually cook us a meal ever, maybe we would have a reason to clear the table."

Maddy, the middle, says, "Do it yourself. I'm your daughter, not your maid!"

I, the baby of the trio, close my eyes and squeeze in, while Mom and my sisters yell at each other some more. And more. And more. Mom walks to the kitchen to make her coffee.

Coffee is always the second thing she does after getting home. I make a habit of preparing it for her before she gets here. I grab her favorite mug from the cabinet, the white supersized one with elephants walking in a ring around the rim, one trunk stuck into the butt of the next—coffee-cup porno. I put the mug on the orange Formica counter. I take out the brown bag from Porto Rico Imports from the refrigerator, grind the beans, and pour the soil-smelling grounds into the paper filter. So all Mom has to do is boil some water, pour it over, and take a sip. A small gesture, it is always worth the try—my attempt to prevent a full-out war between her and my sisters. Because, well, Mom always seems to shift for the better with a cup of coffee in hand.

Mom takes a big gulp of steamy brew and says, "Ah, thank God for you!" and scurries to the back of the loft to hide in her room.

I am not sure if she is referring to me or the coffee, but either way, it works, so I let it be.

"She's fucking nuts!" Lisa says. "The lady is sick. I just can't with her and her hyperactive ways!"

Maddy chimes in, "I know; she's psychotic."

I join in with Lisa and Maddy to poke fun at our mom behind her back. "Yeah. Yeah. She's crazy."

Poking fun at Mom is our connective tissue, the same skin wrapped around our shared sisterly skeletons. They joke about needing to lock her up in a loony bin. I laugh, but in my belly, I feel the truth in my sisters' claims. Something is certainly off with our mother.

I feel sorry for Mom. We are three against one. And she is so skinny! She has little help with us, no husband to speak of, no child support with money or otherwise, and we are a handful. And Mom has zero control. Lisa smokes pot in the playroom, and Maddy sneaks out to parties. We are more like the Four Horsemen of the Apocalypse than we are family, New Testament style: Sword. Famine. Wild Beast. Plague. Each of us on our own mission to somehow survive the palpable angst that lives within the four walls of our loft. A mom and her three daughters, two already bleeding, and the third, me, on the verge of filling a training bra, all under one tin-tiled ceiling.

"This loft is drenched in female pheromones," Mom often says. "It's just too much estrogen for one home."

And she's right. Even our cat, Bri, is a girl. As a matter of fact, there hasn't been a boy born in our family since Grandpa Stanley, and he is almost eighty years old.

My mom is one of those fiercely independent New York City broads. Our friends call her "fly," and adults call her "dynamic" and "magnetic." Mom buzzes like a bee, she rarely eats, she barely sleeps, and she is wired with both arms raised in the air. When we were babies, she raised her voice for women's liberation and raised her fist for the Black Panthers. Now, she raises us on occasional food stamps and a whole lot of adrenaline. She's always on offense for the next thing to fight for, with, or at.

She must have passed the gusto to us through her breast milk, because the three of us are stubborn, strong-willed, and defiant. We love hard; we do. But we fight even harder.

Lisa, five years older than me, is the lion. She loves hugely. She is 80 percent heart and the only one of us who openly cries. She piles up stuffed animals and extra blankets to watch Snoopy's Halloween special, even as a teen. She is the only one of our family who hugs with both arms. On those 80 percent days, she is the lion in *The Wizard of Oz*. Cuddly. Harmless. Protecting me as if I am her own cub. She calls me her Baby Bug Out and I even have a shirt to prove it. It is a purple tee with fringe cuffs around the sleeves and white, fuzzy, velour iron-on letters. I wear like it is my security blanket or a badge of honor.

When the other Lisa shows up, the other 20 percent, she has sharp teeth and a temper like a grenade with three-quarters of the pin pulled out. I always know *that* Lisa is coming by the flair of her nostrils and the gasp of air she takes in and holds right before losing her shit.

I am lucky to be on Lisa's good side. I know she has my back, and she makes sure everyone knows it. I walk around with an untouchable stride in my step. *No one* in the neighborhood fucks with me.

"Yo, leave her alone," they say when I walk by. "That's Lisa Drapkin's sister."

Mom told me the 20 percent Lisa started coming around when Dad left, when Lisa was six. She said Lisa would wait by the front door sobbing, gripping the knob, begging for our father to come back, and when Mom would try to pick her up, Lisa would kick and punch. By ten years old, Lisa's tantrums had turned into unpredictable outbursts of violence. She'd flip the furniture over, knock the photos off the wall, and throw the frames, breaking the glass.

By thirteen, Lisa had taken up with the wild crowd. She and her friends swallowed pills, swigged beers, spent nights flip-flopping between dance clubs and street fights. Now, it's rehabs and relapses. Mom tries everything: Interventions with my Grandpa Stanley. Social workers. Nothing works.

Lisa is strong, and she's bigger than me and Mom and Maddy. Mom is obsessed with Lisa's body size, always on her case about losing weight. Sometimes I feel as if Lisa eats more just to spite her. I probably would, too, if I were Lisa. She is the only daughter who inherited our absent father's frame and face. Maybe that is why they have such a rough go at the mother-daughter thing. Maybe every time Mom looks at Lisa, she sees the man who left her in New York City to raise his three daughters alone.

Their fights are terrifying. Lisa pushes; Mom falls, curls her body into a corner, covering her face with her hands. I run in the middle and wrap my arms around Lisa's waist, risking a punch in the face. I beg her to stop, which usually works.

Except for the times it doesn't. Like last year, when Lisa came home high and furious, she spun out of control after Mom confronted her.

"Back the fuck up," she said to Mom. "I'm not playin'!"

But Mom didn't listen. She charged after her.

Lisa slammed the door. Mom's fingers got caught. They bent around the doorframe, and there was a whole lot of blood. Lisa kept slamming and slamming.

Mom screamed, "Sherry, call the police!"

So I called the police.

The police came and put Lisa's fisted hands behind her back, cuffed her, and took her away.

Yeah, that was a rough night.

Maddy, my middle sister, lives in her own world. She's out most of the time or in her room with the door closed. She takes to her friends' families and plush Upper East Side apartments as if they are her own. She goes with them on vacations to Jamaica and the Bahamas and spends weekends at their second homes at the beach. She acts as if she belongs to those families, not ours—as if she is better than us.

We are only two years apart, and we are close. It is good for me that I have Maddy to bully me out of my serious side. I'm the kind of person who says no before even considering a yes. She calls me tightly wound.

"Just try it, Sherry," she says. "Don't be so stuck."

Maddy forces me to be free, at least freer than I am without her. With her, I feel like I am given a VIP invitation into some special place called Maddyland. We toss Glad bags of cat poop out of our eighth-story window, just missing the people walking by. In late spring, we skip school and sunbathe on the roof, slathering ourselves with her homemade concoction of Coca-Cola and baby oil. Maddy pushes what little furniture we have in the loft out of the way, so we can practice roller skating backward before going to the Roxy Rink.

Over the opening horn section of Michael Jackson's "Don't Stop 'Til You Get Enough," she shouts, "Keep your left leg straight, and roll your right in a figure eight! Now jump! Who cares if you fall?"

At Dad's, when we were still going to see him during those mid-1970s summers, we'd go into the woods and invent magic royal kingdoms. Maddy always played the queen, and I always played her slave.

Mom bends over backward for Maddy. She glues dollhouses for her at Christmas. She writes Maddy's school papers and folds her clothes in neat stacks and places them on her unmade bed. She never does that for Lisa or me. When either Lisa or I am nearby, Mom pretends to get stern for a minute to put Maddy in her place. But Maddy has mastered the art of argument. Man, can she spin a web of facts proving without a doubt that she is forever right about *everything*. She can always bulldoze Mom into getting her way.

"No, Mom . . . you do it," she says.

And Mom does it.

I am jealous of the special privileges Maddy gets. But I am even more jealous of her carefree "I don't give a flying eff about anyone but myself" attitude. Not to mention Maddy got the long legs and straight, reddish-brown hair I always wanted.

When I say it's not fair, Mom says to me, "Now, now. Don't be bratty about it, Snaps, your sister needs extra." Maddy is oblivious to her own special treatment. She acts like she is the center of the universe, and Mom arranges the planets and stars to orbit her.

"I guess the whole world revolves around Maddy!" Lisa says, slamming her door. But under the masquerade of bossing around, twirling in circles, and living the high life, Maddy is insecure and anxious. All four of us are. She's somewhat helpless when it comes to problem-solving. She can only make it halfway through just about any real-life task before she gives up, so I also take it upon myself to carry her to the finish line. She needs me. At least this is what I tell myself. I summarize the how-to instructions of her games. I am the one to alphabetize her baseball card collection and rub cream over her eyes when she burns them on her tanning lamp.

If I were more like Maddy, I would probably be more relaxed, or more focused on myself instead of taking on everyone else's problems. But at the same time, if I were more like Maddy, I never would have learned to budget my allowance.

All four of us got the voice—the raspy, scratchy, comes-from-deep-in-the-throat voice. It is a strong voice. A voice that makes it sound like what we are saying must be true, even if most of the time we have no idea what we are talking about. A voice you can recognize from the other side of the diner. A voice that wins arguments. Except when we argue with each other, because then the separate voices muddle into one rolling thunder roar that just gets louder and deeper, and everyone sounds the same.

Worn Soles

I am told the voice belonged to my great-grandmother Alice Asher, but I imagine it belonged to the mothers that came before her too. Alice was only granted thirty-five years to speak with it before she died of breast cancer, when my Grandma Elise was only eight years old. Grandma Elise uses it to sing jazz while she paints or puts on lipstick in the star-shaped mirror that hangs in her foyer, or to weave fables of her technicolor life that keep me on the edge of my seat.

Grandma Elise gave the voice to Mom, who uses it to counsel her therapy patients during the day, argue with my sisters during the evening, then cry to me at night. Mom passed it to us. On good days, Lisa uses her voice for cracking jokes and making everyone laugh, and Maddy always uses hers to be the boss. I sometimes use my voice to practice the vocabulary words I've memorized so I may sound like the grown-up I feel I'm forced to be in this loft. But mostly I use my voice to circle up Mom and my sisters for the come-to-Jesus make-up sessions I need to mediate after the raging fistfights.

Each generation was born with an octave lower than the one we inherited it from. All of us love to sing, but this voice can't hold a note for the life of it.

Music is our glue. Lisa throws an album onto the record player, the Sugarhill Gang's *Rapper's Delight* or the Rolling Stones's *Sticky Fingers*, and turns up the volume to a nine. The four of us break out in song, roll up the rug, and dance our asses off. Lisa leads. We try to match her moves.

Lisa can do the Bus Stop like it is nobody's business; her hands clap to the rhythm, her feet stamp front to back. She has a way with her hips, as if she is born to sway them side to side, so the Bump comes naturally for her. And during "How Low Can You Go," Lisa's ass hovers just inches from the floor.

That girl knows how to "get the shit off, burn one down," and "get the boogie on"—Lisa-isms for dancing. Lisa holds my hands and pulls me in, spinning me under her arms and flinging

me down into a low dip. Maddy and Mom synchronize steps to
"The Hustle."

The good moments are great.

But our family dance time is sparse, and although Mom
works more than she does not, so are our finances. As the third
daughter of a single mother, I am used to walking in my sister's
shoes. Lisa leans heavy on the heels, and Maddy has an instep
that eats up the arches. By the time they get to my feet, the shoes
are always worn way down to the sole.

Among the Plants

After the fights, Mom and my sisters go into their rooms to do whatever it is they do in there. I finish my lo mein, alone at the dining table doing my schoolwork. I like having homework to do. I like to get lost in whatever assignment I am working on.

I keep great care of my notebooks. I rewrite my notes from class, so that every word lands perfectly on the lined pages and every homework assignment is put in order by date in the folder sleeves of its correlating subject matter. Even though I keep my room messy, organizing homework, whether it is the long-division equations I lay out on the page like poems or penciling punctuation marks for my English class essays, fills me with worth and purpose. It's the perfect antidote to whatever chaos is happening at the loft.

Next to my schoolbooks is a wicker basket filled with a stack of take-out menus clumped together by a leaky packet of sweet-and-sour sauce. I sit so I look out toward the rest of our open loft, like a mobster. *Never put your back to the door.*

Our loft is one long space with a high ceiling, lots of windows, and barely any walls. The furniture tells you what room you are in.

Couch + TV = living room
Books + desk = study
Beanbag chairs + chalkboard = kids' playroom

A Smoke and a Song

All of it is covered in cat hair.

Between the kitchen and the couch, there is a long row of plants where I have my sit spot. Waxy green leaves in clay pots filled with dark earth are huddled together. All taller and wider than me, they make creepy shadows on the brick wall at night. I climb through the plants as if I am roaming the forest. I nestle myself amid them, to give myself a minute—the thing I do when I need to shut things out. Turn the switch off. Pretend that whatever just happened, didn't. I pretend that Lisa did not swing the vacuum cleaner pole at Maddy earlier, missing her head by an inch. I pretend that Maddy did not pull out a handful of Mom's hair and then laugh in her face. I pretend I am a family-less fairy, free and sheltered from the loft-storms.

I sit among the plants and breathe and hum.

"Hummm, hummm, hummm. Hummm hummm hummm . . ."

I have been humming this tune my whole short life, on instinct. Like the time I tripped over my favorite stuffed animal Lammy's blanket and went tumbling down the stairs when I was four and ended up in the hospital with thirteen stitches across my bottom lip. Or the summer when I got attacked by bees upstate and got so many stings I was swollen until September.

Among the plants, I taught myself to pray. I am not sure if God is a thing. We weren't raised as believers. We have no book to tell us when we sin. We do not light candles on the menorah, nor do we go to church or synagogue, like my friends do. But I pray anyway. I know there must be something more than I can see with my eyes. I feel it inside.

I use my body as a prayer stick and my humming as prayer. I lower to my knees, eye level with the soil, and place my palms together at my chest. There, I speak with the God I feel in my body. From the altar of my hands, I open them apart like they are the Bible, and I pray for my sisters to be less mean to Mom. I pray for Mom to get some balls, or better friends, so I don't have to be the one to rescue her from my sisters' wrath. I pray for somewhere else to be, somewhere other than the loft, or school, or my homework. Somewhere quiet where I can just be me.

"Hummm, hummm, hummm. Hummm hummm hummm . . ."

Inside the plants, it smells like Prospect Park. It smells like puddles in the morning after rainfall. Inside the plants, it smells like my dad's.

We used to take the Greyhound two and a half hours upstate to see him. Three sisters crammed in two seats, each with our own bag of candy. Lisa and I always finished our candy way before the bus pulled out of the Port Authority, but not Maddy. Maddy would make one lollipop last the entire ride, taunting us with each lick.

Dad would pick us up in his rusty white pickup and drive us the long way home, down hills with vast views, farmed Christmas trees, and curves that made me carsick. I sat on Lisa's lap sideways, smelling Lammy's soft fur, with my back pressing on the window, facing Dad. Maddy sat in the middle. I would look at our father down and up: His thick-soled, brown boot pressing on the gas pedal, jeans torn by the knee, T-shirt tight around his beer belly. His hands calloused and hairy, at a quarter to three on the steering wheel. His shoulders waved in figure eights as he took each turn, like a dare. The same face each summer, seasoned a year. Deeper laugh lines, looser curls, bushier beard. Country looked right on him. Much better than the black suit, rimmed glasses, and short hair he wore in the photograph of when he and Mom were together in Brooklyn.

Dad would ask a few questions. "How was the bus ride?"

"Good," we'd answer.

"How's school?"

"Good."

"How's your mother?"

"Good."

The rest of the ride we'd sit in silence, shedding off New

York City, mile by mile. By sundown, we'd arrive at the bumpy dirt road with the wooden gate that was never closed. Behind the wooden gate was his red cabin with the porch that was bigger than the cabin itself. Behind the porch were the deep, dark woods—birch and pine, bramble, willows, and oaks, and under the trees, the trailer where he made the three of us sleep.

It was an old metal trailer, kind of like an Airstream, but not as cool. It was more like a walk-in refrigerator. There were no lights, no windows, and one door. Just three mattresses on the floor, a deck of cards, and a few raggedy board games. At night, my sisters and I played Monopoly by flashlight with only one die on a board that was warped and peeling from being left out in the rain a few too many times. We heard insects and animals crunching leaves and sticks outside the trailer, through the metal siding, even when the door was closed.

Dad didn't have a job that I know of, nor many friends. He was a Jewish Brooklyn boy that Mom says "went expat" tucked in the back roads of Accord, New York. A loner, in a cabin with no running water, on two acres he and my mom bought on auction for $3,000 in 1970, the year I was born—the year before they split up.

The first few summers we visited him, Dad took us on truck rides through corn mazes or to the Buddha Hole, the local swimming spot, to cool off. Both my sisters learned to backstroke before I could walk. Dad taught them, back in the days when he took time to be with us. But by my turn, he was already a shell. His arms and legs were with us, yes, but his heart had already left.

I was four when he told me to take off the Styrofoam swimmy bubble. I was wearing the ugly turquoise bathing suit that rode up my crotch when I kicked—the suit that used to be Maddy's, and before it was hers, it was Lisa's. I had really wanted the black bathing suit with the rainbow straps I saw while shopping at the A&S before we were sent to Dad's for the summer. I begged Mom for it. But she said, "Absolutely not. Why would we buy a new one when we have a perfectly good one at home? Anyway, you're too young to wear black."

Dad tucked me under one arm and walked waist-deep into the water. "Ready, set, go!" And he threw me in.

No instructions, no encouragement. I remember feeling the cold punch and then sinking straight down to the rocks and squishy bottom. I could see the shapes of my sisters' legs treading under the murky water and hear splashes and screams of the townies playing. They sounded like Charlie Brown's teacher. It was a strange and mysterious place down there. I was tingly, the water was silky, like the sheets on Mom's bed. There was an electrifying zap in my body. At first, I felt like my Olympian Barbie. Then, I dissolved. I became the water. I was the Buddha Hole. I could've stayed right there forever. It wasn't until Dad scooped me up and lifted me into the open air that I felt the shock of not breathing. Then I became afraid. I coughed and spat and cried.

By the time I was five, we were left on our own. Dad gave us an endless routine of chores to do while he was out. I was too young to feed the chickens and pigs, so that was Maddy's job. My arms were too weak to pump and lift buckets of water from the well. That was on Lisa. My job was to pull the Radio Flyer wagon off the mossy path behind the metal trailer and pick up sticks and pine cones that Dad used as kindling to start the woodstove.

One day, when we were feeling stuck and rebellious, my sisters and I stockpiled our dimes and quarters and set out for a midsummer bike-about to Kerhonkson, the country store, to fill our pockets and fatherless day with gumballs, Swedish Fish, and Mounds bars. As we biked home, high on sugar and candy-less, the chain on Lisa's bike derailed off the ring.

Lisa and I pulled over to the grass. Maddy continued to ride around in circles on the empty road, up and down, up and down, until she eventually said, "See ya, wouldn't wanna be ya," and took off by herself.

A Smoke and a Song

As Lisa fixed her chain, I had an impulse to spin her back wheel. I wanted to watch the spokes go from separate lines into a whirling *whoosh*, like wheels do when they are spun. I put my little hand on the rubber tire and whizzed it around. Lisa's candy-coated hand got caught in the spokes and they sliced a deep gash in her pointer, middle, and ring fingers.

"Oh my God!" I screamed. "Oh my God, Li, I'm sorry!"

"Get some help!" she cried. "Find somebody. Hurry!"

I ran down the road shouting, "Help!" and looking for a house with someone, anyone. Lisa wailed and tried to stop the bleeding with the sock she took off her foot. But there were no houses anywhere. Just a road with trees and fields and small pine-needled paths that led to streams. No humans in sight.

It took us hours to get back to Dad's property. Lisa walked in front of me, moaning, drops of blood marking her one-barefooted, one-socked step. I was desperately struggling to keep the two bikes upright, steering the two handlebars with my two small hands, pedals scraping the front of my shins every other step.

We arrived after dark, queasy from August heat and blood. While Dad patched Lisa's fingers with homemade butterfly stitches cut from masking tape, he gestured for me to come closer, so close that I could hear his teeth click and smell his cigarette breath.

"How could you be so stupid, Sherry?"

"I'm sorry," I said. "I didn't mean—"

"Sherry the stupid, the stupid little girl," he said.

Lisa's fingers never did set quite right. Good thing she's a lefty, like Mom. To this day, both Lisa and I wear the scars from our trip to the Kerhonkson Country Store: Lisa, the scar from the spokes and shoddy butterfly stitch. Me, the scar from being sent to the metal trailer all by myself with no dinner, where I climbed into a ball at the bottom of my brown sleeping bag and hummed myself to sleep—the scar of terror and shame.

Among the Plants

But those days are long gone. It has been years since we've seen or even heard from him, years since his name, Warren Drapkin, has been spoken out loud in the loft. So I rely on the plants to tell me my story. I lean in and bury my head inside the overgrown, tangled geraniums and dig my fingers into the wet dirt inside the clay pot and smell them. The backwoods of upstate rushes to my nostrils; the scent of ferns and Dad's breath resurfaces. I am five again, pulling the Radio Flyer over mossy paths.

Oh yeah, my body reminds me. *I once had a dad.*

Time Line Homework

Mrs. Wasserman, my fifth-grade teacher, gave each student a piece of graph paper and instructed us on how to draw a time line with a color-coded key on the bottom right-hand side of the page as an extra-credit project. I take out my ruler and markers and try to remember. *A time line?*

This assignment has me stumped. I have a difficult time making sense of my memories. To me, time is not a line. Each day does not just neatly follow the last. Instead, what I remember about life, and all the bits and pieces that make me, bounce, go 'round, and scramble in my head. Time feels like a handful of rubber bands that have been tangled together into a knotty ball.

I want to scribble squiggly marks, spirals, and crosses on my life map. But I am a goody-goody, so of course I'm going to do what I can to get a couple of extra-credit points. I follow Mrs. Wasserman's steps. I iron out a few significant memories that I can add to the line and assign a date to them.

Mom comes into the kitchen in a raggedy T-shirt and saggy underwear, so skinny that her knees are the widest part of her legs. She picks at a chunk of cheese, one cracker, and a slice of apple, standing up by the counter and not over a plate. She chews like an afraid rabbit, short, slow chews, eyes darting side to side, as if waiting for a predator to loom around the corner. Her hands are still shaking from the fight she had earlier with Lisa. It bothers me that she doesn't, or maybe can't, sit down, not even to eat.

"How's your homework?" she asks.

"Good. I'm working on my time line," I say. "Wanna see?"

I hold up the loose page of graph paper with my ruler-drawn arrow across the page, starting at 1970, the year I was born, all the way up to now, 1980. The line is colored by dots.

"The green line goes from 1970 to 1977, for when we were in Brooklyn." I trace my pointer finger across the arrow. "Red is for the loft."

I go over a few dots.

Purple—Spring 1976: Adopted Bri the cat.

Orange—Summer 1977: Lost my Lammy.

Yellow—Fall 1978: Saw the loft for the first time.

I don't dare tell her the dark blue dots are for the days at Dad's.

"Nice job, Snaps."

But I can tell she isn't really listening. She seems as if the inside of her skull has been hollowed out. There's a look of shock, or confusion—as if she has suddenly lost her hearing after a loud explosion.

She scratches the top of my head. "Come in to say nighty night before bed." And then: "And straighten the table. I'm sick of looking at everyone's shit."

She goes back to her room, and I pick up the green marker, for the Brooklyn days. In the brownstone in Brooklyn, we had a staircase that led to our bedrooms on the third floor and a back-yard with an apple tree that produced the sourest of apples. In the brownstone, we had a real dining room with four walls and a table that stood still. In the brownstone, at least for the first year of my life, we had Dad.

In our Brooklyn neighborhood of Cobble Hill, folks called each other by name. If they didn't know you, they'd give you a nickname like Precious, or Pumpkin. In Cobble Hill, Dom Leoni, the old man who owned Dom's Deli, would even let us take Ring Dings and cans of Yoo-hoo on credit.

"I-a bill your mama at the end a da month," he'd say in an Italian accent.

A Smoke and a Song

Almost every brownstone within a three-block radius from ours had the name LEONI on its front door buzzer. The Leonis owned the hair salon where Debbie Leoni did Mom's hair. Debbie forever tried to convince Mom to dye her grays. She would snap the smock around Mom's neck and shout, as if Mom were on the other side of the salon and not sitting in the chair in front of her. "How you gonna meet a man looking like this? You-a beautiful lady! But you're starting to lookin' like a grandma!"

Mom would laugh it off, but she wouldn't budge. She didn't need to color her hair, she said. I agreed. Mom has the smoothest olive skin that turns a perfect amber on the days we take the F train to Brighton Beach and roast under the sun. And her thick, black brows frame her wide, brown eyes and German Jew nose like an arbor.

"Not today," Mom would say to Debbie. "I earned these white hairs." She'd nod her head in my direction and roll her eyes.

The Leonis also owned the bakery on Sackett Street, where my friend Teresa's mother, Angie, worked. Angie would sometimes sneak us a little brown bag of black-and-white cookies or a couple of rainbow cookies when we'd stop in the mornings after sleepovers. I was on to her. I knew she gave us the cookies to shut us up. She certainly did not want us telling anyone in the neighborhood about her husband, Sal. Sal used to pull Angie by the hair down the stairs at night after he came home boozed and bothered. Sal also used to come into the bathroom to watch us when we took baths and towel dry us off with his scary sausage hands. We never told anyone about Sal. Not one word about how, during sleepovers, Maddy would make us a bed on the bay windowsill, so that if Sal came in to try to touch us again, we'd be able to jump out the second-story window and escape.

Mom borrowed the down payment for the loft in Manhattan from my grandparents after someone threw a brick through our Brooklyn kitchen window. They wrote "Get the N off our block" in white spray paint all over our stoop. At the time, Mom was dating a drummer named Leon. Leon gave me piggybacks and wore keys on a chain that bounced off his jeans as he walked, making a clinking sound. One day, out of nowhere, the clinking just stopped. Mom said she got rid of Leon because she no longer liked funk music. But later I found out it was because of the brick. Apparently the Leonis did not like black men named Leon.

So when Grandma Elise saw the FOR SALE sign on the front door of the building down the block from her painting studio on Fifteenth Street, she insisted Mom buy it and move us to Manhattan.

"Brooklyn is so far behind, Babetty," Grandma said to Mom, as Grandpa Stanley signed the check. "It's unsophisticated, unworldly, and artless. Don't raise the girls in that."

I put down the green marker and pick up the red. Manhattan.

Getting adjusted to Manhattan life that first year was not easy. A new school, new friends, new neighborhood. Manhattan was crowded, and people were not friendly like in Brooklyn. No one even looked up as they passed you by. In Manhattan, Mom made me hold her hand as we walked down the streets. Sometimes, if I were daydreaming, she'd tug me closer and say, "Pay attention, Sherry. This is the city!"

I was eight when we first went to see the loft that stormy day, just Mom and me. We skipped up Sixth Avenue, my right hand squeezing her left. I can still feel the cold metal of the silver rings Mom wore on four of her five fingers.

"We are upgrading! Just wait until you see this place!" Mom said.

"Three more blocks!" I said, counting as we walked.

It was nine blocks total from where we had been staying on Washington Place, with a woman named Nat, someone "special," as Mom called her. Nat took all four of us into her two-bedroom apartment after Mom sold the Brooklyn brownstone and we needed a place to camp out while the loft was being gutted.

A Smoke and a Song

Mom said it'd only be a few weeks, but it turned out to be all of third grade.

Nat had a short blonde crew cut and wore tight, white T-shirts with high-rise Levi's. Nat was nice enough, but I didn't think this or that about Nat. Except when she would rub Mom's thigh at night. Those times, I thought Nat was weird. Not weird because of the thigh-rubbing, but because she spoke to Mom in a squeaky baby voice while she did it.

As we walked, Mom was trying to open a folded piece of paper that had the address and front-door key taped to it with her free right hand. She passed the note to me. It was Grandma Elise's ever-recognizable handwriting on the paper: "#58. Always great! On the Fifteenth Street, how neat!" Like a line in a Dr. Seuss poem.

I could spot Grandma's crooked longhand from a mile away. Our walls are covered in her artwork, and her artwork is covered with hand-painted words. Grandma's words lean to the left, and the lower half loop. Her letters dangle like overly ripe pears about to fall out of a tree. One letter bumps the next, with barely any spaces between them. It takes a determined detective eye to decipher Grandma's words. But I am a pro. I learned my ABCs from her paintings—especially from the one that hung on our Brooklyn bedroom wall. It was a large frame, with purple-and-orange blotches, with a tiger's face in the middle, and words scribbled all over the canvas.

Maddy would say to me, "I spy with my little eye, the letter *D*."

I'd hold up my alphabet book from school on the page with the letter *D*," Lammy resting on my lap, to study the lines and curves. I'd look at the painting, let my eyes cross because it was easier to see the letters when I blotted out the other stuff. Eventually, I'd see the *D*. I'd run to the painting to point.

"There it is! *D*."

"*D* is for doofus!" Maddy would say and throw a pillow at my head.

Time Line Homework

The first thing I noticed when the elevator door opened to number eight—after its shaking, the rattle, and the pause upon landing—were the floor-to-ceiling windows half-covered by metal shutters that went *bang*! with the wind. It was a sound that reminded me of the door of the metal trailer at Dad's. From the front of the loft, on the elevator side, the right side, through the dirty windows between metal shutters, I saw the Empire State Building. Green lights on the top, red in the middle, and white lights toward the bottom told us Christmas was coming. From the left side window, there was a redbrick building with a clock on it. Behind the clock were the Twin Towers.

"Can you believe these views?" Mom asked.

The views were awesome, but the place was not. There were cardboard boxes, typewriters, and stacks of books not written in English scattered on the floor. A huge printing press machine took over the middle of the room. Behind it, there was an old man dressed in brown corduroy and a beige beret, just like the one Grandpa Stanley sometimes wore.

The man looked up at us.

"Ello," he said, with an accent.

"Hi, I'm Babette, the new owner," Mom said with a proud pitch.

"Ello," he said again and went back to the printing press.

Mom and I walked around the space, mapping out our new life with each square foot. I hadn't seen my mother that excited, not ever—at least not in a long time.

"Your rooms will go here," she said, shouting over the machine noise, "and my room will be over there."

She pointed to the opposite side of the loft, which, to my eyes, seemed really, really far away. Behind the printing press and Mom's enthusiasm, my heart dropped to my feet. *Thump thump. Thump thump.* I scoped out the location of our imaginary new bedroom and then hers and thought, *I'm gonna need a flashlight.*

In our brownstone in Brooklyn, her room was just on the other side of the walk-through bathroom. Almost every night, I'd slip in bed next to Mom.

"Not again, Snaps," she would say. "I need my alone time."

But she always gave in, pulled me near, and wrapped her leg around my body, tucking her big and second toe around my heel.

"We'll put a long dining table with six chairs over here for dinners," she said and pointed to the space in front of the elevator. "Just in case *we* meet someone special."

I remember thinking, *Isn't Nat our someone special?*

But two years living in the loft, and I can count the number of times Mom has cooked us a meal on one hand. There are so few, I can give them their own color and add them to my time line! A couple of pasta dishes, maybe some burgers or fried baloney, but never a casserole or lasagna or a warm cake in the oven. And a house never really feels like a home until the oven is turned on.

I wonder if my dad still likes to cook. Does he have a signature meal? Is it baked lemon-garlic chicken, cooked in a square glass pan, garlic crisping so you can smell it from the third floor? In my fantasy of what life would be like had he stayed, we'd still be in Brooklyn and things would feel normal, like how families feel on television. I'd sit with him while he orchestrated the meal, music on full blast, his curly salt-and-pepper hair dancing as he dashed herbs and spices in with the chicken.

In Accord, Dad butchered and cooked meat in a cast-iron pan on the woodstove. The entire cabin filled with the scent of burning flesh, Rosie the chicken and Fred the pig—and other animal friends Maddy had fed and I had played with all summer.

I'd cry, refusing my plate. "I can't eat them."

But Dad hovered. "Finish your dinner, Sherry. Now."

I hid my bites between my cheek and molars, so that in the

moments when Dad turned away, I could spit my friends into a napkin and stuff it in the pocket of my Lee jeans. Later, I'd throw the scraps into the woods behind the metal trailer and say a prayer. "I'm so sorry, Fred. Please forgive me, Rosie. Thank you. I love you. Hummm hummm hummm . . ."

I collect the markers, put them in their case, and slide the unfinished time line into my homework folder. I take one last bite of my lo mein and throw my paper plate away. Time to check on Mom before I go to bed.

Most nights when I check up on Mom, she cries to me. I say things to cheer her up. I move my facial expression to match the story line she shares, to make it look like I care. But inside, I am seething. My organs cramp, and I go numb. I want to jump out of my skin and shout, "You're the therapist, not me!" But my tongue gets caught on the roof of my mouth, too thick to work, and limp like a fish. And words, a million of them, just bounce around inside my skull, like pinballs popping from lobe to lobe.

Mom usually says something like, "Please talk some sense into your sisters tomorrow, will you?"

"I will, Mom, I will."

And I do. I uphold my promise on days I feel daring. "Come on, guys, let's try to be nicer to Mom," I say to my sisters.

But it always backfires. Lisa throws her pack of cigarettes at me and says, "Oh, so you're trying to be the boss of the family now?"

Maddy pushes me down and straddles me, pinning my arms with her knees to do "the typewriter" on my chest. "You better mind your own business!" she says slowly, poking and bruising my breastbone while pretending to type. She slaps the side of my face and says, "Ding!" as if my cheek is the carriage return and she is sending it back to the starting position.

Apparently, my big sisters do not like it when their baby sister tries to talk sense into them.

A Smoke and a Song

Tonight, when I walk toward Mom's room, I hear her gagging from the other side of the bathroom door.

I knock. "Mom, are you okay?"

"Go away, Snaps," she says.

The toilet flushes. I wait, but she doesn't come out.

So I leave her a glass of water on the floor outside the bathroom door, as I do on these types of nights, before I go climb among the row of plants, to hum and pray.

First Drag

I am the only other person in the world who has keys to her studio.

"Not even your grandfather is allowed here," she says, holding a gold ring with a Cupid charm and two keys dangling off it, "but you, darling, get your own set. And you can come here anytime you want."

She must know I need a break from the loft, from my older sisters and Mom. Grandma Elise can see this, and see me, and possibly see parts of her own story in mine. So she gives me a set of keys and a wage of three dollars an hour.

My first real job, and I even have a title: studio manager. On Tuesdays and Wednesdays after school, I change into overalls and call her on the yellow phone by our kitchen window, so she can give me her list, which is always the same:

Fig Newtons
16-ounce Canada Dry ginger ale, in the glass bottle
Two Granny Smith apples

"You're a lifesaver, darling," Grandma says. "You know I find going to the store dreadful."

At her studio, I sweep the floor, fetch her supplies, or help frame while she paints. She works on several paintings at once, adding brushstrokes from one to the next, while sitting on top of a small foldout ladder, her canvases set in threes on separate easels in a semicircle in the middle of the long room.

A Smoke and a Song

She collects her skirts from behind, layers of shorter over longer ones, ruby red floral print on top of sandy stripes, pink polka dots over purple paisleys. She wraps the material around the top of her thighs, legs wide, using the fabric that hammocks between her knees as storage for tubes of paint, brushes, and sharp-edged tools while she works.

"Always add texture," she says, as she lifts a foot that wears only Birkenstocks with thick wool socks and rests it on the first step of the ladder, "to give the painting depth."

Grandma Elise scrapes hard lines into the thick slopes of acrylic or oil creatures and calligraphy on her canvases. She calls me close, smelling like rose and turpentine. "See how the light shines more brilliantly through all the dark cracks and edges?"

Sometimes, she falls into her zone, waving a long wooden brush in her hand, singing, while I make myself useful. I'll adjust the pillows on the pullout couch, tidy the kitchenette, or clean the bathroom, which is my favorite place in her studio.

I have many private little moments in the bathroom among her floral hand towels, rose soaps, and carved wooden statues of Cupid that hang on the bathroom wall. I peek into the one small, round face mirror on top of the old-fashioned shaving kit. The kit has a long iron stem with a hook for a brush and a plate for the razors—the real razors that you sharpen and reuse, not the disposable kind like my mom uses. There is an ivory cup where Grandma keeps her makeup. I lean over the speckled gray-and-white marble sink, which she has set atop her old Singer sewing machine legs, and smear her orange lipstick over my lips. I make sure to pucker and pout as I have seen models do in magazines.

"Darling!" Grandma calls. "Fresh water!"

I rub off the lipstick with the back of my hand, making a long smudge up to my fingernails, and run to her with a pitcher filled from the faucet. She puts her hand out like a surgeon. When I pass her the pitcher, she sees my lipstick-stained hand and places the pitcher on the piano.

First Drag

"That's not your color, darling. Red is much better for your terra-cotta skin. Next week I'll show you how to put on a face."

My grandma knows how to put on a face. Hers is the most beautiful one I've ever seen: She has the tallest, thinnest neck on earth. Blushed cheekbones as high as the Himalayas. Hazel eyes you can see through. And no matter the time of day, even first in the morning, her lipstick, Revlon #710 Orange Flip, is perfectly on point.

She dips in the tip of the brush.

I watch the clear water take a hit of indigo blue. Color clouds stretch until they erase the clear water in the pitcher. She passes me the brush and asks me to add a dot to one of her canvases.

"A collaborative masterpiece!" she exclaims.

Despite the curve that bends her spine like a wilted flower, Grandma moves across the studio like a tango dancer, graceful, with dignity and elegance. But outside, she uses an empty grocery cart to help steer her bunioned feet up the streets of the West Village, as if she can trick the public to think she is just on her way to the store. But if you know her, you know she never goes to the store, not to mention that using a cane or walker is not an option for someone of her beauty, or her pride.

After cleaning, we reward ourselves with Fig Newtons and ginger ale. She weaves tales of her colored past, speaking into the pauses and low notes of the jazz playing in the background. She makes her voice higher and lower with the trumpets and percussion, as if she is Ella Fitzgerald herself, in syncopation and scat.

Grandma is certainly not the chocolate chip cookie–baking type. She is eccentric, a dreamer, and she has lived lives. She learned to sculpt during a pilgrimage to Israel and took a cross-country railroad from Chicago to Big Sur to live on a writer's commune, where she played Chinese checkers with a famous writer named Henry Miller. She was married three times. She had to travel to Reno to end the first two, because divorce was still illegal back then, at least in the state of New York.

A Smoke and a Song

"I've always thought they had it backward, darling," she says. "They should make it much more difficult to get married and easier to divorce."

Grandma Elise met her match with her third husband, my Grandpa Stanley Kunitz. They are the painter and the poet. The two host cocktail parties at their Twelfth Street apartment, the likes of which friend and poet E. E. Cummings once read to the guests. The walls of their West Village digs are covered in paintings from their famous artist friends, guys I've heard her talk about so many times, I have their names memorized by heart: Motherwell, de Kooning, Rothko.

Grandma and Grandpa are the center of the circle in Provincetown, Massachusetts, where they spend their summers and where we visit every year. In the early sixties, with what little savings he mustered on a poet's salary and the bit of inheritance that was left from my great-grandpa Lou, Grandma's dad, the two purchased a two-story cottage on the west end of town. It is just a five-minute walk from the half-mile jetty that separates the Cape Cod Bay from the Atlantic.

"Rumor has it," Grandma said to me, "the house on Commercial Street was once a popular brothel visited by salty dogs who found themselves at the tip of the Cape at the turn of the century."

With his own delicate hands, certainly not made for construction, Grandpa Stanley tore open the walls of the basement rooms and built a painting studio for her, and a one-windowed study for him. Grandma's Provincetown studio is filled with beachy natural light. Grandpa's study is dark, barely big enough for a desk where he writes from dusk to dawn on a typewriter he bought at the thrift.

In the summers, Grandma fiddles around aimlessly while Grandpa mentors aspiring writers at the Provincetown Fine Arts Work Center as part of an artist-in-residence program he started. Grandma is a private person. She detests when Grandpa's adorers, of which there are many, come by their cottage in the afternoons to get, as she says, "their daily dose of the poet." Enthusiastic to recite their latest pieces, they sit with him in the corner living room overlooking his garden while he drinks his Beefeater Gin martini. Extra dry, three olives, poured into a jam-sized mason jar, which he hides inside his blazer breast pocket and drinks every day at three in the afternoon, as soon as he hears the cardinal call from Grandma Elise's bird clock over the dining table, signifying "martini time."

Grandma Elise calls his admirers "the coven of big hairs." When they arrive to see and be seen, she hides in her studio. Before making her exit, she always puts on a fresh coat of orange lipstick and says, "Stanley, sweetie, don't bother me. I'll be downstairs, painting."

When Grandpa Stanley isn't writing, or at a reading, or hosting his fans, he is in his garden, his prized possession, and the bane of Grandma's Provincetown existence. "His other wife," she calls his garden. "He tends to the plants better than family. The roses, his children. The trees, his elders."

Grandpa Stanley had sculpted what once was, as he claimed, "just a sad slope of sand" into four tiers of decorative grasses, roses, spiked veronica, hydrangeas that bloom three seasons long, and the largest juniper tree known to man. Tourists trek to the very end of Commercial Street just to peek at Stanley's garden.

The slow-moving Cape Cod sky and waiting on Stanley's flowers to bloom from spring through summer and into fall is not Grandma's thing, like it is for Grandpa. He is in his element. She is not. My grandma is a city gal.

"The sand is treacherous to walk on," Grandma Elise says to me when talking of their summer home. "I always miss my concrete!"

But she loves him, and it is where all the artists go for the season, so she agrees to make a life of it for four months of every year. But not without complaints.

A Smoke and a Song

"It's absurd, Mon Sherry. It takes me all winter to pack for the summer in Provincetown and then all summer to pack back up for New York."

At the end of every Wednesday shift, Grandma hands me an envelope with my pay and says, "Well earned. I couldn't do this without you."

I keep the envelopes in a small jewelry box that used to be hers. It sits under my bedside lamp. It's painted white pine, with pink, pillowed silk on the inside and a little ballerina that pops up and spins to the tune of the "Tales from Vienna Woods" waltz by Strauss when opened. Every couple of weeks, I tear open the stack of envelopes and spread the cash out on my comforter in piles. Singles, fives, and a few tens that I count and recount, fondling my merit, before carefully wrapping rubber bands around each pile, the money warm from the heat of the lamp. My first savings account. Validation for my efforts. Energy flow that finally goes both ways. Give and take. Worth so much more than the money itself.

One Wednesday, with "Summertime" from *Porgy and Bess* blasting, Grandma singing at the top of her lungs and me dancing with the broom, she takes out a red pouch from her desk drawer and lights a cigarette with a long match from a skinny glass vial. She holds the cigarette between her lips and takes two long drags in a row before exhaling. I watch her in awe, the smoke puffs around her beautiful face, rising to the high ceiling, circling the water pipes to her sultry notes.

"Come," she says, coaxing me closer. "Try it, darling."

She passes me the cigarette. I inhale and cough it out. I take another puff, cough again. I feel like a movie star.

"This will be our little secret," Grandma says, as she slips her pointer and middle fingers over the cigarette in my hand and places it between her lips for a drag. "Don't you dare tell your grandfather."

First Drag

"I won't tell a soul," I say, staring at her blushed cheeks. Grandpa must know. He must smell it on her hair or taste it on her lips. I imagine, if he ever found out, Grandpa would care a lot more about being lied to than Grandma's smoking. But if he does, he gives her this secret to have for herself. He gives her a studio to paint, smoke, and dream in. Grandpa is a generous man. When I ask why she doesn't tell him, she says, "It's a womanly thing. We all deserve to have something just for ourselves."

I think I understand. Grandpa Stanley is the famous one. She goes along as a supporting character in his one-man show. She makes his martini and pours it into his jam jar to slide into his breast pocket. She warmly welcomes the PBS crews when they come for interviews. To them, she is just the poet's wife. But to me, she is so much more than this. And in her studio, she lights up! She is the grandma who sings, makes art, and has lived all these interesting lives. She is the person who sees me, likes me, and treats me like a grown-up. To me, she is much better than chocolate chip cookies!

Grandma and I make a habit of sharing one Camel Light every Wednesday at the end of my shift. I don't tell anyone, and neither does she. I love having something special with my grandma. But I don't like keeping secrets. I worry we will get caught.

When I mention it, she says, "In public, we can be one person. In private, someone else. It is a lot like when we stand in a mirror. We think we are seeing ourselves correctly in the reflection, but things aren't what they seem. Right is really left, and left is right. We see a backward reflection of ourselves."

"But isn't that a lie?" I ask.

"Let's not be dramatic," she says. "Don't stress yourself about it, darling. Not another thought. We aren't telling anyone that we are *not* smoking. We just aren't telling anyone that we are."

Manhattan Misfits

When I am not at school, the loft, or working for Grandma, I spend my days with The Crew, a scrappy blend of downtown Manhattan misfits that I have become friends with since starting junior high. None of us in The Crew have those perfect family units we see in the movies—a mother who follows recipes and a father who carries home a briefcase from the office. None of us do homework by a warm fire. We are the children of divorcées, struggling artists, recovering addicts, and washed-up theater actors who are just trying to keep it together.

We kids are given all kinds of freedom to do the things New York City kids like us do. We stroll the streets, joyride the subway, start a band, BMX bike on the mounds at Washington Square Park, or sneak up to the roof of one of our apartment buildings to play manhunt and sip on a fifth of blackberry brandy that one of us manages to score. We go to the Horatio Street Bar, where the woman bartender lets us play *Ms. Pac-Man* and sip beer from the tap. We kick over garbage cans and roll them down the curbs until the streets are full of trash. Sometimes I go over to Grandma's studio and find her cigarettes. I take a few of them to my friends, and we smoke on a stoop by the streetlight.

I do these things because it is better than being at home with Maddy, Mom, and Len. Len is Mom's boyfriend. Len tries to tell me how to behave. Mom lets him, and she lets him boss her around too. She always does this when she first dates someone new. She loses herself and becomes whoever they want her to be.

Now, suddenly, she listens to classical music and cooks. Give me a break.

I do these things because it makes me feel closer to Lisa. These are the things Lisa would be doing if Mom didn't kick her out of the loft. Lisa now lives at Phoenix House, a rehab for troubled teens in Westchester, and she loves hearing about my shenanigans when we talk during her once-a-week call. She can't do things while living at the group home. So I do them for her.

"Li, guess what I did?" I whisper into the phone.

"Oh, tell me!" she says.

"We found a wallet on a bench in Washington Square Park. There was a one-hundred-dollar bill in it. We took the money!"

"Oh snap. What else?"

"I've been taking Dexatrim. It gives me a good buzz."

"Try NoDoz, it works better. What else?"

"I heard Mom and Len having sex in the shower."

"Ewww, barf, what else?"

One night Mom shakes me awake in the middle of the night.

"Wake up, Snaps, we have to talk."

"What?" I say, rubbing my eyes, still half asleep.

Her grays seem glow-in-the-dark, iridescent loops of moon-white opal that wrap her frizzy, shoulder-length ringlets.

"Stop acting out. Enough. You got it out of your system." She leans down to kiss my forehead. "This is the best thing for your sister."

"How can you just throw her out, like she's trash?"

"I love your sister. I love all three of you."

"And why do you let Len walk all over you?"

"I certainly do not!"

"Whatever."

She climbs into bed with me and pulls me into her.

Part of me wants to pull away.

But the part that yearns for my mother always wins. I inch

closer and lay my ear on her braless chest. Her exhales are long and slow, hot, like the way the air feels after the subway passes at the outside station at Coney Island. Each breath she takes in, her chest rises and meets my cheekbones. Each breath out, her chest pulls off my cheeks. She collects a clump of my knotted hair into her hands and attempts to run her fingers through it, but can't, so she detangles her hand and kneads the top of my hair instead, just like Bri the cat does when she's "making muffins" on blankets.

"And the smoking and drinking," she says. "Enough. You're not even thirteen years old, for God's sake."

I don't say anything. I curl into her, sleepier than I have been in months.

As I drift into deep sleep, I hear Mom whispering to me. "You're my stubborn one, Snaps. Len is a decent enough man, you'll see. You have got to let things go, really. Holding on only makes us suffer."

Minus the Smell
of Wet Paint

Mom gets home particularly late, and she's annoyed. Maddy is not doing her homework like she should be. She is on the phone with a boy instead.

"Hang up the phone, Madeleine."

Maddy looks up at her and laughs. Mom tries to yank the phone out of Maddy's hand. The two of them wrestle with the receiver until it slips and conks Maddy in the face.

"You're out of your mind!" Maddy says, shoving Mom away with her foot. Mom goes in for more. Maddy starts punching.

The fights between Mom and Maddy are getting louder, more physical, and often impenetrable. No longer able to keep peace, I have a new tactic at the loft. I do not try to stop them, nor do I hide in the plants as I did when I was younger. I let Mom and Maddy have at it like wild dogs; then the next day, when they are licking their tails, I circle them up for the hug-it-out session.

They push and slap and scream. My mother's inability to stand up for herself and take control of the situation is too unbearable, and quite frankly, too embarrassing to witness, so I grab my set of keys, throw a coat over my flannel pajamas, and escape over to Grandma's studio, three buildings away. The studio feels as it always has, minus the smell of wet paint.

It's been months since I've shared a Camel Light with Grandma. I'm no longer working for her now that I am fourteen and legal working age. I can make some real cash as a hostess at Chelsea Place, the bar on Eighth Avenue. Plus, Grandma's cataracts have advanced, and her back is so hunched that it is hard for her to paint. She does go to the studio weekly, feeling her way up the three blocks from their apartment on Twelfth Street, her empty shopping cart and cellular memory serving as her compass. But most days, the studio sits unused. Except by me.

The smoking kit is still in the top drawer of her wooden roll-top desk: The red clutch, with the vile of matches, Camel Lights arranged in a row in an old-fashioned, gold cigarette case. Rose perfume in a refillable glass spray bottle, a travel-size Crest, and of course her lipstick.

I turn the dial on—WGBO, jazz public radio—put on her lipstick, and light up a cigarette to smoke out the window. I stare at the lights on the Empire State Building.

I love the flickering lights outside the picture-frame window. I love how the lipstick makes a Hollywood imprint on the filter. I love that smoking takes my appetite away. I love the pause and peace, the delicious silence of these moments alone in Grandma's studio. It is the one place where I can indulge in being quiet, where I have a place to think and smoke and be me. The real me.

I call Grandma on the phone, to see if she needs me to do anything for her while I am there.

"Oh, not again," she says, referring to the chaos between my sister and Mom at the loft. "Your mother has always been weak."

I agree, but it hurts to hear. Grandma's tone of voice always gets sharp and her words stingy when she speaks of my mother. I find this confusing and uncomfortable, but I am curious. I wonder what my mom must have done as a kid to bring out Grandma's mean side.

I have seen it in person, too, at holidays in their apartment. Mom tries to connect to her by talking about something Grandma Elise cares about—the latest installation at the Guggenheim or a travel piece on Egyptian art she read about in

Minus the Smell of Wet Paint

National Geographic—and Grandma barely acknowledges her. Instead, she turns her chair sideways, so her back is to Mom, and when Grandma does speak to Mom, her sentences are short and her toes curl under the strap of her Birkenstocks. The tension is thick. Grandma scooches her chair closer to me, leans in, so she can loud-whisper in my ear. "What is *she* talking about?" she asks and nods over in Mom's direction.

How can Grandma be so kind, so funny, and so caring with me, but so harsh to her own daughter? It is as if Grandma's loving skips a generation.

"Well, you just take some time to be you, Mon Sherry," she says. "Let your mother fend for herself. And say hello to the kiddos for me," she says, referring to her art.

Telenovela

Grandma Elise is the only one who I tell about my fantastical double life with Joaquin. She finds it exciting and amusing.

"It's like your own telenovela," she says. "A real-life Mexican soap opera."

I am fifteen; he is twenty-nine. We met while I was on a parent-free spring break adventure to the island of Cozumel, Mexico. "There's no drinking age there!" my friend Josie said, convincing me to join her.

"I'm coming," I said, before even asking my mom. I had saved my own money. I could pay for it myself.

When I told Mom I was going, she was unphased. She is so worn down to a mom-nub from my older sisters that she does not seem to care what I do in my spare time.

Joaquin and I met at the guest services desk at Playa Azul Club, the resort at the end of the hotel zone, where he is the manager. Josie and I were staying there, and I noticed him on our first day. Although he was rather plain looking in his beige Tommy Bahama hotel uniform, when I walked closer to him, under the enormous open-air *palapa* lobby, he had a vibe. As he handed me the blue-and-white-striped beach towel across the counter, our fingers touched. He said something professional, in perfect English, like, "Take the two chairs by the rocks. It's the best spot at the beach." He pointed across the powder-white sand, where two lounge chairs sat halfway in the clear, turquoise Caribbean Sea.

Then he winked. "Nice to finally meet you, *Sirena Morena.*"

I didn't know a lick of Spanish yet, but I liked that he had given me a nickname, as if we already had a past, and said the word "finally," like there was destiny ahead for us.

On our third night in Cozumel, Josie and I were getting ready to go out to the disco. As I slithered into my favorite tight, black-and-neon-pink-striped Guess dress, there was a knock at our door. It was Joaquin in short shorts and high socks, like a Mexican Harlem Globetrotter, only shorter. There was a U of sweat around the collar of his tank, and he was panting. His round cheeks were reddened, and his light brown hair, which was spiked during the day, was flat down on his forehead.

"Hi," I said, surprised.

"Hola," he said, catching his breath. "Would you like to go for a swim?"

I looked at Josie, who gave me a nod. "Duh! Go!"

I grabbed a towel and followed Joaquin outside.

There we were, in the down-lit infinity pool, under an almost-full Mexican moon, Joaquin treading water by the ladder and me sitting on the ledge with my calves dangling over the side. He said, "I have not stopped thinking about you. My feet ran me to you tonight, seven kilometers, my fastest run to date."

I laughed a little, a nervous laughter. I wasn't yet used to the corny romanticism he seems to weave into every sentence. City boys don't speak like this. But then again, Joaquin is no boy. He is a man.

With the tension of a possible touch filling the pool, we talked through the night. As the sun was peeking out from the pool's horizon, he said, "You should know this about me . . ."

He paused to wrap my towel around me. "I'm married."

I did not know what to say.

A Smoke and a Song

He took my hand in his and said, "But the juice from the orange has run dry. We aren't in love anymore."

I believed him. And I let him kiss me.

When I am in the city and he is in Cozumel with his wife, he writes me letters filled with yearning. A letter arrives, and I climb up to Lisa's empty loft bed, with the Empire State Building in view, to read his letter two, three times in a row. English sounds more colorful coming from him. He has a way of describing everything as if it is magic realism, a real Carlos Castaneda. He writes things like "Someday we will share the same one breath" and "We will let our love slow cook."

But my favorite three words are ones he speaks in Spanish— my nickname.

Mi Sirena Morena. My brown siren.

What girl wouldn't be swept off their feet to be seen by a man in this way?

Grandma is right. It is like my own telenovela. In one life, I am this older Mexican man's mistress, planning secret trips where I will fly off to Mexico to have late-night visits in a fancy hotel. And in the other, I'm just a regular teenager, drinking blackberry brandy with my crew and studying for the SATs.

Köln Concert

Mom built a half wall in front of the elevator and converted our old playroom into her office where she has a private therapy practice. She moved her albums and periodicals in there and placed speakers in every corner of the room. I packed up Maddy's dollhouses and tanning lamp and took over her room.

We make a ritual of curling up in her office after her last patient has left, with cups of coffee to listen to the album of the evening—me on her therapist's chair, and Mom on the chaise she has set up for her patients. Mom's record collection is bigger than Nashville, and way more diverse. Classical, folk, opera, jazz, blues, world music, classic rock, and Dolly, Willie, and Patsy, the obligatory country, of course. It takes us months to travel the long rows of albums in alphabetical order—from ABBA to Frank Zappa.

We are on letter "J," and today's album is Keith Jarrett's *Köln Concert*.

"Close your eyes, Snaps," she says. "Listen to how he tears up the piano here."

I lean back, put my feet on her desk, and close my eyes. Jarrett's live concert is a fusion of jazz and classical, one man on a piano in a packed concert hall. The music is hypnotically rhythmic. I can feel the high notes tickle my kneecaps. In the suspended lows, my shoulder blades fan and my lower lungs lift under my armpits. When his skip on the piano keys gets quiet, I can hear the pause at the top of his inhale. I can practically feel the audience on the edges of their seats, as if every single person in the auditorium is also holding their breath, waiting for Jarrett to exhale and rev up again, so they, too, can breathe out and clap and cheer and emote. The music gets louder and more intense—the pounding turning into wildfire or tsunami sounds—and explodes in my groin and belly. It is as if Jarrett's fingers coming down on the ebony and ivory are a vessel for transmuting all the hidden stories held in the dark of all the humans in that concert hall.

"That was a full-body experience!" I say at the end of the record.

Ever since Maddy left for college last fall, things at the loft have turned around. There are no more fights for either of us to escape from. We take space in *all* the open rooms of the loft. We are buddies. We go to concerts together: Crosby, Stills & Nash at Radio City, Chico Hamilton at Lincoln Center, the Metropolitan Opera. When we go out, Mom waits for me to get dressed. Then she goes back to her room and comes out with an outfit like mine. When we go to bistros, where she eats a whole meal right in front of me, she has me order first. Then she says to the waiter, "I'll have what she's having, only I'll have mine extra-rare. Still mooing if possible."

One night, over burgers at the Corner Bistro, I tell her about Joaquin and my hopes to move to Mexico after high school, if things are ready for us. He and I have managed to keep our affair going for almost two years through letters and my occasional jaunts to Mexico. He's still with his wife, and I'm hanging out with a moody bass player named Cyrus, but I know Joaquin and I will end up together, when the time is right.

"That worries me, Snaps. A married man?"

"I know, but that will change," I say. "They aren't in love anymore."

Mom asks me to apply to college anyway. "Things usually don't go as we hope," she says. "Especially when it comes to men. Men disappoint."

"Not Joaquin, Mom. He's romantic, and kind."

She laughs. She takes a bite of her burger. Red meat juice drips off the bun and splashes on her plate. "Men are hunters and gatherers," she says, still chewing. "Strong and steady until they get the prey. Then they get soft. Then all they want are their mommies."

She pauses between bites and puts her burger down, bun soaking in a pool of wet. "I'm still waiting to meet someone who can man up to me."

I have seen it in every relationship she's had—with men and women, with Leon, with Nat, with Len, now with Bob, and who knows how many others in between. There have been too many to count. She is all in for a few months. Then the yelling starts. Then she throws out her lovers like they are used paper towels—only good enough to keep around while they clean up her latest mess.

"The term 'soulmate,'" she says, "is a Hallmark marketing scam."

Not long after the burgers, I start to notice a couple new books about Mexico on her nightstand. The same cocoa butter kinky hair–cream products I use are on her bathroom sink. I see a twin of my checkered army green bag from Canal Jeans by the elevator.

Mom is slowly taking all the things I love and making them hers. She is living through me. I find it cute, and admittedly, it boosts my pride at first. But when everyone around us thinks it is she who introduces me to these things and not the other way around, it starts to bother me. I do the legwork. She takes the credit.

I confront her about it. "Mom, stop copying me. Let me have my own thing."

She denies it. She's defensive. "Don't be ridiculous, Sherry. I have always been interested in Mexico."

I can't quite understand why she needs to lie about it. She lies about bigger things too. I overhear her tell stories to her friends on the phone that aren't even hers to tell. "When I was young, I fell in love with an older, married man." These stories are mine. But in her version, she's always the main character. It infuriates me. I am finally out of my sisters' shoes and now I have to share shoes with my mother?

Little by little, I distance myself from her. I shop at second-hand stores, so she can't copy my outfits. I throw away my cocoa butter and start to blow-dry my hair straight. I wear all black, all the time. I find new music to play, music I know for a fact she doesn't listen to: hip-hop, reggae, hard rock.

But she's sneaky, and she is subtle. Not easy to detect, but hard to ignore. Like a missing limb, invisible to the eye but still felt. The more I separate myself from her, the slicker she gets, tying a clear codependency cape around my neck. She knows how to keep me attached. She uses my affections as a bargaining chip to keep me close. She takes me shopping and pays for my clothes. She books my tickets to Mexico to visit Joaquin. She lets me and my friends smoke in the loft.

"Don't tell your sisters," she confesses, "but I left you all the albums in my will."

I don't tell my sisters.

Kunitz and Kahlo

Grandma Elise has been sketching with charcoal and writing poetry in a little room off the kitchen in their Twelfth Street apartment. I stop by weekly to bring her groceries and check in on her spirit. When she gets distracted by her art and forgets I am there, I walk around and snoop.

I look at the framed photos that hang on their hallway wall—photos of Grandma and Grandpa at readings, at parties, walking the beach, when they were younger but still old. When Grandma was able to stand upright. Many are of my aunt Gretchen, Stanley's daughter from his second marriage, now a doctor who lives in Oakland.

There is the one family portrait from a few summers ago—all of us girls and Grandpa's cat, Celia, scrunched together, sitting on the front steps in Provincetown. Grandpa is the only one standing, the trunk of our family tree.

I peek through the open door of Grandpa's study down the hall. There are books from floor to ceiling and even more open on his desk, at least a dozen for every year he has lived. Wearing his signature brown corduroy pants and jacket, which match his eyes, and in his favorite writing chair, Grandpa Stanley hunches over his typewriter, fixated on his latest poem. He is wildly stylish for his age, with thick white sideburns, which meet his mustache, curling across his cheekbones. He's in a paperboy cap and suede Hush Puppies that look older than he is.

Grandpa drifts in and out while he writes. His eyes roll to the back of his head, his chin lifts, as if he is visiting some otherworldly realm, waiting on a message from the abyss. When a phrase hits him, he snaps back, and tacks on the typewriter feverishly, afraid the words might leave him faster than they can slap the page.

I knock on the door. "Hi, Grandpa."

Without his eyes leaving the poem, and without hesitation, he says, "What goes, dear?"

I wait for him to invite me in, which he does. "Come," he says, patting one of the empty chairs on the long side of his L-shaped desk. "Come."

We mostly sit in silence, which I find odd since words are his thing. But Grandpa Stanley has always been more of the listening type.

After a few minutes, he cups his warm hands around my face and asks, "Tell me, what exhilarates you? How is your heart today, my dear?"

Truth is, what exhilarates me lately is him—my Grandpa Stanley Kunitz. I have been looking for excuses to converse with him ever since my English teacher had us read his poems my junior year. I am fascinated by how he takes words about seemingly insignificant things—a cricket trickling underfoot in the garden, or the labor of a compost heap churning new life from rot—and somehow arranges them in a way that makes me think about how complex the simple things are.

My favorite of his is "The Long Boat." I have been reading the second stanza over and over, as if it were written just for me.

> Too tired even to choose
> between jumping and calling,
> somehow he felt absolved and free
> of his burdens, those mottoes
> stamped on his name-tag:
> conscience, ambition, and all
> that caring.

Kunitz and Kahlo

His poems feel like word-filled windows into his mind, and somehow, I feel, into my mind too. Even if he isn't Mom's father by birth, he is the only grandpa I know. Even if we don't share the same genes, it is as if Grandpa's DNA has been injected right into my very own veins through his poems. I appreciate that he is level, calm, quiet, and although not overtly masculine, he is the only man in our family. Being around him balances me in a way I need, being fatherless and all. Even though I am considered the grounded one of the family, I can never quite get my footing around all the women. At least, not on the inside. And spending time with Grandpa feels more natural to me than time with anyone else with whom I share blood.

Grandpa Stanley and I grow closer as I find more pockets to sneak off to sit with him, human to human. A man, a grandfather—and me, a budding woman, his granddaughter. I dress up and go to his readings at the 92nd Street Y, or at Poets House, where his followers probe me with questions like, "What is it like to have such a brilliant grandfather?" I know how lucky I am to see the quirks of a man at home that others yearn to get a piece of out in the world. I smile and nod and sip my sparkling wine, always turning back to check on Grandpa as his small five-foot-eight frame gets swallowed by his fans. Even when I can barely see his cap in the crowd, I feel him. He radiates and fills the room.

Grandpa agrees to help me edit my college entry essay. As usual, my paper is too breathy, and I need to pare it down to five hundred words. I am writing about the 1978 protest led by the American Indian Movement called The Longest Walk, a transcontinental trek for justice and tribal sovereignty. I figure if I decide to go to college instead of moving to Mexico, I will at least study something that eventually gets me closer to the border.

The Longest Walk is a great topic for an aspiring cultural anthropology major and one I think Grandpa will be pleased with, as he is a die-hard human rights advocate. I read in a review of his book *Passport to the War* that he spent two years shoveling shit out of latrines during World War II after being denied as a conscientious objector, because he refused to hold a gun.

But when reviewing my essay with me, he does not mention the content, only the technique.

"You've used 'therefore' three times on this page," he says after reading through my first draft. "Use. Words. Sparingly."

Grandma Elise interrupts us. She can never leave the two of us alone for very long. She rolls up on the extra office chair, the wooden one with the cranky wheels, and slides herself right in the middle while Grandpa is speaking.

"Replace it with 'hence,' or 'consequently,'" he says, face so close to the paper, as if he is inhaling the tobacco from the peace pipe in my essay right off the page.

Grandma Elise kicks me under the desk and smirks. "Therefore! Hence!" she speaks in my ear. "Consequently, please wake me up when it's over."

She snorts and drops her head, as if she's a narcoleptic and falls out flat. It's funny but distracting. I just want some Stanley time. But Grandma can hardly stand Stanley's and my intellectual things. She has thin skin for such seriousness.

Grandma kidnaps one of Grandpa Stanley's plants and takes it to the studio—a fern, which she hangs in the front window in an off-white crochet hanger with wooden beads on it. Every couple of days, she calls me to check if I have watered it. "How's Frida doing?" she asks about the plant.

"Still growing," I say.

She isn't fooling anyone. I know she puts Frida there to make sure I still have a reason to go to her studio, and to keep three blocks of distance between Grandpa Stanley and me.

During one of my weekly watering visits, I notice a book I haven't yet seen on the windowsill. It is a thick paperback, with hues of deep ocean green and a portrait of a dark-haired, dark-eyed woman with a thick black unibrow on the cover. The woman has a light mustache, and red ribbon braids through her bun, trailing off her left ear and noosing her neck. The other end of the ribbon is connected to a monkey perched on her shoulder. I immediately take to her face. I can practically feel the woman's soul.

I flip through the book, a biography, by someone named Hayden Herrera. Each page is accompanied by self-portraits of the woman. There is one with chicken wire tied to her torso, her sitting on a bed of calla lilies, and several of her lying down on a bed with a back brace from waist to ears. The most curious one is of her in midair in an industrial setting, factory-stack smoke forming a heart—the organ, not the valentine kind. She wears a similar expression in every painting. Assured. Serious. Broken. Pained.

On the first page of the book is a note from Grandma: "Darling, meet Frida Kahlo, our fern's namesake. I thought you would like her, given your trips to Mexico. She's not my preferred artist; I find her obsession with herself as subject matter a bit monotonous. However, I believe you will appreciate her story. She was a revolutionary. A communist. A feminist. She reminds me a little of me, and a lot of you. With love, Elise."

I eat the book up. Gobble it. Chew every portrait into tiny pieces and savor every page. I earmark, sometimes double folding, the top and the bottom of the pages. I learn that Frida was in a trolley accident as a teenager that left her with a broken spinal column and pelvis, and a crushed foot. Bedridden for much of her life, her self-portraits were painted by mirror, which she had attached to the ceiling above her bed.

Grandma is correct—something about the artist's aloneness and her strength helps me feel better. Her portraits are eerie, gloomy even, but they give me comfort. The darker side behind her face helps me feel at home with my own darkness. Plus, she, like me, was in love with a much older Mexican man. For Frida, it was famous artist Diego Rivera. For me, it is Joaquin, the manager of the big resort at the end of the hotel zone.

A Smoke and a Song

Frida's portraits exude a message of independence, a need to self-know, self-realize, and actualize that into something tangible—her own face. I admire her ability to take her pain and make something beautiful from it. I haven't yet found my thing. I have no art form to speak of. My self-confidence is still intertwined in supporting everybody else. I feel the pain; I just have no way to channel it. I am well adjusted, for the most part, well received by others. I know my elders appreciate my hardworking nature. My sisters call me for advice. My friends compliment me for seeing the humor in things.

But I carry around, hidden within me, a lingering sadness, a self-doubt, and a neglected resentment. I'm always feeling as if something is missing, stolen from me, or forgotten, but unable to place what it is. Like a backpack filled with boulders labeled "Loneliness," "Rejection," and "Lacking" has been sewn to the skin of my shoulders.

Frida's portraits inspire me, and I start to write. I light up one of Grandma Elise's cigarettes and turn to a yellow legal pad where I put down questions I have inside me but am too proud to ask.

Do we ever stop loving those that left us?

When do we get to be the person we are inside, out in the world?

Eighteen Mixtapes

It is the day before spring break, my freshman year at Hampshire College. My buddy Jeremy and I are smoking a bowl in my dorm room. We are in deep, listening to Richie Havens's *Mixed Bag* on record. It's what we do most nights—have a smoke, listen to a song. We chat about the musician's life and the lyrics. We study the album cover, highlight the chords. We sing the chorus.

Jeremy is on my bed, leaning against my tapestry-covered wall that has a Miles Davis *Kind of Blue* poster tacked on it, using my one pillow from home. I am on the floor, cross-legged, my extra-large maroon sweatshirt pulled around my knees and tucked between my ankles and the scratchy, stained carpet. The low lighting from my one lamp is haloing Jeremy's face. He looks like an overgrown six-year-old, his plump cheeks and enthusiastic smile hidden behind his peach fuzz.

Jeremy is also a True Yorker, as we call ourselves, those of us from Brooklyn. He, too, is a straight shooter. He doesn't take it personally when I say exactly what I mean, no filter. I like to argue, to prove my points. With Jeremy, I do not have to edit my speech, sugarcoat my words, or take out my "fucks" like I have to do with the others in our posse who grew up in the suburbs or the Midwest. It is refreshing to have a friend like Jeremy at school.

"I love that you brought your record player," Jeremy says as he gestures for me to pass the bowl.

"Dude, of course I did. Music on tape sounds so whitewashed,"

I say. "Too clean, too overly produced." The smoke exits my mouth and floats toward his frizzy hair, like mist over mountains. "I want to hear the grit, dammit," I say. "I want to feel the angst between the notes."

"Word!" Jeremy says.

We nod in agreement, really getting each other, in that super stoned way, as if it's the most profound thing we've ever heard. He packs another bowl and lights it.

"Wait," I say when the song "Follow" comes on. "Shh, I fucking love this song."

I sprawl across the floor and put my bare feet up on the growing stack of albums beside my bed. On weekends we go on record hunts. Amherst, Massachusetts, is a great town for this. There is Mystery Plane, an old hippie's home collection converted into a record store, and The Infectious Harmony, where they serve you coffee and let you listen to records on headphones before buying. And when we are feeling adventurous, Jeremy and I catch a ride to the Olde Hadley Flea and search for albums through the mile-long rows of antique wheelbarrows and trunks from World War II.

I pull my blue fleece blanket off the bed and drape it over my chest and shoulder. It's April in New England, and it's chilly outside. We have opened the window of my single dorm room to get rid of the smoke, although on my hall, no one seems to mind the smell of weed.

I sing along. My voice is even raspier than Havens's. I close my eyes. It helps me hear the music better. I picture the long floor-to-ceiling shelving unit that separates Mom's office from the living room. She may be a psychotherapist by trade, but she's a music lover by heart.

Before I came to college, she gave me a short stack to take with me to school. "The essentials," she said. "Bach for studying. Joni Mitchell for rainy days." And her favorite album of all times, Aretha Franklin's *Lady Soul*.

"I have *no* idea what kind of music he listens to," I say.

"Who?" Jeremy asks.

"My dad."

Without skipping a beat, Jeremy says, "I don't have any plans for this week. Let's go find out."

I wake up early with a jolt. Going to see him is risky. What if he slams the door in my face? What if he isn't home, or worse yet, what if he doesn't even live in the cabin anymore?

The urge to see him is stronger than the fear. Why not? Why not go find out what kind of music he listens to? There is little to lose. I am an adult, almost nineteen years old; I can handle it. It is time to face him again.

I take a shower and pack an overnight duffel, just in case. Jeremy is still asleep in last night's clothes on my dorm floor. I don't wake him. I write a note: "J—This is something I'm gonna do alone. Catch you on the flip side my friend—S."

I leave the note by his head. I go to the public phone down the hall and call collect. Grandpa Stanley answers. I can easily tell it is him by the amount of time between when the receiver is picked up off its dock and when I hear a voice say, "Hayyyy-llo" at a molasses pace. It is a good ten seconds at least. If it were Grandma Elise, she would be talking into the air before she even got the phone to her face, already in mid-conversation.

Grandpa accepts the call. We catch up for a few minutes about my classes, and I tell him my plans to go see my father. I ask if he has the address. I hear his feet walk across his study, a drawer open and close, and papers being fiddled with. He comes back to the phone, another long pause. He takes a breath in and out, and finally says, "Ready, dear? Ninety-eight Tug Road, Accord, New York."

I scribble it down. We map out my route.

"Does he know you're coming?" Grandpa asks.

"No."

"Practice listening," he says. "He's just a man. And men have limits."

"Okay," I say.

"Remember, his truth may not be your truth or the truth at all, for that matter. Everyone has their side of the truth."

Grandpa's advice makes sense; it always does. We hang up.

I walk to the student hall in the spring rain and hop the Five College shuttle to downtown Amherst. When the bus comes, I find an empty row in the back. I take out my Walkman and put on one of the tapes I have been making all month for my upcoming move abroad. I won't be able to bring my records, so I have been manic about getting all my favorites on mixes. In June, I am off to Mexico. Things are finally ready for Joaquin and me to start a life together. I have already started to DJ the soundtracks that I will later play in the background while I explore unknown parts of me, in a foreign country.

In Joaquin's last letter, he wrote, "She filed for a divorce." His wife saw a *bruja*, or a witch, as the people who I know in Mexico all seem to do. The witch told her that her husband has fallen for a foreigner, a young brunette who wears silver rings on four of her five fingers. She went looking for evidence and found the stack of handwritten letters from me that he kept in a drawer in his office.

He wrote, "I did not deny it, and she was relieved."

Apparently, she, too, wanted out of the marriage. I guess he was right—the juice from that orange had run dry.

His letter said he rented us a little house a couple kilometers inland from the town square and opted for two waist-high speakers instead of a couch. He left his furniture behind when he left her and doesn't have enough money to furnish the whole place.

"But I promise you surround sound, my brown siren."

The bus whips down I-90. This morning's tape is called Upbeat Jams. I need all the help I can get for my mission ahead. Bowie's "Modern Love" kicks off the playlist, followed by a throwback, "Night Fever." I close my eyes. The music pulls me into some half-dream daze, and for much of the ride, I am merely on the bus in body. The rest of me is riding the easy groove of the electric guitar and smooth harmonies of the Bee Gees.

The last time I saw my father was in the city, in winter, in junior high school, years after we stopped going to Accord for the summers. Dad never made it to the closed-casket service at Sherman's Flatbush Memorial Chapel for his father Sam's funeral, but he did ring our buzzer a couple hours after we got back to the loft and asked, "Any of you girls want to get a bite to eat?" I was the only one of my sisters who said yes.

The two of us sat awkwardly side by side at the Hollywood Diner around the corner, eating grilled cheese-and-tomato sandwiches. We picked at a shared order of fries placed on the red-and-silver speckled countertop between us.

"This is good, isn't it?" he asked, stuffing his sandwich into the mouth hole somewhere hidden inside his scraggly beard, looking straight ahead, not at me.

"Yeah, it's yummy."

"I like that they use cheddar and not American cheese," he said.

"Me too," I said and took another bite.

After dinner, he walked me to our building, put his hand on top of my head, and said goodbye. I wanted to ask him if I would see him again, *ever*, but I didn't. We never got past the small talk.

Upstairs, no one asked me how the date was. So I tucked the dinner with Dad away, into my belly, to decompose in digestive juices along with the fries and grilled cheese, as if it hadn't even happened.

I must have dozed off, because next thing I know the bus is pulling into Kingston. I grab my bag and rush off and transfer to the smaller, local bus. Accord is only three stops away, so I find a seat by the front. I flip over the tape, hoping my mood will match the music—pumped, positive, and full of purpose for the pilgrimage. *Yes, perfect*, I think when I hear Prince's "Purple Rain" kick off side B.

I take a taxi from the Kerhonkson Country Store to his property. The road seems shorter than I remember; the forest on either side is less dense this time of year. I notice a handful of new houses on the road.

I stand on his large, rotting deck, which is bigger than the red cabin itself, just as I remember. I look around. There are no chickens in the coop. The fence to his vegetable garden has fallen over. I stare at the woods behind the house. The metal trailer where we used to sleep is still there, but the pathway to the trailer is covered in ferns, fallen branches, and prickly sticks. I feel a chill down my spine.

My last summer in Accord was 1977, the summer of the big New York City blackout, the summer that the Son of Sam was caught, and we no longer had to worry that he might kill Mom while we were upstate. It was just Maddy and me in the metal trailer. Lisa had already stopped going. She left the summer before, after Dad slapped her across the face with the back, and then the front, and the back of his hand again during a fight. Lisa ran into the trailer and packed her duffel. She said, "Fuck this jail!" and stormed out. I followed her to the open wooden gate where she gave me the longest, warmest two-armed hug and said, "If he ever, I mean ever, tries to touch you, I will kill him."

I believed her.

I left the next summer, the morning after the night Dad locked me in the trailer by myself. The night he invited Maddy to sleep inside the cabin with him but did not invite me. I remember the door to the trailer closing in slow motion. What little light that shone from Dad's porch went dark. I went to the door. I tried to open it, but the door was locked. I pulled and pushed and banged but could not get it open. I ran to my mattress with Lammy. I hummed and cried, wishing Maddy would come back, wishing that somehow Lisa would magically appear, spoon me, and rub my back.

But no. No one came to save me. I stayed up all night picturing every scene from every scary movie my sisters made me watch: Damien from *The Omen*, Regan from *The Exorcist*, the shark from *Jaws*. I was so full of fear, waiting for the attack.

The next morning, I walked from the trailer to Kerhonkson all by myself. The man working helped me call Mom collect in the pay phone booth that stood outside the store. I begged her to let me come home early.

"Absolutely not," Mom said. "I have plans. What will you do in the city this month?"

I promised I'd entertain myself. I promised I'd stay out of her hair. "Mom, pleeease!"

She gave in.

That afternoon, Dad drove me to Kerhonkson, and I got onto the bus. Before I did, he said, "Always the unhappy one, aren't you?"

I looked down at my feet, kicked a rock, brought Lammy to my nose to smell her, and jumped on the bus.

I push my bag strap higher onto my shoulder and fold both arms around my chest, bracing myself for the next step. I look to see if the taxi is still there, hoping it is not too late to jump in and tell the driver to drive away as fast as he can. But he is gone.

I cannot summon the courage to knock, and I am too proud to walk away, so I put my hand on the doorknob and wiggle, to see if the door is unlocked, which it is. I open it. There he is, bending over the woodstove, a teakettle in his hand. He is tall, with hunched shoulders. He is much slenderer than I recall. He turns to face me. His gray hair is cut close to his head. He looks good. *Healthier*, I think.

Under his sculpted beard, I can make out his double dimples, which are carved into his left cheek only. I inherited one of those dimples and wore it for much of my early life. Somewhere along the way, the dimple filled in, or fell off my cheek.

Dad seems unsurprised to see me. He puts the kettle on the stove and holds out his arms. "Well, lookee here. Come in, kid."

Grandpa Stanley must have warned him I was coming. But how? I never knew my dad had a phone.

"Peppermint or Earl Grey, which will it be?" he asks after our awkward, loose hello.

"Umm, do you have any coffee?"

"Not sure. Lemme look."

He spends several minutes squatting next to the one cabinet by the stove, removing a box of Raisin Bran, Rice-A-Roni, and several packages of ramen. "Aha!" he says as he holds up a glass jar of instant Chock Full o' Nuts. "How's this?"

I nod.

"I don't have any milk or sugar, but I have local honey fresh from the hive," he says. "Gave up caffeine, dairy, and sugar months ago." He shrugs. "Doctor's orders!"

I take in those last two words, "doctor's orders," and say, "Black with honey is fine."

As the water heats up, he gestures for me to sit down. I put my bag on my lap and look around. It doesn't look that different from when I was little, only a bit cleaner. No couch, just two navy La-Z-Boys in the center of the one room with a crate between the two and a beige, circular rug with a black ring around it. There is a pile of firewood next to the TV and an axe on the floor next to a pair of muddy boots and clean running shoes. Silence fills the rest of the space.

"I've been waiting for this day for years," he says.

I say something small, like "uh-huh" and look around for more clues to tell me who my father is. On the opposite corner of the room, there is a shelf full of albums and a phonograph.

"I actually just came to find out what kind of music you listen to," I say.

"So," he says, "you're gonna go easy on me, huh?"

The first album he puts on is Bob Dylan's self-titled debut album, 1962—track four, the song "Man of Constant Sorrow." We both start singing.

"Oh, you know this song?" He's surprised.

"Yes. Great tune. Mom loves this song."

"We used to listen to this song over and over. Did she tell you that?"

I want to say, "No, she never talks about you. None of us do. You are a family taboo." But I do not. I just shake my head.

The first half of the day goes by quickly, for the most part. I learn he has recently taken up swimming and does laps at the local Y on Monday and Wednesday evenings after work. He has a part-time job with social services placing foster kids with foster families.

He places foster kids with foster families.

"Cool," I say. "That must be rewarding."

He then talks about the case he is working on—a teenager named Jaime who is smarter than a whistle but sadly has been in the system for years and will never be placed in a real home with forever parents because he is too old.

I feel my face get warm. *Why is he talking about some kid I don't even know?* I want to interrupt him and scream, "Forget Jaime! What about us?!" But instead, I ask him to play me more music.

He swaps records—Ry Cooder's "Teardrops Will Fall."

"Does your mother still have all my albums?"

"*Your* albums?"

"Yes. There were hundreds of them. I left them when I came to live here."

That's not all you left. Mom never mentioned the albums were his.

A Smoke and a Song

He continues, "I always regretted leaving them behind."

Did you regret leaving us behind too?

He stacks a few pillows from the chair where he is sitting onto the rug on the floor and sits down to face me.

"You look good, kid. A lot like your mother when I met her."

I do look a lot like my mother. Everyone says so.

"Has your mother ever told you how you got your name?"

"Yeah. I'm named after your mother, Sherry. She died the week I was born."

"There's more to the story than that," he says, laughing. "We wanted to name you Alexandra and call you Sacha for short. But everyone in my family said to name you Sherry because it was the right"—he puts his hands up, gesturing quotations—"Jewish thing to do."

"We weren't close," he says. "I didn't like her very much, or her name. She was always so disapproving."

Ouch, that hurt.

I was told that my namesake had a sharp-as-a-knife wit with, as Mom loved to describe, "Bold boundaries for a woman of her time. Sherry never let anyone walk on her. Much like you."

I always found this view my mother had of me at odds with the way I felt about myself. I always felt more like the family doormat.

My dad continues with his story.

"A few hours after you were born, I was taking a smoke break by the nurse's station when what comes on the radio? Frankie Valli's 'Sherry Baby.' Can you believe it?" He sings, "She-eh-eh-eh-eh-ehrry bayaybee. Sherry baby."

I hate that song. Everyone sings it when they first meet me.

He stops singing. "I took it as a sign and gave in. My mother was still bossing me around, even from the dead." He laughs. "Babette was pissed at me for filling out your birth certificate without her consent." He shrugs. "But I had to."

I never felt much like a Sherry. I have always felt like I got the wrong name. Sacha would have suited me much better.

He gets up to change the record and hands me the cover: Taj Mahal's *Mo' Roots.*

"Good one."

"My daughter has good taste," he says and smiles.

I don't like that he says *my* daughter, as if I am his.

"Come here." He pats the rug on the floor, but I stay on the La-Z-Boy and stare at the album cover. He turns more serious.

"I was drinking a lot back then, kid. Smoking too much pot. Doing drugs. City life was just too much for me. Your mother was too much for me too. Having three kids was too much for me. Anyway, I thought she could do a better job with you girls without me." He pauses. "But I have thought about my daughters every day." He chokes up, and his eyes water. "I do speak to your Grandfather Stanley from time to time. He fills me in on you girls. Anyway," he says, brushing his hands through his hair. "I have something for you."

It's an open shoebox that he lifts from the crate between the two chairs. Inside there is a row of handmade tapes, each labeled with a blue marker: 1970–1971, 1971–1972, all the way to last year, 1988.

"Eighteen mixtapes. One for each year of your life. Number nineteen is still in the making. I have another month to make it before your birthday."

I am surprised he even remembers my birthday. So many May sevenths have passed by with not even a call from my father.

He hands me the box. I look at him; he looks down at his lap and fiddles with a loose thread on his sweatshirt. He ties a knot around the thread and then tears off the extra string, rolls it into a ball, and tosses it across the room.

"I've been making these music mixes since I got my diagnosis, seven months ago."

A Smoke and a Song

I say nothing.

The cancer started as a spot on his throat and has spread to his lungs and stomach. The doctor says it is too far gone for radiation or chemo. There is no treatment for him.

"I'm dying," he says.

It takes me a second to register the bomb he just dropped. *Dying? He is dying. How dare he die! I finally find him, and he tells me he's dying?*

He slides closer to me and reaches into the crate next to the La-Z-Boy. He takes out two more boxes.

"Will you give your sisters these from me?" he asks.

"Sure," I say and set them on my duffel, which is still on my lap.

"Making these tapes has been fun," he says. "Therapeutic. I was going to mail them off to you girls, but now I don't have to." His voice cracks. "I'm glad you came."

I look outside the window and see the sun setting. I am suddenly so damn tired, and my back is sore from sitting so long. I am hungry too. We haven't eaten anything all day. And I have to pee.

On my way to the bathroom, I pause by him. He is on the floor. He looks defeated, slumped over like a schoolkid at the principal's office. I put my hand on his head and say, "It is okay, Warren." His name feels weird in my mouth, like a foreign language. "I get it. We all have our sides of the truth."

I stand in the bathroom looking around. There is no faucet attached to the sink, no plumbing. A jug of water is on the vanity, so I pour some into my hand and quickly splash it onto my face. I look up into the mirror, which is hung on the wall extra high, so I can only get a glimpse of the upper half of my face. I eye gaze with myself for a minute. I look different from how I looked this morning.

I do not need my overnight bag. It is time for me to leave.

Eighteen Mixtapes

There is a 5:41 p.m. bus back to Amherst. Grandpa Stanley and I did our research this morning, just in case. I go back in and ask him for a ride to Kerhonkson.

"Won't you stay the night?" he asks.

I look around. *Where would I sleep?* I gather myself. I ask him. "How come you locked me in the metal trailer all by myself?"

His brows furrow, carving a thick wedge between his eyes. He says, "What are you talking about?"

"My last night here. How come you locked me in, to sleep alone? How come you didn't let me sleep in the cabin with you and Maddy?"

He raises his arms up to stretch, circles them back, and places his hands on the floor behind him. He leans into his arms, like kickstands on a bike, cracks his neck to the left, then to the right, and says, "I never locked you in; of course I didn't."

I look at him again and say, "Yes, yes, you did. I tried to get out, but I was locked in."

"That's crazy. There's no lock on that door. Go see for yourself."

I don't go look. I don't need to. I know it happened. Why would I make that up?

I tell him I have a test to study for. I say I will come back in a month or so. He doesn't know I am on spring break, nor that Hampshire College doesn't even give exams. He doesn't know I am moving to Mexico and visiting him will be impossible. He doesn't know anything about me. This man has not asked even one question about me all day.

"You should give these to them yourself," I say, pointing to the two shoeboxes, the ones for my sisters, that I had set down on the floor next to my bag.

As he puts on his coat, I say, "You were right. Mom did a great job raising us by herself."

He pulls his head back a little. "I would have stayed, you know. If your mother weren't so crazy, I would have stayed."

A Smoke and a Song

I feel gut punched, a sharp tug on the invisible umbilical cord between me and my mother. How dare he talk about my mother like that! She didn't abandon us, like he did, the coward. I want to take a bus straight to the city instead of back to school. I want to hug and apologize to Mom for all the times I sided with my sisters and told her, "You suck!"

He asks again. "Will you come again soon? I don't have a lot of time."

The drive to the bus station is quiet. He pulls his truck in front of the store, and we sit waiting for the bus, just me and this man named Warren, in the silent space of the front seat. No music. No words. No past. No future. Just the hum of the motor. Our farewell song.

He is the man who was supposed to love me the most. I never felt the love.

When the bus pulls up, I walk away. My legs feel loose, as if my femur bones are no longer in my thighs. My feet are heavy as I lift them up the bus stairs. I take the first empty seat I see. As the bus pulls away, I look over my shoulder and watch his truck drive away.

I will not tell my sisters, nor Mom, that I came to see him. There is truth that heals, sure, but there is also truth that hurts, and I do not think they can decipher the difference. I do not want to open a wound for them like seeing him has done for me.

I take out the first tape, labeled 1970–1971, and put it into the Walkman.

At least I got what I went for. Without knowing, I already knew what kind of music my father listened to. I have been listening to his music my whole life. Maybe Mom couldn't bear to talk about the man, but she kept a thread. She wove us to our father through music.

I press PLAY and turn up the volume. I know it well—Jackson 5's hit "I'll Be There." As the bus whips down I-90, I picture the stranger I spent the day with, the man I probably will never see again, and think, *Sure you will. Sure you will.*

Eighteen Mixtapes

ꣿ

Dad died on July Fourth—of all days, America's Independence Day, being the expat, antiestablishment man he was.

I hear the news over a scratchy telephone connection from Cozumel, Mexico, where I am living. Mom offers to pay for my ticket home if I want to join her and my sisters at the funeral. None of them know I saw him just months ago. I say, "Thank you, but I will not make him more alive after being dead to me all these years, just because he died."

"He was your father, Sherry. I just don't want you to have any regrets. It may be a good closure for you."

"I have already let him go, Mom, but thanks. Haven't you taught me that holding on only makes us suffer?"

Ixchel

"**S**hould we have a party?" Joaquin asks as he twirls one of the
longer strands of hair on my head, as he does when I am
being distant, and he tries to tenderize me.

I look up at the sloppily painted Creamsicle-colored ceiling,
tracing the long crack that goes from above our bed to the wide-
open window. I kick the sheet off our damp bodies. It is sticky
hot, probably ninety degrees, even at night. I set the book I am
reading, Isabel Allende's *The House of the Spirits*, on the nightstand
and climb to my side of the bed to put my bare feet on the floor.
Concrete is as close as we get to air-conditioning in our casita.

I turn over my shoulder and say, "A party? Really?"

My twentieth birthday is coming up, and maybe Joaquin
thinks a party will help me feel better. But I don't feel like talking,
not about my birthday and certainly not about a party.

See, when Joaquin throws a party, he throws a party. Cleaning up after one of those all-nighters sounds like way too much
work, especially since we are leaving the next day for our big
travels through the country. We will have to spend all day cook-
ing, because food is the centerpiece of any celebratory gathering
in Mexico, and I haven't yet put in any effort to learn the regional
fare. Plus, who will we invite? Joaquin's people are all nice enough,
but they are his age, with kids and spouses and adulting conversations that I can translate into English but still can't understand.

I love living in Mexico—I do. I love the colorful interchange
of modern and pre-Columbian culture and history, the long

stretch of white sandy beaches, and the spicy food that lingers on my lips for hours after the meal is over. People are humble and have reverence for family and community here. I don't even mind the firecrackers that explode from the Cathedral de Corpus Christi every night to honor one of the zillion saints that Mexicans pray to, as if every one of them has right reason for its own celebration, even if the sound keeps us up all night. But I am not feeling great. And I am homesick. Despite all my attempts to escape the place and people of my past, I miss my friends, my language, my city—even my family.

Joaquin has been planning a trip through the country for months, to show me the "real Mexico" where tourists do not dare to go. He is eager to introduce me to his family, who are spread out between Mexico City and Monterrey. I am jazzed to see his country, to get out of the tourist zone and have an adventure, but I am apprehensive about the family part. We have known each other for four years, and I have been living here for ten months. I still haven't met any of his six older siblings, nor his parents. To them, I am just the young American who broke up his marriage.

"Think about it—a party will be fun." Joaquin pulls me back onto the bed and kisses my forehead. "Twenty *is* a big year; we should celebrate."

"Maybe." I turn off the light. "Let me think about it."

The next morning, I put on my work uniform: a knee-length black skirt, black flats, and a white, short-sleeve button-down pinned with a plastic name tag. I tie my curls in a tight bun and open my makeup bag. I brush one full sweep of mascara onto each of my eyelashes, right eye top and bottom lashes, and then the left. I apply some blush. *Am I supposed to start at the nose and swipe up to my ears, or is it the other way around?*

I look at the mirror and laugh at myself. I dress the part—I try to look older, so I am more believable than an American girl who just wants to play grown-up abroad. But seeing my reflection, I

A Smoke and a Song

think, *Who am I kidding?* I've never worn makeup well. I never learned. Mom didn't wear makeup. Grandma Elise forgot to show me. Whenever I try, I look more like a kid who snuck into her grandmother's makeup dish, or like an untrained drag queen. As they say in Mexico, *"Aun no tienes alas y ya quieres volar."* You don't even have wings yet, and already you want to fly.

I bike to my job at the Island Museum, where I give tours of the history I am still learning about, for college credit. I don't know if I'll ever go back to school, but I'm keeping a line connected to my professors, just in case. My job at the museum is to relay the facts I have read in the archives to busloads of tourists. Facts that some want us to think are true, about the Spanish sailor Hernán Cortés, whose ship landed on the tip of this island in the late 1500s to conquer a fresh land.

Cortés's journal, which sits open on display in a plexiglass box in the entrance of Gallery A, describes how the Spanish were warmly greeted by the indigenous Mayans, and how his descendants turned the island into a bustling port economy of chicle, the sap from the sapodilla tree used to make chewing gum. The gallery walls show glorified images of the new arrivals and natives living peacefully, breaking bread together and exchanging traditions. It's like an olden-day Mexican Thanksgiving, only much more colorful, and people are dining on roasted boars instead of turkeys.

But I am a cultural anthropology major, and I have learned a much different, more brutal, history of colonization—one in which the Spanish waged wars, robbed and raped, spread disease and famine, and enslaved the Mayans. So I make it a point to insert my own bits into the tours, information I have gleaned from conversations with local folks or by studying on my own. I look over my shoulder to make sure my lady boss, Lucinda, who often roams the halls to check on my tours, isn't anywhere in sight, and then I slip in marvels about the Mayans.

"Did you know the Mayans were the most highly advanced astronomers on earth?"

"Mayans were the ones who invented basketball."

"We have the Mayans to thank for chocolate!"

My hope is that when the tourists are dropped off to purchase loom-woven ponchos, stretched-leather *huaraches*, or other handmade souvenirs before they reboard their cruise ship, they might look into the eyes of the surviving Mayan peoples and treat them with the respect they deserve. Fat chance. But I am determined to do my part.

Today, I am not in the mood for truth sharing. I've had a stomach thing going on all week. Montezuma's revenge, or maybe I caught one of those bugs the tourists carry off the cruise ships. Today, I simply paraphrase the tour punch line written on the plaque on the wall at the last stop of the tour.

"By the late fifties, the Mexican government sold most of the chicle farms to the American chewing gum company Wrigley. The infamous Juicy Fruit gum comes from the trees of Cozumel."

I get my usual oohs and aahs from the tourists, as if history is more important once they find out there is an American name attached to it.

Usually, when the island shuts down from noon to four for siesta, I go to the beach. I change out of my uniform, put on my bikini, cutoffs, and a tank top, and bike the five kilometers to play tourist where Joaquin works. I lie on a fancy white beach chair immersed in the calm Caribbean waters and read a book I borrow from the museum library, or listen to one of my many mixtapes, and tan.

Joaquin is the big honcho at the hotel, and being his lady, everyone refers to me as *la mujer del pato,* or "the duck's woman." I don't understand the expression, but the staff treats me like royalty, so I take it in stride. Apparently, calling the boss "duck" is a good thing.

Kinich, the daytime waiter, delivers my colada and club sandwich directly to my beach chair. I feel bad for him, schlepping heavy trays in a long-sleeve shirt and pants in the hot sun and sand every day, sweat dripping into the frozen cocktails. But he is always kind enough to stand by me and chat for a few minutes. He likes that I ask about the traditions his family still practices, those which have survived colonization and tourism. He teaches me expressions in Mayan.

"*In lak'ech*," he says. "I am you."

"*A'la k'en*," I reply. "And I am another you."

Kinich is trying to help me grok the Mayan calendar, a pre-Columbian system of geometrical etchings to tell time.

"See the three stone wheels?" he says in English, pointing to the drawing in my book. "One depicts the lunar cycle, and the other the solar. The large one on the bottom is for the long count of Venus."

I cannot seem to wrap my mind around it; math has never been my strength. One must be a calculus major to even begin to understand what the Mayans learned just by looking at the sky.

But I'm not up for biking or beaching today. I'm going to sneak in a nap in the museum garden display, called *el ejido*. I stop by my office to get the crackers and ginger ale I packed earlier. On my desk is a small package covered with stamps and worn-out corners. I appreciate that Mom stuffs manila envelopes with Swedish Fish and my favorite bagels from the Hollywood Diner, even if her needy letters make me cringe. Mail takes weeks, sometimes months, to get here, so by the time the packages arrive, the bagels are inedible, rock-hard stale. But it's cute that she sends me relics from home anyway.

The ejido is a thatched hut with a hammock and dirt floor next to a sculpture of painted wood made to look like a burning fire and a clay pot with a replica of *elote*, the traditional street food—corn on the cob, roasted in its own husks and sprinkled with cheese and chili pepper salt. Behind the hut, there is a rock replica of what the tourists call "ruins," but the Mayans call "temple." Atop the temple is the aging statue of Ixchel, the Mayan priestess of birth, death, and rebirth.

Ixchel

Ixchel is depicted in a white tunic, for purity, with flowers embroidered around her collar. I read that the orchids and hibiscus symbolize the abundance she offers with the land. She stands barefoot with thirteen toes, thirteen being the sacred number of the Mayans. Her toes are adorned with half-serpent, half-jaguar creatures shaped on silver toe rings. Her hair is black, braided, and wrapped in colorful threads on top of her head in a high pile, representing her connection to the heavens. She has an ardent profile, with a classic Mayan noble nose and lips spread apart so you can see her silver-painted teeth. She holds a rabbit, the animal of fertility, in one hand and a staff with jade snakes in the other.

She reminds me of a less angry, much more beautiful Medusa. She also kind of reminds me of Frida Kahlo.

I have been especially drawn to studying this ancient matriarch since living in Mexico. I feel her pull. Ixchel represents the archetype of a woman I hope I'll someday be: loving, strong, giving, purposeful.

The story goes that Ixchel inhabits three faces: of maiden, of mother, and of crone, and has the power to change face in the presence of her devotees. Back in the day, Mayan women from all parts of the Yucatán Peninsula would pilgrimage to Cozumel on the new and full moons, to bathe in the fertile waters of the underground wells called *cenotes*. She is known as the protectress of women, and if they come to pray to her, she gives back to them.

Maiden Ixchel assists young girls ripening into women. Ixchel gives beauty, menstruation, and productive men to marry. Mother Ixchel fills women's uteruses with healthy babies, the muscular strength needed for childbirth, and plenty of breast milk to feed their offspring. Crone Ixchel promises long, wisdom-filled lives, long enough to grandmother their children's babies.

Ixchel also has a tough-love side. Along with the gifts, Ixchel impregnates women with the lessons they need to learn in this lifetime.

A Smoke and a Song

"When you bow to Ixchel," Kinich the waiter says, "be careful what you ask for because you might just get it."

If you ask Ixchel for unconditional love, all your ideas about what love means will be tested. She will break your heart over and over, teaching you first what love is not. If you ask Ixchel for material abundance, she will first take everything away from you, strip you naked, so that you realize everything you need is already inside. If you ask for understanding, she will make you doubt all that you think you know to be true.

I turn over the package and realize it is not my mom's left-handed scribble. The return address, written in boxy blue marker, reads Accord, NY. There is so much tape on the package it is impossible to tear open with my bare hands. I fondle the outside for what might be inside. I know exactly what it is! It is the nineteenth mixed tape! *But how did it get to me?* He's dead.

I have been listening to the eighteen mixes my father made me all year, especially during my bike rides. My favorite is number sixteen, an anthology of Tom Waits raspy, rugged blues, the perfect soundtrack to the potholed roads of Cozumel.

I go to my office to get scissors. Joaquin is sitting at my desk. He looks pale and even older than his thirty-three years. I give him a kiss.

"Hola, *amor*, you're never going to believe what I got today!" I hold up the package from my dead father.

He puts out his hand, in a "stop talking" motion, and asks me to sit down. "Morena, you're never going to believe what I got today."

I am busy cutting open the edges of the package; I cannot get it open fast enough. But the tone in his voice tells me I better stop and look up at him. He wipes his brow with his forearm, and then holds up a little white piece of paper. My eyes scan from his mouth, across his cheek, over his small shoulder, and all the way up his right arm to his hand.

Ixchel

Oh no.

Results from the blood test I had taken at the doctor's earlier in the week.

Ixchel must have mistaken someone else's prayers for mine.

"Morena," he says, "we're pregnant."

Filling the Gaps

Joaquin tries filling the gaps—the gaps of age difference, language, culture, and the loud silence between two people that takes up the space after *that* kind of choice.

Six months after it, I am still not right. Still nauseous some days, full of guilt, anxiously waiting to menstruate again. I tell myself it was for the best, but I'm not sure I believe myself.

I swap out my feelings with hard discipline. I quit smoking. I train for a 5K, even though my knees buckle and I can barely walk without cramping and my insides feel as if they are falling out. I run anyway, as if running can take it away. I diet, allowing myself three clementines and a handful of carrots during the day, a salad at night with one chicken taco, minus the tortilla. I lose fifteen pounds that I don't really have to lose. On the outside, I look svelte, my ab muscles defined, and my new bikini bottoms are two sizes smaller. But inside, I am punishing myself, removing one pleasure at a time, determined to control what I can control—my body.

I wrote about it only to Grandma Elise. Somehow, I knew she would understand my choice, and my decision to do it here in Mexico instead of coming back to the States.

When her reply arrives, I go to the wild side of the island, the side with no hotels and no sand, the side with roaring waves and jagged limestone. I run to the water's edge to read Grandma's legendary longhand, out loud to the wind.

On the page is a sketch of a curly-haired woman, on a horse, riding toward the moon. Under the sketch:

Filling the Gaps

Darling Sherry,
    Everything here is the same. New York is still New York-ing. I am still Elise-ing and your grandpa, well of course he's Stanley-ing. We are two ships. He scurries into his study overnight, I fall asleep to the tapping of his typewriter, a sound I find rote and irritating. (Oh, you know me, ever hard to please, easy to agitate.) Pen and paper are still my preferred tools.
    I got your letter. Mexico, and the man you are with, were meant to be an experience, not a life. We all look forward to your return.
    Your biggest fan,
    Elise

Joaquin quits his job at the hotel, and I do the same at the museum. We roll up our clothes and leave Cozumel to backpack through central and northern Mexico. We visit his six siblings in five different cities. We eat *queso menonita* up north, *pozole* in the Pacific, *mole* in Oaxaca. We stroll through art museums in the capital and lose our breath up the steps of the Aztec city of Teotihuacan. We take a tiny boat filled with flowers and candied skulls and tombstone-shaped bread as we glide past a colorful coastal cemetery on the Day of the Dead.

We spend an entire week visiting Frida Kahlo's house. I stand in awe, practically pinching myself, inside the infamous cobalt blue home, with its courtyard of ferns, in the Colombia del Carmen neighborhood of Coyocan. I stand beside the very bed, with the mirror above on the ceiling, where the artist herself was pained and painted all those self-portraits. Grandma's book, taken from the window ledge under the fern, thick and misshapen from all the earmarks and extra notes of paper I have written into it, the book that helped shape-shift me out of my head and into my creative heart, is tucked under my armpit. It is the only thing that helps. I am broken, in body and spirit, just like Frida Kahlo.

A Smoke and a Song

After months of travel, I convince Joaquin to come with me to the States. I need medical help. It's now been almost a year since the procedure. Grandma takes me to her doctor. They give me a D&C and put me on hormones. The doctor says my uterus is covered in scar tissue and that my chance of having babies in the future is slim. I put on my big-girl pants and accept my fate. I will never be a mother. And maybe that is best.

I reenroll at Hampshire College to continue my cultural anthropology studies. Joaquin hides out in my dorm room for the semester. He buses tables under the table while I go to class, write papers, and map the rest of my independent study with a committee of professors so I can graduate from Mexico, which I eventually do.

We move to San Cristobal de las Casas. It's a city in the mountains of Chiapas, the most southeastern state of Mexico, next to the border of Guatemala, where Joaquin's mother is from. We live in a month-to-month A-frame on a hillside, with the woods behind us where we forage magic mushrooms and trip in the underground caves of Grutas Del Mamut. We make friends with locals in San Juan Chamula, a village where they speak a Mayan dialect called Tzotzil and where Joaquin starts leading cultural tours to university students.

We even adopt a stray cat, with gray-and-white stripes and two extra toes on his left paw. I name him Marley. After Bob, of course.

Despite our adventures, our trying, our love, Joaquin's caring attention, and my adoration for Mexico, it is impossible to make a real life together after the loss we shared. Every time I look at Joaquin, I think of May 7, 1990—my twentieth birthday, of all days. That was the day he walked me down a dusty dirt path to the back nook off the kitchen of the so-called doctor's house, in the city of Merida, in the country where abortion is still illegal. I laid down on the doctor's kitchen table, naked from the waist down. I do not remember much, except that they did not even have a sheet on the table, and the doctor couldn't get the IV into my arm. He kept slapping the inside of my elbow, laughing, and calling me *obstinada*. Stubborn.

When I woke up, she was gone. In her place, I was left with an infection that had me curled in a ball on the bed for weeks. And still, I am not right. I haven't had a period in almost two years.

I do not know if she was a girl; there is no way to prove it, but I *know*. I daydream daily about her. It is as if the doctor forgot to scalpel out one tiny piece of her, and she has lodged into the back side of my heart. I picture what she would look like. Curlicues and big brown eyes? Maybe she would have inherited one of my father's dimples, or my mother's bold nose. Would she be walking? Eating solids?

I did not give her a name. She deserved a name, but I did not give her one. I made up a couple, during those weeks she was living inside me. Elisabella, after Grandma, with a Mexican twist, or Alejandra, after my middle name. But I could not let myself name her because, if I did, it meant that she was real.

Instead, I keep her a nameless cluster of cells, and I call her regret.

Banna

Banna and I meet on the steps of the Santo Domingo Cathedral in San Cristobal, where she and her five children, all under the age of nine, sell sweet potatoes and handwoven dolls to tourists. I go to the steps to write in my journal during breaks between the English classes that I teach to the upper class at the fancy language school. I sit next to Banna and her kids. Rosa, Banna's middle child, draws with me daily. It leads to a beautiful friendship between Banna and me.

Banna says it will take thirteen days under the hands of Don Miguel to repair the wound in my womb. She is convinced that someone has cast the evil eye on me, and Don Miguel is the one to help. I admire her spiritual beliefs but do not agree with her superstitions. I did this to myself.

"*Los milagros solo suceden cuando estás de rodillas,*" Banna says. (Miracles only happen when we are down on our knees.) "*Es hora de aprender a orar.*" (It's time you learn to pray.)

I tell her I used to pray all the time as a kid, but the praying stopped somewhere along the way. She gives me a list: a dozen eggs, shaved bark off the pine tree, and a bottle of pure, clear liquid, which I have in a used Fanta bottle in my bag.

We stand in the white-and-blue arch of her village church door, taking in the scene. The floor of the church is covered in a carpet of pine needles, spread throughout the main hall. There are no pews. No finished floors. No electricity, either. Pillows of smoke from the amber incense called copal, made from the crystallized sap of the evergreens, makes it hard to breathe at such high altitude.

There are skinny white candles sticking straight up from the ground, some thigh high, others burning inches from the earth. The wax melts in pools and mixes with the pine needles and dirt. Flames from the candles cast shadows of adorned saints that stand upright along the periphery of the room, creating larger-than-life, moving mirages of spirits against the walls and a warm glow onto the stoic faces of their believers.

Catholic saints—Christopher, Augustine, Francis, and the like—are dressed in the uniform of the village: black, handwoven, wool wrap skirts on the bottom half, tied with a thick red sash at the waist, and potato-sack-shaped cloaks on top. Royal blue with bright-colored petals are embroidered across the collar for the women, plain white for the men. If it weren't for the fresh flowers around the crowns, the puffy tasseled bracelets and mirrors tacked onto the bellies of the plastered statues, it would be nearly impossible to decipher between the saints and the people who are here to pray to them.

The men, women, and children are of similar stature—under five feet, broad backs, long arms—regardless of age, it seems. They walk slowly in patterns, zigging and zagging through the church while chanting a rich, low-bellied sound in their native tongue. It is so baritone, it sounds as if it comes from the underworld. Everyone is barefoot, each shoeless step a drumbeat of devotion on the great Mother Earth's back.

Those not walking sit in front of the saints, staring into the mirrors, trancelike. They move only to take a shot of the same clear liquid I have in my bag, called pox. The fermented sugarcane and cedar root, full-proof moonshine, which is distilled by the village priests and sold for six pesos at the door, is believed by the San Juan Chamulans to be a nectar from the gods, plant medicine unifying spirit with her devotees.

We walk through the open prayer space to a small shack

behind the church and wait in line with the others here to see the medicine man. He comes out from behind the doorless threshold and calls the entire group inside. He is small with a welcoming smile. I find it funny that he is wearing a Pittsburgh Steelers T-shirt over his tunic.

He walks over to us. He stands close and leans his forehead to touch Banna's forehead, and after, does the same to me. He and Banna speak in Tzotzil for a minute before he moves on, going from person to person to greet them the same way. She explains to me he asked her to leave and for me to put my bag of offerings in the middle of the space and follow along the best I can. She leaves.

He has us sit in a close circle on the dusty floor, knee to knee. In the center of the circle is an altar with our offerings, plus a live hen, a bowl of cracked eggs with their shells floating on gooey yoke, bushels of red-leafed plants, and a blue wooden cross. He opens the ceremony by calling in the Spirits of the Four Directions—North, South, East, and West—a ritual that I have seen Banna and her children do in the morning market to initiate fortune for their daily sales. Don Miguel walks around the circle behind us, chanting and waving a ceramic pot of burning copal over each of our heads. It is like a slow-motion version of shamanic Duck, Duck, Goose. He stops chanting at the same moment his hand lands on my head, where he pushes down, to help himself step over my left knee. It takes everything in my power not to jump up and start chasing him around the circle.

We carefully pass around the plastic bottle of pox several times, sipping the clear alcohol at each pass. It is sweet with a bitter aftertaste and burns my belly. Don Miguel commands; I look around and imitate the others. He instructs us to open our arms out in a T and place a hand on the back of the heart of those on either side of us. He holds up the hen by her two feet and draws a large cross with her in the air. She wriggles and wrestles with the smoke-filled space, but as soon as Don Miguel chants, she goes limp, her beady eyes staring at me.

Banna

For many hours, Don Miguel and the hen pace the inner circle, eyes closed. He is deep in worship, stopping in front of some of the others, where he dips his hand into the bowl of eggs, and slathers the dripping yolk onto their bodies while they cry and moan and raise their arms up to the adobe roof. I watch him put the hen on the blind woman's eyes, her face and head covered with feathers. She wails and stands up, then falls to the ground, facedown.

After that, things get blurry. I can't feel my body. I am a floating mind in space. Don Miguel kneels in front of me. He places his hand on my low belly and starts to sing. Everything spins and spins; I am Dorothy from *The Wizard of Oz*, taken by some tornado. I pass out.

I return for the ceremony every day for the next eleven days. Each ceremony takes place from morning to night. It is the same ritual daily—the copal, the chanting, the hen, the eggs, the pox, the passing out. The other hours of the night I spend sleeping on a mat Banna makes for me on the floor of her one-room hut or purging into a bucket she leaves outside the door. She and the kids check in from time to time and feed me chayote stew. Rosa rubs my back. But mostly I am left alone.

On the twelfth day, Don Miguel takes us into the main hall of the church to join the other villagers. He walks each of us to the saint where we are to sit for the rest of the day.

I am in front of Santa Ana. Don Miguel tucks an itchy blanket around the back of my hips and places a bottle of pox between me and the saint. I do my best to sit upright, my weakened body aching. "*K'opo*," he says. "Pray."

As I look into the mirror tacked on Santa Ana's belly, the face I see is no longer mine. My nose and mouth have almost disappeared, melted down like candles, dripping off my chin. I take a breath in, exhale, and gulp a shot of pox. I feel the warm potion slide down my spine to my tailbone and then rise like a bolt of lightning until it sits on the back of my skull, directly behind my eyes.

A Smoke and a Song

I look straight ahead, zoom into the left eye of my reflection. The eye in the reflection shape-shifts. It is the eye of a mountain lion, then it becomes my mother's focused eye, and at some point, the eye of an eagle. I feel the pine needles and dirt and the weight of my long curly hair, but I lose sensation of everything in between. I want to close my eyes, float, dissolve, but I lean forward to take another shot of pox, sit back, and refocus.

I see a barely formed eye, that of a newborn mouse or day-old puppy, unable to open yet. Then I hear it, in a little girl's voice, the familiar tune, the one I have been singing all my life. "Hummm hummm hummm."

I don't remember anything else.

At night, I dream I am holding my daughter. She has curly blond hair and puffy lips. We are on the grass in an open field. It is sunny. She is lying on me, her tiny hands cupping my face. I playfully tickle her, and she rolls off my lap onto the grass.

"I'll be back, Mama," she says.

She flips over and rolls down the field. I watch her little body, tangled in a purple dress, covered in grass clippings, rolling and rolling, getting smaller and smaller until she disappears.

I wake up on the thirteenth morning in a pool of blood. I flicker and blink my eyes, noticing every detail of the room with precise clarity, the hues of the corn kernels in the pile on the side of the room, the piercings of sunlight through adobe walls, the wavy hairs on the handmade broom by the door.

Banna walks in with a pail of steaming water and a cloth and washes me. I move my fingers around and make a fist and then release it and reach down to touch the sticky blood. It is still warm.

"*Levantate*," she orders me. "Stand up."

I stand up. My legs are solid, earth strong, like the trunks of the evergreens on the mountains of San Juan Chamula, Mexico.

Banna

From that day onward, on the third Thursday of every month, I menstruate like clockwork. For the first couple of months, I return to the memory of the thirteen-day ceremony with Don Miguel. Over time, that memory sinks into gray matter. It is replaced by my monthly hair appointment to color my roots, which have already started to turn white, at twenty-two years old.

Revolution

Joaquin's cultural-tours company is growing, but in order to make some real money, he needs a van. I go to New York City every three or four months to waitress for a month at a time to make extra cash. I can make more money in one shift than he brings home in weeks.

This trip, I have a gig cocktail waitressing at Mickey Mantle's Restaurant, an upscale sports bar on Central Park South. I go out after work with the trendy waitstaff and bartenders. Tipsy, we Rollerblade down Fifth Avenue, from Central Park all the way to Washington Square. We grab burgers and beers at the Corner Bistro, where I find my name carved in the wooden booth in high school handwriting.

I borrow Mom's high-heeled leather boots, even though they are too tight on me. It feels great to stomp on concrete again. I am back in my element, back in the city. Feeling like me.

I stay longer this trip than I am supposed to. This is partly because I am having fun but mostly because of Lisa. When Lisa went to her final prenatal appointment, just two days before her due date, they could not find a heartbeat. They said that her water must have broken without her knowing, and my sweet little nephew suffocated. His name was Matthew.

Lisa is beyond devastated. Destroyed. She goes to work in Manhattan and makes the moves of life, but inside she is dead, like he is. I take the Q out to Bay Ridge, Brooklyn, on nights I'm not waitressing, to cheer her up. Those nights are long and exhausting. She cries and says, "All I ever wanted is to be a mother."

I rub her back like she used to do for me and say, "You are still a mother, Li."

Mom barely acknowledges Lisa's loss. When I talk to her about Matthew, she says, "It's terrible, but Lisa has to move on." I think Mom is secretly relieved, given that Lisa would have been a single mother.

I argue with Mom, tell her she needs to be more empathetic. Although Lisa's loss is worse than mine was because it was not her choice, I have my own version of a dead baby. I feel Lisa's pain in my own body. I'm just not allowed to cry about it.

I go out to Brooklyn to see Lisa and this time Mom tags along. That is a mistake. Instead of consoling Lisa, Mom talks about her patients, as if that is appropriate under any circumstance. When Lisa starts crying, Mom says the worst thing she could say. "Stop it, Lisa. You can have another baby someday when the situation is right."

I hear Lisa take a gasp of air in and hold her breath.

Oh shit, here it comes.

Lisa starts to rage. "You're loveless!" And rage. "You're not a mother!" Lisa is screaming. "You can't even mourn your own grandchild? Do you even have a heart in your chest? Get out!"

We leave. Mom cries to me the entire subway ride home.

When I get back to Mexico, Joaquin and my relationship is like a framed photograph left out in the sun: worn and faded, only the edges remaining sharp. We start to fight all the time. He accuses me of being cold, and I call him too needy, "especially for a man of your age."

Our fights are nothing compared to the war that starts on New Year's Day. We wake up to find out our town has been seized by bandana-clad, machine-gun-carrying revolutionaries protesting the passing of the North American Free Trade Agreement, a trilateral trade bloc signed by Canada, the United States, and Mexico, enacted the first of the year, 1994. The Zapatista National Liberation Army consists of a couple hundred men, mostly indigenous, who stand post around the town square. City Hall is on fire, and boxes and papers are being chucked out the windows. We civilians huddle in the town square as the Zapatistas take orders from Comandante Marcos, their leader. We can see behind the ski mask eyeholes that he is light-skinned, and by the way he speaks through the megaphone, clearly very educated.

By midday of the takeover, we realize that the machine guns are made of plastic or are hand-carved sticks and that the "men" are young boys. I spot Banna's eldest, Mario, in the archway of a hotel. He sees me too. I wave. He does not wave back. There is fear in his prepubescent eyes, but he proudly stands with both of his hands behind his back, his spine as upright as the cornstalks that he and his male siblings tend outside their adobe hut.

The Zapatistas do not stand a chance against the array of army tanks that roll in later in the day, crushing the cobblestone streets into pebbles. Soldiers jump out of their tanks with real machine guns that they fire up into the sky and command, *"A la casa!"* (Go home!) And do not come out until instructed.

We barely leave our house for a month. There are constant gunshots in the distance. The stay-at-home curfew starts before dark. The government has closed off the borders of the city. No one is allowed in. Those of us inside the city are not allowed out. We have no idea how long this revolution will last, or if we'll get out of here alive. Joaquin clings. I let my edge soften, because, well, fear can make us forget.

Six weeks into the revolution, a *New York Times* reporter who I have befriended knocks on our door. She tells me they've opened the borders for media vehicles. "We're leaving in an hour if you want to come."

Revolution

I quickly throw some things in a suitcase and say, "I have to go—you understand, don't you?"

Joaquin doesn't understand. "Your life is here, with me."

"My life is also there."

He lifts a section of my hair and brings it to his nose, takes a whiff. "Come back to me, Morena."

I hug him tightly and say, "I will."

I kiss him and climb into the van of reporters and American travelers, and I go. I leave my house on the hill. I leave speaking Spanish and immersing myself in all things Mexico. I leave my friend Banna and her children. I leave Marley the cat. I leave Joaquin, the man I was in love with since I was fifteen. I leave the remnants of our what-if baby girl.

The van drives down a long winding road, past the military checkpoints and the small fires that burn outside the adobe shacks by the side of the road. At the airport, I board a plane: Tuxtla Gutierrez, Chiapas, for Mexico City. And then another one: Mexico City for JFK.

Truth is, I had been plotting my exit way before the revolution. I had already outgrown my Mexican life and the man that came with it. Grandma was right all those years ago. Mexico was meant to be an experience, not a life. It is time for me to go home.

Toward the Void

G randma calls this one *Toward the Void*. It is the signature piece at her exhibit, the image on the opening invite card. It is a big deal—her own solo show. We all get dressed and go to the reception. Maddy is home from her cross-country travels. Lisa is pregnant again, and so there is another reason for everyone to celebrate, even if the father of the baby is not in the picture. I even bring my "special friend" Rob as my date—the bartender I met last fall while waitressing at Mickey Mantle's.

The opening is packed, with artsy types and aspiring writers, most of them only pretending to admire Grandma Elise's paintings while they inch their way closer to exchange some words and wine with Grandpa Stanley. Grandma doesn't seem to notice. But then again, maybe she is just used to it.

Toward the Void hangs in the center of the gallery, on a wall all by itself. The painting looks familiar, a lot like the drawing from Grandma's letter, the sketch of me on a horse riding toward the moon—living my rite of passage in real time. But seeing the sketch hit the large canvas and come alive with color, it is obvious that it is of my mother. On the woman's head, seen from the back, there's a puff of frizzy white locks, just like my mother's head of hair. She's riding a black horse, toward a yin-yang moon without the dots. The two are placed in a mangled meadow of rusty red and deep yellow grasses with a large sundial tipped on its side, and a red barn in the distance.

Toward the Void

To my knowledge, *Toward the Void* is the only painting Grandma Elise made of my mother.

As Mom and I stand in front of the painting, we overhear two women discussing it.

"Solitude, but not peaceful," one woman says, sipping her white wine.

The other woman chimes in. "Ominous. It renders a sense of despair."

I ask Mom what she thinks of the painting.

"Well, it is not flattering, that's for sure," she says, lifting her shoulders. "But fitting of our relationship."

I know what Mom is referring to. I, too, read Grandma's autobiographical pages that she wrote to accompany the show. Twenty-plus pages of her life story, and *not one* mention that she has a daughter. Grandma does not acknowledge my mom is even there at the opening. She walks past her as if she is a stranger. And yet the painting she made of her daughter stands front and center. It doesn't add up.

"My mother cast me off. Literally," Mom says and then points to the painting and sighs. "And apparently figuratively too."

Mom smiles a fake smile and looks away. Something across the room catches her eye, and she gestures for me to look. Grandma is next to my date, the two of them smiling. Her hand is on Rob's shoulder, the flowy material of her bright green dress and her many bracelets hanging in space like a suspension bridge between them. He is holding both of their drinks in one hand.

Mom rolls her eyes. "Better watch out, she's flirting with him."

It makes me laugh. My grandma is a big flirt.

"I know everyone thinks she is charming," Mom says and shrugs. "But to me, she has always been so bitter, so absent of affection."

A Smoke and a Song

When the exhibit comes down, Grandma Elise gives Mom the painting.

"For the loft," she says, "so it can continue to get some sunlight."

Mom takes down her framed photographs of her trip to Senegal and hangs *Toward the Void* on the wall directly in front of her bed. I wonder why, of all the artwork she owns, she hangs that painting there, in her bedroom, a place so intimate.

"Isn't it a bit of a slap in the face?" I ask.

"Well, it inspires me to get up every morning and prove that I belong," Mom says. My mother does operate as if she has something to prove. She lives as if it is her duty to do as much as humanly possible in one day. She wakes up before sunrise and goes to bed later than I do, and I am in my twenties. She fills her days with African dance classes, aerobics, a second master's degree in ethnomusicology, trips abroad, her patients, and coffee dates with whatever friend group she happens to be buzzing through at the time. As Lisa says, "That bitch can run circles around all three of us."

Sure, it is admirable to see a woman of her age remain so active and full of life. Everyone compliments her for it. But it drives Lisa, Maddy, and me bananas.

Lisa says, "Mom, take a chill pill. You're almost a grandma now."

Maddy says, "Seriously, Mom! It's crazy!"

I chime in and say, "I'm dizzy just looking at you."

"Leave me alone!" Mom says. "Stop judging me, girls!"

It makes me sad that Mom cannot slow down long enough to enjoy any of her activities. She acts as if her bones will fall into a pile on the floor if they aren't wrapped in overly engaged muscle. It is as if she will literally disappear "toward the void" if she dares slow down, even for a moment.

Toward the Void

I read once that busyness is a coping response—a strategy some people take on to disassociate from whatever pain they are avoiding inside. It makes me curious. What is my mother always running from?

Jumping Off Points

R ob and I are in Grandma Elise's studio, photographing her artwork for the slideshow part of my master's thesis at New York University's Museum Studies Program, where I have been studying for two years. I am curating a mock retrospective of Grandma's artwork for my final presentation. I am calling it *Jumping Off Points*, Grandma's expression for good poetry.

I am explaining to Rob that Grandma says a well-written poem is like a diving board, some good *oomph* to push off, and spring to plunge you deep under the waters of your consciousness. She says a poorly versed poem is like trying to dive off a floating rowboat—clumsy and shallow.

Rob is not really getting what I am explaining. He is a simple guy, uncomplicated, not artsy, not a college grad. But it doesn't matter. He lets me indulge in my headiness, even if he does not always follow.

He props up one of Grandma Elise's paintings on the easel we have set up under the track lights. His white T-shirt lifts off his beige corduroys just enough to get a glimpse of his lower abs contracting in a perfect V at the waistline. *Damn, he's hot*, I think, *and he's all mine*. I bend down to bite his low belly. I can't help myself. Despite my claims to just have fun when we first met, we have been hanging out for over two years, and I am in love.

"You said she was a poet first and then got into painting these?" he asks, referring to the canvases.

"Yes, and in between she had a decade or so of making these

plexiglass sculptures," I say, pointing over to the side of the room where I put her large standing books and cylindrical human-sized jars.

"I think those are my favorites," Rob says.

"Mine, too, but she stopped making them when she said they got too pretty."

It feels great to breathe life into the studio again, to put Grandma's art under light after sitting in the dark for so long.

Rob has spent time with my grandparents—at her art show, at his readings, and at holiday dinners—but I haven't yet shared with him the studio, this long room on the fourth-floor walk-up, with sculptures scattered across the creaky old wood floors, canvases of all sizes eating up the brick walls, and little glass jars with dried-up paint on every tabletop. All of this is new to him. So are the drawers of acrylic tubes squeezed and pinched with Grandma's arthritic hands.

I have not yet shown him the place where I learned as a kid to see with my whole soul and listen with every pore that covers my skin, the one place where I always seemed to breathe best. And being here, with him, is like bringing the best two parts of my life together.

"It makes me sad that she no longer comes to the studio to paint," I say. "Her essence has faded from these walls."

"I bet, but it's cool that she's writing poetry again," he says. "Kind of a full circle for her."

I suppose, yes. I haven't thought about it this way. I spend more time feeling melancholy about her not using the studio that I haven't acknowledged how well my grandmother is adapting to her limitations, as old people do when they must.

I have everything organized in three piles, each one for her three creative periods, which I am highlighting in the retrospective: Poems. Plexiglass. Paintings. Each period also coordinates with her three husbands: Arnold, Nanno, and Stanley.

My grandmother started writing poetry to escape her boring

suburban life in Rochester, New York, with Arnold, her first husband, my mother's birth father, a Harvard-educated lawyer who never practiced law. He sold men's hair products and ran the books for a couple of small businesses. He even grew and roasted peanuts in their backyard. She was miserable then. She called that her duplicitous period.

"She promised herself that when she had a solid collection of twenty-five poems, she'd leave Arnold, and Rochester, and go to New York City, where she was meant to be," I say to Rob. "It took her almost a decade, but she did it. She moved to the city when Mom was nine."

"I cannot imagine your grandma living anywhere else but NYC," Rob says. "She's as New York as Lady Liberty herself."

"After Arnold, she met Nanno, an abstract expressionist, at the Bleeker Street Bar. She used to go there to listen to William S. Burroughs, Allen Ginsberg, and Kerouac read poetry. Before they were legends."

Rob smiles. "Cool."

I don't think Rob has heard of these poets. Stanley is most likely the only one he knows.

"I don't know much about that time with Nanno, except that they traveled out to Big Sur, and that was when Grandma Elise put down the pen and picked up plexiglass. She said that writing was too two-dimensional, and life with Nanno was not."

"How long were they together?" Rob asks.

"Seven or eight years. I'll have to fact-check that," I say, making a note on a Post-it.

I continue, "She met and married Stanley after Nanno left. That's when she started painting on canvas. She used to say that life with Stanley was quiet, and she needed a new surface to paint on. The canvas was softer—it had more give, just like Stanley."

Rob picks up one of Grandpa Stanley's books, *Passing Through*, and studies the back sleeve. There is a black-and-white headshot of him, wide-eyed, big-eared, mustached, in a flannel shirt.

"Stanley's just a flat-out cool dude, such style, such swag," Rob says, taking a swig of his beer. He throws his feet up on the desk, Converse Chuck Taylor All-Star high-tops, scrambling one of my research piles. I give him a look.

"Relax, Berry," he says in his laid-back tone. "It's all good."

"Grandma thinks my project is silly," I say.

When I told Grandma I was doing the retrospective, she told me, go forward, not back. She asked, "Why would your class-mates be interested in an old, cracked tune like me? When the clock looms over us, none of it means a thing. All we are left with are cramped knuckles and too many regrets."

Rob places a palm on my neck, slides his hand up the back of my scalp and scratches my head, lifting my curls up off my shoulders. With his other hand, he sections off a lock, the part that is extra curly, shorter than the rest of my hair, and loops his finger around a spiral.

"I bet deep down she appreciates the validation," he says, swig-ging his beer again. I open the window. It is a breezy, late spring evening, that multiple-personality season in New York where you can wear tank tops during the day but step over frozen piles of garbage that are still trapped under hardened snow at night. I open my bag for my Marlboros and light a smoke. I look at Rob.

Rob has the perfect acting face, chiseled jaw, green eyes, blond hair, and a ski-slope nose. No matter what he wears, he makes it look sexy. He can rock Kurt Cobain grunge in a flannel one minute or give us Tom Cruise sleek in a black blazer and dark sunglasses the next, and later be classic, young Paul Newman Western in fitted jeans and work boots.

And doesn't he know it. Never have I known a man with so many face creams and such a large mirror. Never have I known a man who takes longer to get ready than I do. Rob has a com-mercial agent and is auditioning but hasn't booked anything yet. In the meantime, he makes a fortune winking at wealthy women while pouring white wine at the Round Bar at the Royalton Hotel.

A Smoke and a Song

I daydream about what life will be like when he gets famous, my arm looped through his at the Emmys, winters in our Los Angeles home, warm seasons on Martha's Vineyard, where we spent last summer with my sister Maddy. Despite having all As, on a full scholarship with a monthly stipend, on a clear career path in the arts, I secretly yearn for a life where I do not have to work so hard at upholding my importance.

Rob turns with a smirk. "For real, Stanley didn't know Elise smoked?"

"For real," I answer, exhaling out the window.

I flick the butt onto the street and close the window, open my bag, and start to pack up the materials, so I can take them to Kinko's and make copies to back up my thesis. "Ready to bounce?"

Rob and I walk down the stairs and onto Fifteenth Street.

"Should we stop by and say hello to your mother, since we are right here?"

"No, not tonight. I'm not in the mood."

I have been distancing myself from my family. When Mom invites us over, I say I am too busy. I have Rob, my studies, two internships, plus managing a restaurant as my excuse. But the truth is, I am just tired of being who I have always been to Mom and to my sisters. I no longer want to be the family's sacrificial Lammy. And family members don't like it when you change your role on them. Old family dynamics stick to us like superglue, impossible to chisel apart. Especially when your connection has been based on some shared suffering. When me, Mom, and my sisters are together, the four of us end up raging like it's 1980. It is easier to make our interactions sparse.

Whenever I talk about my family, Rob says, "Don't be so hard on them. Take out the good parts, leave the rest."

He loves that I come from feisty women and artsy elders. "Children and tuna-macaroni casseroles were my family's only masterpieces," he jokes.

Rob is great at taking the good parts of his childhood growing up in a trailer park in Southern California, and even better at forgetting the not-so-good parts. His mother, Karen, got pregnant at fifteen, and by the time he was born, his biological father was already gone, sent away to finish high school. Tim, the man who raised him, came along fresh out of jail at nineteen, when Rob was just five months old. He met Karen and her baby boy and picked up from there. He became a hardworking car mechanic who drove a tow truck at night to make extra cash; he did what he had to do for his family.

"Art and education were not part of my upbringing," Rob says, "but loving and keeping it real was."

Rob has told me stories about how his uncles would pile in the back of his dad's pickup, honk the horn, and hoot and holler while drinking beers at his Little League games. "Man, that was embarrassing," he said. "But it's how they loved. They were teenagers."

Rob's childhood stories sound dreamy. I would have paid big money for a family like his.

As we walk past the loft, Rob asks me a question: "What was it like for your mother to grow up with Elise the artist as her mother?"

"I don't know." I look at Rob, then to the giant blue-and-yellow painted mural of a ten-speed above the bike shop on the corner. "I've never really asked."

What was life like for my mom before we came along? I know she is an only child. I know when Stanley came into the picture, he embraced her as his own daughter. And I know she and Grandma are strained—that is obvious. But that is about it.

Somewhere along the way, I separated my mom and my grandma, set them apart as two distinct women, rather than a mother and daughter who have almost six decades of history together. I guess I only saw them in relation to myself.

"Why don't you interview her?" Rob says. "Doing the retrospective gives you the perfect excuse."

Herstory

Mom and I sit over a cup of hot coffee. Milk and a little honey for me, black for her. I press PLAY on my recorder.

"What was it like . . . growing up with Elise as your mother?"

"Well, you know your grandmother—she is a rare breed."

I give her a "yep, I know" smile.

Mom sits silent for a while, reflecting. The skin around her lips purses tight, lines stretching halfway across her cheeks.

"She certainly didn't win any mother of the year awards." She checks herself and takes a breath and sits up taller, fixes her shirt, leans back into her stool. "How much do you want to know?"

I shrug. "As much as you want to tell."

She sips her coffee, both hands cupping her favorite supersized elephant mug. "Elise was the child in our trio."

Mom talks about their backyard in Rochester, where they had a red barn and a rope swing. Mom would beg for a younger sibling to play with but never got one. "Childhood was lonely; instead of a younger sister or brother, I got her. Elise would come out to the swing and tell me to get off, insisting it was her turn." She tells me how her father, Arnold, swindled a membership at the local country club, where they played tennis, even though they couldn't afford it.

"Elise was very competitive and a great tennis player," Mom says. "But she refused to wear tennis attire, and they eventually made us leave the club."

I laugh, picturing Grandma playing tennis in her layers of multipatterned, long dresses.

"When I was very young, Elise and I painted together. She called them E and B masterpieces and hung them on the refrigerator."

I think about the times Grandma invited me to add a dot or smudge onto her paintings. A tiny ping of jealousy hits the center of my chest. But at the same time, I am glad to know our collaborative masterpieces were part of a lineage, and that my mother had special Grandma Elise moments too.

"It annoyed my father, all those pages tacked to the fridge door. Once, when they were fighting, he ripped them off and threw them in the trash." Mom frowns. "Elise couldn't handle anger, and he was an angry man. She hated life in Rochester; she hated him. He was a lot to hate."

This is the first time I've ever heard my mother talk about her father.

"His words were like arrows. Piercing and mean. He berated her in front of me. And mocked me in front of her. He started the divide between Elise and me." She pauses, then continues. "When they would fight, which was often, she'd hide in her room to write."

She takes a sip of coffee. "By the time I was five or six, all my nights after dinner were motherless. He made me his surrogate wife."

Is she saying what I think she is saying?

"His hugs were always too tight. As if he could squeeze some Elise out from me. But she just hid. She left me with the wolf."

I do not like the story she is sharing, not one bit. My skin feels itchy. I regret interviewing her for the retrospective. I shut off the tape recorder.

"I thought things would get better when we moved to the city, but things only got weirder," Mom says. "She dragged me around like an accessory, to readings and parties. She never introduced me as her daughter, always as her companion Babetty. God, I hated that name."

I have heard Grandma call her that many times. I always thought it was endearing, Babetty, a sign of affection.

"When Elise met Nanno, we moved to a small apartment on Christopher Street with no privacy. Nanno painted in the living room where I did my schoolwork. He would sometimes paint me, and Elise would critique his portraits. She'd say that he made my hair too straight or that my nose was bigger in real life. That I was much fatter than he painted me. She'd say, 'Stick to abstract. Realism isn't your forte.'"

Mom stands up and goes to the refrigerator, sifts around, and then closes the door. She puts the water pitcher under the faucet, fills it up, and starts watering the plants. "I studied extra and graduated high school two years early. Vassar College was my ticket out," she says. "At least that was what I thought."

I look at her and the plants. I want to climb in and hum.

"Anyway, none of this is relevant to your retrospective. Let's talk about her art."

I have already heard more than I want to hear. But I have opened Pandora's box; it is too late. I have no other choice.

"No, it is okay," I say. "What happened when you went to Vassar?"

"She disappeared," Mom says. "Happy to have me gone so she could live the artist's life. But Nanno would show up at my dorm room. I was proud to have him meet my friends. He was so handsome. He'd take me out to lunch and talk to me about his dying romance with Elise. He'd say she was too aloof. That all she cared about was making art."

I drift out of body and to her. Grandma is singing "Love Me or Leave Me." She's tiptoeing around her apartment, sneaking a hand into the candy jar. She's kissing my cheek with her gooey lips.

I hear Mom say, "That's where it happened."

I must have missed something big. "Where was what that happened?"

Mom tips the spout of the pitcher from one plant to the next, shaking. She grips the pitcher with both hands.

"That's where Nanno had sex with me."

"Oh God." I missed the details, but I don't inquire. No one wants to hear this about their mother.

"I was confused, guilty, young, and I got lured. I held our secret for over a year. When I finally told her, all your grandmother said was that it was okay because they were not getting along anyway and not to come home for break. And then something like, 'And put on a longer skirt, will you? Look at you. You're wearing half a dress. And you don't have legs for half a dress.'"

Mom sits down again, this time on the stool next to me. I imagine her as a teen, with her exposed collarbone, irresistible to an older man. I am mad for her, and I am mad at her. How could she let that happen?

"When it all came out, Nanno left my mother and me without a word or backward glance."

I'm doing my best to be here, with Mom. But I want to run, stick rocks in my ears, and pretend I have not heard any of this. I want to be one of the characters in those Choose Your Own Adventure books we used to read when we were kids. *Turn to page seventy-five if you want to go back to the beginning of this story, or page one hundred if you want her to keep talking.*

But you can't unhear a story like this one, no matter how hard you try. "Oh, Mom. I didn't know."

Her mother's instinct kicks in. "I've come a long way since then." She puts a hand on my shoulder. "It's fine. I'm fine, Snaps."

Mom and I spend the afternoon together, sitting on the couch with coffee. She tells me more. Following her confession to her mother about the rape, Mom grew increasingly anxious and hostile, dissociated and delusional. Feeling fat and afraid of being too feminine, she ate handfuls of amphetamines and drank mustard water to make herself throw up. A few months later, she tried to kill herself. The college nurse called Grandma Elise for five whole days before she came to get Mom. When she finally came, she showed up at the infirmary with her new boyfriend, Stanley.

"She had no idea what to do with me," Mom says. "Stanley convinced her to bring me to High Point Hospital, where his friend worked."

My mother spent four years in and out of several mental institutions, under strict supervision due to ongoing suicidal attempts. She was diagnosed with schizophrenia, manic depression, and affective dissociative disorder. She was treated with shock treatments and insulin coma therapy, a technique they used then, but one that has since become illegal.

"When Elise and Stanley visited, Elise would spend all her time with my doctor. I think she cared more about convincing him she was not a bad mother than being with me. Stanley and I would sit on the garden bench and talk." She pauses. "If it weren't for your grandfather, I don't think I would have made it out alive."

Grandpa Stanley and Mom have always been bonded. It was Stanley who put out extra olives, Mom's favorite, on holidays, or snuck Mom envelopes and said, "A little something to help you and the girls."

I turn to Mom and ask, "Do Lisa or Maddy know any of this?"

Mom shakes her head.

"Will you ever tell them?"

"Probably not," she says.

I do not want to be the only daughter to know my mother's story. Her story is too heavy for me to carry alone. And yet, I always knew this story, or that there was some story. It's why I instinctively felt the need to check in on or rescue her. Now that

Herstory

I know her story, I am glad I did. She is my mother, and nothing compares to the love a child has for her mother. Nothing.

Except for the love that a child has for her grandmother.

As Mom reveals all the cracks in her foundation, my own earth quakes. All the rose-painted walls I built around the Grandma Elise from my story begin to crumble. She has been the world to me—the woman who saved me and paved paths for me. She is the woman who handed me a set of keys, and let me breathe, and told me stories. And gave me art.

How can I possibly stand up in front of my professors and classmates and present her art? I have more questions, ones that I'll probably never ask.

Why did Grandma choose me to coo over and not my sisters? Am I just a pawn in some mixed-up mother-daughter chess game?

"I'm sorry," Mom says. "I know you and your grandmother are close. I haven't wanted to get in the way of that."

"How can you still love her?" I ask.

"We just do. We love anyway. It is not what happened to us, but what we choose to do with it that matters the most. It helps to see the way she is with you. She adores you, Sherry; let that be what you remember. What you heard today is my story—don't make it yours. She is the only mother I have. Family is family. We forgive. We let things go. Now I use my past to help other survivors. This is what we do to heal. We find a way to use our hardships and give it back."

I sit with her answer for some time. It helps. I have a new, deep respect for my mother. *My mother is a super woman!* I must find a place to put all these new pieces to my family puzzle, compartmentalize them. Take out the good parts, so I can put those back in the box. Let the other ones drop to the floor to sweep under a forgive-and-forget rug. She is the only grandmother I have. Despite what I now know, my love for her is unwavering. I can't give up on her. Maybe she did the best she could with what she was working with. She never had a mother to teach her how to mother. And back then, women didn't have a lot of support for these things. She is human, and humans make mistakes. Hell, look what I did to my daughter.

Maybe, by loving me, Grandma has been able to right her wrongs of motherhood—by "grandmothering" the girl who wears her daughter's face.

And I do it. In early May, I stand up in front of a committee of professors and my classmates, the projector displaying image after image, and speak of my magnificent Grandma Elise's art. And I get a certificate, with my name, the purple New York University torch emblem, and the words "Masters of Art" printed on it.

After the presentation, we all celebrate together—Rob, Mom, Grandma, Grandpa, and me, over a glass of giggle water, Grandma Elise's affectionate name for champagne, at their apartment. We sit around the living room table and hold up our flutes of Veuve for the cheers.

Mom says, "You did it, Snaps!"

Grandma Elise says, "To you, darling!"

And I think, if they can sit and celebrate together, my mother and my grandmother—accepting their herstory, smiling, drinking champagne, forgiving, celebrating me—then the least I can do, even if it is just for one night, is kick back and enjoy the moment.

Fool's Gold

"Use your key," Grandma says. "Robert can have mine."

She has the keys in a little white box with a handwritten label that says, "September 12, 1998," along with a pair of cuff links for Rob and a dress pin for me. Both are made of fool's gold—Grandma's favorite stone. Grandma takes out the pin, a teardrop-shaped clump, raw and sparkling, set in a copper backing. She unclasps it.

"Oh, Sherry. I'm pleased for you. Our Rober-to is the loveliest of men." She pins it to my ivory lace shoulder strap. "But are you sure you want to take his name?"

I pull up on the straps, now weighted by the pin, realign my slip with the lace, and drop the material over the back of my shoulders.

"Yes, I am sure."

I can't wait to be a Sidoti. I am done carrying around the last name of a man who never cared enough about his daughters to check in from time to time. Plus, Tim went through the trouble to legally adopt Rob at twenty-eight years old so that I can take the family name.

"Sherry Sidoti has a great ring to it, doesn't it?"

Grandma undoes the pin, takes it off the strap, and repins it lower, down by my heart. "Much better." She turns me around. She smooths out the extra fabric that had pooled on my upper back and then spins me back to face her.

"You have to make sure not to lose yourself in him. Most

days, it'll be just you and you. You'll need to lean back onto something that is all yours."

"Thank you, Grandma," I say, "for the pin. For the keys to the studio. For your advice."

I give her a hug. I tower over her. She can barely stand up alone without collapsing her entire body into mine.

I go upstairs to the second-floor bedroom. We are at Mom's country house in the Berkshires. It's a small white clapboard that has a running brook behind it. She bought the house a few years ago, something she had wanted to do ever since losing the two acres she shared with my father in Accord.

The second-floor room is a mess, with wet towels and clothes all over the floor, half mimosas on every dresser and end table, coffee cups, too, and a bottle of giggle water sweating on the bathroom vanity. My bridesmaids—Lisa; Maddy, who is nine months pregnant; and my three best friends—put on the finishing touches. Makeup, hair, shoes. Each is dolled up in different shades of purple. Mom looks stunning in her pale violet, satin maid of honor dress and matching shoes.

Lisa, teary, pins Mom's curls up in a loose bun. "I can't believe my Baby Bug Out is fucking getting married!"

"To Sherry and Rob." Mom lifts her glass. "And to true love! It does exist after all!"

Everyone in the room cheers and makes their way downstairs. The ceremony is about to begin.

"Have a peek out there," Mom says, before leaving. "Look out the window. Take it in, Snaps. Today is your day."

I look out to the wide lawn and the backyard scene. There is a beautiful afternoon light, warm sun on the mums that line the aisle, casting an early-autumn, orange hue on the cornstalks we chopped down from the field across the road and stuck inside the planters. The mason jars of wildflowers have opened themselves in fans of colorful arrangements against the off-white linen tablecloths. Framed photos of Rob and me are on the cake table next to a two-tiered, white buttercream cake with nasturtiums in a ring around the upper layer. All our friends are here, sipping on cocktails. The actors, models, and writers who we have met working in restaurants over the past five years and the old-school Crew are all dressed to the nines. The men of Rob's family are parking cars. The women are helping the caterers set up tables. I see my nephew Justin, Lisa's boy and our ring bearer, three years old in a three-piece black suit and tie, swinging in the hammock with my cousin Ariana, our flower girl.

Grandpa Stanley is waiting for me by the front door. Before he walks me down the aisle, his purple button-down matching my bouquet of lavender, violets, and irises, he stops and asks, "How is your heart today, my dear?"

I loop my arm through his and say, "Couldn't be better."

The ceremony is short and sweet. The justice of the peace asks everyone for a moment of quiet to hold our love in the light and to remember to do the same if Rob and I ever find ourselves in a difficult patch, which we inevitably will.

"They will need all of you around them, just as you're doing today," she says.

Rob cannot hold back his emotion. He is barely able to say his vows. Every few minutes he squats down and places his hands on his knees and takes a gasp of air and comes up and says, "No, I'm good; I'm not crying. I just have something in my eye."

Our people whistle and clap and hold his emotion in a safe container, saying things like, "You got this, Bobby boy!" It is sweet, and it makes me steady, and it makes me smile. I am full of joy.

Grandpa Stanley closes out the ceremony by reading a stanza from one of his poems, "Touch Me," which makes even our toughest-skinned New York City people cry.

> What makes the engine go?
> Desire, desire, desire.
> The longing for the dance

A Smoke and a Song

Stirs in the buried life.
One season only,
And it's done.
So let the battered old willow
Thrash against the windowpanes
And the house timbers creek.
Darling, do you remember
The man you married? Touch me,
Remind me who I am.

After the wedding, Rob and I move into Grandma's studio so we can save money for our move to Los Angeles. We snoop through Grandma's drawings of owls, water creatures, and chairs with three legs—figures that she birthed, but never found home on any of her paintings. It's her pile of misfits, her orphans.

We find a shoebox of old love letters from her first two husbands and spend hours reading through them.

"Can you imagine being this in love and then, someday, you're just not?" Rob asks me.

No, I certainly cannot fathom it, I think, staring at my handsome husband's face.

One night, while Rob is out bartending and I am bored, I check to see if her smoking kit is still here. I promised Rob I'd quit before we got married. And up until now, I have kept my promise.

I open the drawer and there it is. I unzip the clutch, take out the lipstick, and smooth it over my lips. The tip breaks off and falls on the desk. I pick it up—it is hard as a pebble—and throw it in the trash bin. I take out a cigarette and go to the window. I swipe a match, hold it to the tip, and take two slow drags in a row: one for Grandma, then one more for me. Then I flick the rest of the cigarette out onto the street. I clean up the smoking evidence with rose oil spray and put a dab of crusty crest in my mouth. I hide the kit back in the top drawer.

Fool's Gold

I won't tell Rob that I smoked. It is not the most honest thing to do a month into our marriage, but I give myself a pass. Maybe we need little rituals, to remember where we come from. Little ways to make meaning of a once-was self. Preservations of a bloodline, too tender to touch with words and outside interpretation.

Those two puffs touch me, like hands on my heart, or wings of a bird flapping in an open sky, or a tap on the shoulder from a long-ago relative. They remind me where I have come from and how far from there I am willing, or not willing, to go.

Nature or nurture. I am still undecided.

TWO

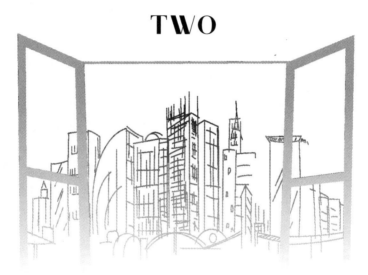

When the Student
Is Ready

We find a guest cottage that is so tiny you can practically flip pancakes from the toilet. But if I am going to live in California, I sure as hell am going to live near the beach, and tiny is all we can afford. The cottage sits just six blocks from the Venice boardwalk, on Marine Street, on the Santa Monica side. It's a three-hundred-square-foot A-frame painted all white, set behind a gate in the backyard of our landlord's house. She is a grumpy woman who barks louder than her three terriers. We have a little side yard with a fountain that makes a soothing sound in the evenings, which we enjoy after the landlord and her dogs finally go inside and stop their yapping.

When Rob isn't auditioning or bartending and when I am not interviewing for museum jobs, we strap on our Rollerblades and hit the Venice boardwalk for afternoon rides. We roll past incense vendors, the skateboard park, and buff gym rats lifting weights at Muscle Beach. We roll past tent communities under the boardwalk.

"If one has to be homeless," I say to Rob, "Venice, California, is the place to do it."

Occasionally, we take off our blades and walk knee-deep in the ocean. The water by the city's edge is sadly so polluted, so full of bacteria, that we never dare a full plunge.

"What a tease," I say. "To have all this ocean right here and not be able to go in."

A Smoke and a Song

"It is what it is, captain," Rob answers, every time.

Southern California life is easy breezy, just like the commercials promise. Everyone seems to move with a lingering stride. Nothing much of anything seems so pressing that you can't stop for a random conversation with a surfer dude or an old hippie in the middle of the day. But the truth is, I have been struggling with a heightened sense of anxiety, dread, and worry that seems to have followed me out west. Something about being newly married and being so in love, even more so *receiving* so much love, makes me edgy and panicky. I'm trapped in some odd hypervigilant state, looking for threats everywhere. I mistake every lowrider muffler rumble as the next big earthquake. I shake Rob at night just to make sure he hasn't died in his sleep. I ruminate that when the clock strikes midnight, our love will somehow vanish. Y2K is looming, and I just learned to drive—at twenty-nine years old. And anyone who knows the 10 Freeway in Los Angeles knows it is enough to send any New Yorker over the ledge. Especially a newly licensed New Yorker.

My anxiety cries out as judgment, harshness, and discontentment. Sometimes it squirts out from me as rage. Yelling helps. So I look for, and find, reasons to yell—socks on the floor, not having enough money, Rob's meandering.

I lash out, but Rob is not a fighter. He's an "it's all good" kind of guy. His method of operation is to try his hardest to butter me up. Up until now, Rob has been the one person who can get me out of my moods and soften. But these days, when he tries, I become an unbreakable stonewaller, and I bite harder. He fails; he freezes. Then he flees, off to play another eighteen holes, leaving me to boil alone in our one-room cottage, proving to some part of my brain that my reaction is justified, righteous.

By hour two, when my body chemistry changes from the hot adrenaline rush of fight to the cold blood-sugar dip of remorse, and I realize he's just trying to love me in his way, it becomes unbearable. I spiral into regret. *Why do I yell?* Regret rolls into shame.

When the Student Is Ready

How could you be so stupid, Sherry? Shame spins into fear that Rob will in fact get fed up and one of these days leave for good. And just the thought of being abandoned brings back the anxiety.

He comes back hours later. He always does. But he returns distant, far away from me, numb, in his own bubble. Desperate to feel him close, I claw, I beg for forgiveness. I own all the blame. I coddle him. I am extra nice, cheery even. I give him free passes to do whatever he wants. I encourage him to play basketball instead of picking up the extra shift at the bar. I bite my lip when he chucks his smelly, sweaty clothes across the room and misses the hamper. Eventually, he forgets the fight and we act like it never happened. And then I see the stack of unpaid bills he stuffed into the junk drawer, and I erupt again. And so we go, around and around. It is a cruel cycle.

About a year into living in Los Angeles, a friend of ours, Wardell, invites us to a yoga class. I have taken yoga before. Back in New York at Crunch Fitness, after the treadmill, I'd go down to the basement into the neon-lit, heated room and join the others— mostly thin white women in short shorts—in the power-hour practice. The teacher would hurry us through a series of sun salutations, standing warrior poses, deep backbends, and twists set to loud music. I enjoyed the challenging postures, the sweat, flipping upside down into inversions, and balancing my entire body on my own two hands—poses I called "party tricks" when I showed them off to friends. I loved the endorphins that gave me that special yoga high after each class.

But California yoga is different. This yoga is not in a neon-lit studio. This yoga is set in a house in a residential nook off Abbot Kinney Boulevard in Venice, an ashram called Sivananda, where people not only do yoga, but live and eat together.

When Rob, Wardell, and I walk into the ashram, a waft of incense mixed with a pungent fart smell meets us at the door.

The house is modest, barely furnished, with lots of pillows on the floor and tapestries on the walls. There is a man chanting in the corner of the living room and playing an instrument that looks somewhat like an accordion. People sway on a rug in front of him with their eyes closed. Bearded men and lightly mustached women wearing yellow shirts and loose white pants mill about in an open kitchen. I feel out of my element in my Manhattan-black Lycra leggings and tight black wifebeater. But I am intrigued.

We say hello, throw three ten-dollar bills into the donation basket, and walk up the ashram stairs, where they hold classes in the two bedrooms—one for men, the other for women. Rob and Wardell go in one door, and I go into the other.

Inside, the women on the mats are in two rows facing each other, with the teacher sitting off to the side on a striped blanket. Everyone has their eyes closed. It is dead quiet except for the chanting coming through the floor from downstairs. I look for an opening and lay my mat next to a robust woman, who opens her eyes and offers a condescending smile when I sit next to her. The teacher, named Sita, begins by saying, "Namaste, sisters. The light in me bows to the light in you."

I think, *What about my dark? Do you bow to my dark too?*

With her wispy "yoga voice," she guides us through an opening prayer and then a series of postures. Some postures are seated, some on our belly, and on our knees. We hold each one for a bit, and between each pose, we lie down in corpse pose, called Savasana. After the series, she repeats the same postures again.

I am impatient and bored. I want her to hurry up, to quicken the pace. I want to sweat. But by the ending of the class, when Sita has us on our backs between a seated twist and the last pose, a forward fold, something in me shifts.

Sita says, "Feel what you feel, without trying to make what you feel better."

This instruction is a revelation to me. *Feel what I feel? Without trying to make it better?* I don't want to feel how I've been feeling. *I thought the whole point of yoga was to feel better.*

I realize that I feel quite regular. I'm not ruminating, anxious, or angry. Something about being in this room and slowing down my breath and taking these shapes in my body gives me space to feel calmer than I have all year.

After the poses, we meditate. It seems like forever, but it is probably five minutes tops. Sita sings a chant in Sanskrit and explains the mantra *om*.

"The om has three parts," she says. "A. U. M. It represents our three states of consciousness. The waking state, the dream state, and the deep-sleep state."

She has us put our hands on our belly to "feel the *A* sound go down from your belly into the legs and feet." The *A*, she tells us, is for the waking state, symbolizing our connection to the earth. The mantra grounds us. It helps us root deeper into how we live our lives.

Next, she instructs us to place a hand at the heart, for the *U* sound that lives in the chest—for our dream state. "Feel how the mantra ripples outward, in all directions," she says, "from your chest out into the world." This part of the om helps us to connect from our hearts to others, to bring peace to our relations. "With people, our environment, and nature."

And then, she has us put our hands on our heads, for the *M* sound in the skull—the deep-sleep state, which connects us to all that is unseen, God, spirit, universal divine. "When we chant om," Sita explains, "we recalibrate, in body, mind, soul. Our feelings of separateness reunify. We remember we are already whole."

She chants, "Aaaaaaaa uuuuuuu mmmmmm. Aaaaaaaa uuuuuuu mmmmmm. Aaaaaaaa uuuuuuu mmmmmm."

"The silence after the om is so important that it has a name," she says. "It is called *turiya*, and it means our 'transcendental state.' It is the space where we go beneath the layer of mental chatter to our true selves—beingness of peace."

A Smoke and a Song

Beingness of peace? That sounds like what I need. I try it on. I'm here; I might as well. I chime in and start chanting, "Aaaaaaaa uuuuuuu mmmmmm."

This is a mistake, at first. When I join my voice with the others, I am overcome with a feeling, like broken glass splintering in my chest. I want to round over myself to cover the feeling. But I'm curious. The promise of peace is too tempting, so I om louder, and louder.

Memories surface, flashing in my mind movie. I am in the bottom of my sleeping bag inside the metal trailer at Dad's. I keep chanting. Mom's bloody hand is being slammed in the door. Lisa, handcuffed, is being taken away. I'm desperately looking for my Lammy. These images I had forgotten, but here they are again, in this yoga room, all these years later. I am weepy.

"Ommmm, hmmm, hmmmm," I keep chanting. The sound starts to fill me, but it changes. I drop the "o," and now I am just humming, my hum, the hum I used to hum. "Hummm, hummm, hummm." The hum is soothing and the feeling of glass in my chest dissolves and everything under my skin is vibrating. I keep humming. I have another memory. We are in a room like this one. People are dancing and singing. They wear orange robes and are bald, with little ponytails on the back of their skulls. I hum louder. My humming starts to merge with the om of the other women here; there is no distinction between their om and my hum. The sounds of separate voices have merged and become one.

As awkward and corny as it is, I feel at home in the room of the om.

"It's true," Mom says when I call her to tell her about the yoga class I took and ask about my memory of the orange-robe place. "We were at the Hare Krishna temple, down the street from us in Brooklyn. They served stew every night at six."

This was years before I started humming.

When the Student Is Ready

"I used to lip-sync the om and pretend to be a devotee, just so you girls could have some supper."

We are in our white-tiled bathroom. I am on the toilet, with my one-piece, navy blue, cotton romper pulled down to my knees, nothing but a black lace bra on top. Rob sits on the edge of the vanity in his still-sweaty basketball clothes and tears open the box.

This past year has been a relief. The world did not end with the new millennium—the year 2000 came and went without a hitch. We upgraded to a two-bedroom on Pier Street, able to afford it since I have secured a full-time job at the Getty Museum and am on my third round of interviews for a promotion. Rob booked a Red Lobster commercial. He has made more from residuals from that one day of acting work than my yearly salary, but I am not complaining! Our finances, our relationship, and both of our senses of worth, have improved. We have become regulars at the Sivananda Ashram yoga classes.

I watch him, excitement radiating through his eyes and smile, and I get a knot in my stomach. I realize that somewhere along these years together, I left out some very important details.

Have I never told him? Did I marry this man without letting him know?

It is not that I have tried to deceive him, really; I don't think I did. I didn't *not* tell him I could have children. I just *forgot* to tell him I couldn't. I had put my life in Mexico behind me, or somewhere deep inside me, as if it were a past life and not this one, or someone else's and not mine. When I left, I left. I forgot—everything.

Rob hands me the stick and I pee on it, going through the motions, already knowing the results. I hand it back to him. I stare at the toilet paper that is propped sideways, sitting on top of its holder. I lean forward to fix it. I slide the plastic tube through the cardboard roll, position it in the holder on the wall, squeezing the springs that allow the tube to fit in place. The springs pop out, and the toilet paper flops on the floor, unrolling at my feet.

I am having one of those brain pauses, a moment of genuine disconnect. I cannot bend down to pick it up, nor can I look up at Rob. I am here, but also not. I should say something, but my words won't work. In my peripheral vision, I see him looking at his watch. The heels of his sneakers are thumping the side of the vanity. "One more minute," he says.

I hold my breath and fade. It is a very, very long minute.

Rob jumps off the vanity. "Two lines, Berry! Two lines!" He is beaming; he blows me a kiss.

I rip the stick out of his hands to look at it myself. *Holy shit. Two lines.*

Later that evening, after the shock wears off and after our celebratory dinner, Rob and I go to Borders on the Third Street Promenade. He buys a book, *What to Expect When You're Expecting.* I buy a prenatal yoga video, taught by a powder-white woman, see-through almost, with a turban wrapped on her head. She looks a bit like a ghost, but the kind of ghost I can trust.

"For the days I can't get to class," I say.

Rob puts his hand on my belly and kisses the top of my head.

In the morning, I wake up early so that I can do the yoga video, still in pajama bottoms and one of Rob's tanks. I am convinced that my boobs are already swollen and that my own tops are already too tight on me, because, well, that is what happened the first time.

I sit on my living room floor and press PLAY. The powder-white woman in the video starts the opening meditation.

"When the student is ready, the teacher appears. Put your hand on the teacher inside you. Take a breath in and exhale out."

The phone rings. It is my father-in-law, Tim.

"Sherry," he says in a panicked voice. "Turn on the TV. Turn on the news right now! New York is being attacked."

"What? What do you mean?"

When the Student Is Ready

"Just turn on the TV!"

I turn off the video and change the auxiliary, and then I see the footage: the smoke, the sirens, the plane flying straight into the second tower.

"Holy mother!" I say and then shout, "Rob, get up! Hurry!"

Neither of us can take our eyes off the crumbling buildings, the people running on the streets, the panic. It's a kind of chaos that not even the news reporters can make sense of.

I call Mom, no answer. Lisa, I get a busy signal. I do the math. It is after nine in the morning East Coast time. For sure, Lisa just dropped off my nephew Justin to elementary school in the West Village. What if they were caught in the subway? I call my grandparents. There's not even a ring. Just silence. I put my hand on my belly, on the new life growing inside me. On the not-empty space of my future. *I knew it. I knew in my gut that something bad was going to happen.*

"I'm sure they are okay," Rob says in his ever-positive California tone. "We have to believe everyone is okay."

The rest of the day is a blur. Work is canceled. We pace. We watch the news, just like the rest of the world. By nighttime, Lisa finally calls. Rob is right—she and Justin are home. She reminds me that Mom is in Cuba on one of her photography trips, our grandparents are still in Provincetown, and Maddy and her family are on Martha's Vineyard. Everyone is safe. They are all fine.

But I am not. I peed on a plastic stick and two lines appeared, just hours before the Twin Towers were blown up from a terrorist attack, and I am not in New York. My whole world has since turned inside out.

The next day, the only thing I can think of doing is yoga. But I cannot turn on that video ever again, that is for sure. I go to the ashram, to a prenatal yoga class taught by a woman named Rocky. I like her right off the bat. She's no fuss, not hippie-dippie like Sita. Probably in her late fifties, she is a short little thing with very toned arms, stud earrings that climb up her earlobe, and silver, straight hair in a choppy pixie cut.

"Let it all go," she repeats three times, very matter-of-fact. "It's out of our hands. Visualize your baby, surrounded by white light. Let everything else go."

Let it go? How can she ask us to let go? How can anyone unclench from this senseless act of violence? How can we not grasp onto the image of all those people upon impact, the moment the planes hit? For sure, those people held on with all their might, with both arms and both legs, while they called their loved ones to say goodbye for the very last time. And how can anyone possibly expect me to practice letting go when there is a new person inside me? After the doctor told me I'd never be able to bear a child. No. No thank you. Not again. I absolutely refuse to let this baby go.

"I will hold on to you," I say to my belly. "I will hold on."

And I think, *Women are made to hold on*. It's in our biology, our cells; it's in our DNA. It is the job of our uterus to clutch the life inside us. It's our destiny to hold on.

Despite my mental arguing with Rocky's instructions, I go to yoga the next day, and the next, and almost every day of my pregnancy. Inside the yoga room, with Rocky's sensible instructions, doing our squats and Kegels, surrounded by the other moms and baby bumps, is the only place that feels safe. Outside, the world is too scary.

Rocky teaches us breath work techniques to slow down our heart rate when worry arises. "Breathe in for three counts, exhale for six." She instructs us to be a witness to the sensations in our body by scanning them. "Cultivate compassionate attention to the feelings. Notice how they move and change. Go toward one thing inside that feels right. Be with your baby." She teaches us how to resource when we feel anxious. "Feel your seat on the floor," she says. "Look around the room, take a breath in . . . now exhale." Her instructions are so simple and doable. "Ask yourself these very simple questions: Who am I? Where am I? What am I doing? And answer them as literally as possible."

I am Sherry. I am sitting on my mat in prenatal class. I am breathing.

I did not know before now that my anxiety had simple needs. It just wanted to be seen, heard, and felt. Just as my baby will, it requires caring for, nurturing, spoon-feeding. Just as my baby will, if ignored, anxiety only cries louder.

Yoga follows me out of the ashram, into my car, and into my days. Eventually, over time, with consistency and care, I can follow Rocky's instructions to "Just breathe. Let go of everything else." Chanting om to my belly on my way to work, my drive becomes a bubble of calm. Counting my breathing before bed, I start to sleep through the whole night. All that matters is keeping my body a safe home for my baby.

"I will hold on to you," I say to my baby while doing my Kegels and squats. "I will hold on."

Blessed One

For the first three days of our son's life, he doesn't have a name. Despite the long lists Rob and I collected during our pregnancy, nothing fits. Not Zander, not Milo, not even Jasper, the name at the top of our list, which is after my Grandpa Stanley, whose middle name is Jasspon.

"Nothing is truly ours but our name," Grandpa says when he calls to congratulate us on the baby. "Choose one with meaning."

He is interrupted by Grandma Elise, who is mumbling in the background, as she always does.

"Don't be a phone hog, Mister Kunitz," I hear her say as she pulls the phone away from him. "Darling," she says to me.

"Grandma. He looks like one of the creatures in your paintings, part old man, part slug."

She chuckles. "Little monsters," she says in her wry tone.

"Don't make me laugh; it hurts," I say, still sore from twenty-six hours of labor and another four of pushing.

I tuck the cordless phone between my ear and shoulder. I look at the thick absorbing pads trailing out from underneath my seat, which we ordered from a medical supply shop. They were on the list our midwife had told us to get for the home birth—along with gauze, peroxide, and a handful of cloth diapers—all of it still in a pile on the bed.

My breasts are so hardened with milk, so engorged, that they take up space under my armpits and rub on the inside of my arms. Each breast is bigger than my baby's head. I look down at my son's face, who is back-down on the Boppy that is resting on my still-round belly. He is looking up at me, face squished like a monkey. His newborn, blue-black eyes are extremely focused, already lifting his taffy-like neck up to wrap his newborn mouth around my swollen nipple. He is a squinting little blob on the outside of me, tiny and new but old and wise. Fresh from the womb, yet somehow I know he has outfitted more lives than me already. My 9/11 baby. My little yogi boy. My teacher.

Grandma keeps chatting away. I brush my hands across my newborn's scalp, which is already starting to crust, exactly like my sisters said it would.

Love fills my pores and my surroundings. It's a free love, a pure love, an oxytocin-induced, new-mother love. Not like love as I know it, but like love is supposed to feel. This love comes from a vast place, a holy place. A love without needing anything in return. And all of it moves from every cell inside my body and pours directly to my baby.

"I cannot believe I am a mother," I say to Grandma.

She makes a gurgling sound and then says, "Neither can I, darling, and I've been doing it for sixty-four years."

However sad her comment is, it's also funny, and so I let myself laugh.

"Now, darling, how are you?" Grandma asks.

"It's beautiful. He's magic. But it's hard. He has been attached to me for three days. I need a shower. I stink."

"Put him down," she says. "Let Robert take him. He'll have to learn to be without you, especially when you go back to work."

I confess that I have decided to quit my job when my maternity leave is over. There is no way I can go back to working full-time and leave my baby boy in day care, not even with Rob.

"The baby has changed me, Grandma," I say, my tone more serious. "It's like all the times I ever questioned my life have just disappeared, and I know why I was born. My baby boy is my purpose now."

A Smoke and a Song

She pauses for a minute, saying nothing. I am sure she disapproves of my words—my sacrifice to give myself wholeheartedly to my son and my decision to leave my career. She didn't do that for her daughter. Plus, she knows how hard I busted my ass for the promotion. She holds my title as if it is her own. She tells anyone she can that her granddaughter is *the* education specialist for community audiences at the prestigious J. Paul Getty Museum.

After a bit of silence, she says, "Well, you are a better person than I am. And maybe it's best. We both know the Getty art collection is a bore."

I laugh. But after the laughter comes the cry. It's one of those new-mother cries, the kind that won't quit, when you're overly hormonal and every single feeling hits you like a roaring river.

"Oh now, darling!" I hear her say as I collect myself. Grandma hates crying. She just doesn't have the skin for it.

"I could really use a smoke and a song at the studio right about now," I whisper.

"So could I," she whispers back.

We say our goodbyes.

I take a sip of wine and close my eyes to listen to Carlos Nakai's flute off *Canyon Trilogy*, the one album I've played every day, all day, on loop these first days of his life. I think about Grandma Elise, the magnificent artist, who can no longer paint or write. Withered down to an old woman, a great-grandmother almost blind in bed, intent on getting a laugh from her granddaughter.

I think about my mother, who is on a plane back to New York City. She had shown up fully these first three days of my son's life. She and Rob's mom made it to the birth, and they stayed out of the way, as we asked them to. They grocery shopped, had coffee brewing all day long, fed us, and hand-washed the cloth diapers. Mom even helped me give my son his first bath, instructing me how to wash inside the creases of his skin. She told me what temperature to make the water and how to hold his arm, palm up, and angle his wrist to get inside the folds.

Blessed One

Mom may have fumbled through mothering my sisters and me, but the lady has the grandma thing down.

I think about my sisters, who are both mothers, and doing it so well in their own ways, perfectly fitting their personalities. Lisa is overly loving and overprotective. We joke that she'll still make Justin heart-shaped PB&Js even when he goes to college. God forbid he ever gets bullied at school. I would not want to be those kids' parents! Maddy has a free-range mothering style. Her three-year-old daughter, Juniper, is one of those *Lord of the Flies* children who runs around naked most of the time.

And I think, *I am a mother now.* It is now my job to pass down the stories of my family to my son. What will I tell him? Will I tell him that even today—as grown-ass adults—the women of his family still cannot manage to gather without some explosion taking place? Or will I try to explain to him that under the masquerade of rage lives pain, and under that hides love, and that none of us really learned how to show love appropriately?

The responsibility of being a mother feels overwhelming.

The baby has fallen asleep on my lap. His little lips release off my nipple, and he sighs, one of those newborn sighs that brings you back into the moment. His warm exhale brushes my bare chest.

I think of what Grandpa Stanley said: "Nothing is truly ours but our name, choose one with meaning."

Rob and I name our son Miles Asher Sidoti. Miles, Latin for "merciful soldier," and for Mom's favorite jazz musician, Miles Davis, of course. Asher, "blessed one" in Hebrew, is also Grandma Elise's maiden name.

Perhaps, through mothering him, this boy, our son, Miles Asher, my teacher, I can rewrite our family herstory. Or better yet, I can let my son write his own. He can craft his own assessments of the characters he was born to, based on his own experience, not mine. Perhaps all the unconditional love that I have for this tiny being, a love that is so much larger than any chapters in my little story, can heal the scars of our family's past. He and I will not fight. I will not make my child hold my emotional pain. I will not confuse him with adoration and then withdrawal. I will not turn my chair sideways or nod in his direction and roll my eyes. I am not Elise's granddaughter, or my mother's daughter. I am Miles Asher's mother.

I take a breath in; I count to three. I take a breath out; I count to six. I bend down to his little ear and whisper, "My blessed one. You and I were made for this. Thank you for choosing me to be your mom. Thank you for being a boy."

FLY

No matter how much we want to stay in Santa Monica, we can't afford it. We won't be able to survive on Rob's bartending tips and no health insurance, nor the prayer that he will book another acting gig. Not since I quit my big job at the Getty, and certainly not now that we are parents.

We decided on Ojai, a quaint mountain town about an hour and a half north of Los Angeles, the town where Rob grew up. It was an arduous search for houses. Every place in our budget Rob said no to. His aunt lived in the pink house that I liked on Chaparral Street; he couldn't live there. He lost his virginity in the adorable adobe on Amber Lane. "No way. Not here," he said. His friends used to throw barn burners in that house down Alomar Avenue, so that one was "out of the question." Even Maggie, our realtor, was growing impatient.

So when Rob said yes to the one-bedroom river-bottom home, we paid a deposit on the spot, in cash. A house on the floor of the flash-flood zone, just outside of town, surrounded by avocado trees and sage bushes, on an arid patch of dirt across the street from an orange grove. "In the evenings," Maggie the realtor said, "the whole neighborhood smells of orange blossoms."

Rob found a part-time job at the local tennis and pool club. His plan was to man the front desk while getting certified as a personal trainer and building a clientele, which I trusted would not take long since Rob is strapping, Adonis-like, and the older tennis-lady types swoon over him. His job came with a free family membership where we could teach baby Miles to swim in one of the lap pools. They even had a day care where we could leave Miles for an hour, if he ever let me put him down, so that we could both work out. I accepted the job as the director of Ojai's history museum. Although the whole reason for leaving Los Angeles and my position at the Getty was to be with my baby, they offered me a package I couldn't refuse: a decent enough salary with benefits, I could start from home for the first three months, and they said I could bring Miles to work with me when it was time to go into the office.

But three days before our big move to Ojai, which was two days ago, while we were sipping on freshly squeezed orange juice at the Tuesday Santa Monica Farmers Market on Main Street, Rob had a change of heart.

"Ojai?" he said, straw dangling off his bottom lip, while rocking Miles in the crook of his muscular arm. "I just don't think I can do it." He clamped his upper lip down onto the straw and took a sip.

I gave him one of my looks, a look that says, *Don't do this. Don't do that Rob thing now.*

I cannot say I was surprised one bit by his quick switch. My husband has a way of changing course midway all the time. "Being in the flow, cruising with life" as they call it in California. In New York City, we call it "flaky, indecisive, and unreliable."

Damn.

We had a house and jobs lined up, and everything was already packed up in boxes to move to Ojai, which was no small feat with a five-month-old. I even mailed out "We're Moving" cards to our people with our new address on it, for fuck's sake.

But somehow, on the seven-block walk from the farmers market to our Pier Street apartment of jam-packed boxes and empty rolls of packaging tape, I convinced myself he was right. I learned in yoga that arguing with reality is a useless endeavor. Suffering comes by forcing an agenda, and thus to avoid suffering, we need to take the path of least resistance. What was the point of moving to Ojai if Rob didn't want to live there?

"What now?" I asked.

"I'm not sure," Rob said. "But it'll all figure itself out."

He went to the bedroom to put Miles down for his nap. I went outside, sat on the top step, and called Maddy on Martha's Vineyard, where she, her French husband, Philippe, and Juniper live.

"Hey, what's up?" she said.

I could hear Juniper singing "Wheels on the Bus" in the background.

"It's Rob. He changed his mind. He doesn't want to move to Ojai anymore."

"What do you mean? Why?"

"He says he can't do it. Too many memories of barn burners."

"What?" Maddy said. "Well, what are you going to do?"

"Not sure. I guess we have to come up with plan B."

"Well," she said, without hesitation, "come to the Vineyard!"

Hmmmm? Martha's Vineyard? As in full-time? Like, even in the winter? I hung up with Maddy. I called out to Rob, "Hey, how about Martha's Vineyard?"

He meandered to the archway of the front door and said, "Martha's Vineyard? Sure. Why not?"

I called U-Haul to find out how much extra it would cost to take the trailer across the country, instead of an hour and half up north. I called the Ojai Museum and quit the job I had not yet started. I called Maggie the realtor. We would lose our deposit on the house, but there was nothing we could do about that. I called Mom to see if we could use her credit card and, thankfully, she said yes. I booked the U-Haul. I booked my flight.

Rob and I say our goodbyes. He leans his head into my tank-topped torso, to kiss Miles, who is smushed between the BabyBjörn and my milk-filled, sweaty breasts. We are on day seven of a late September, Southern California heat wave. The hot Santa Ana winds are blowing something fierce today. I can smell the residue of smoke from the Topanga fires that smolder over the mountains past the city, above the Pacific Ocean.

"Be good to Mama, my boy," he says. He lifts his head, kisses me, raises both of his arms into the air and shouts, "Road trip, baby!" He climbs into our blue Bronco II, U-Haul hitched to the back, and drives off with all the things worth taking, plus his floundering teenage brother, Vincent, who Rob's dad had convinced him to take on the drive.

I am standing below the steps that lead up to our apartment on Pier Street. In front of me is the stroller. Inside the stroller is my overstuffed overnight bag, filled with a stack of cloth diapers and rash cream, the breast pump and two bottles, one change of clothes for me and three for Miles—three, in case he throws up, as he has been doing all week. In the front pocket of my bag are all the important things: wallet, phone charger, his birth certificate, my hair products. Enough hair products to last the seventeen hours before Miles and I are to fly out to New York tomorrow morning, where we will stay with Mom while Rob finds us a place to live on Martha's Vineyard.

The straps of the Björn crisscross my upper back and dig into the tops of my shoulders, yoking into the grooves in my flesh that are becoming permanent from carrying Miles on me. He is growing fast, already twenty pounds, in the ninetieth percentile for his length and age. My big little bean sprout.

I am bouncing, a slow methodical bounce, the one I learned in baby-and-mommy yoga that gets him to relax. *Bend knees a few inches, hover, sway to the left, sway to the right, stand up straight. Repeat.* I hold the back of Miles's head, which is cradled in the thick, blue padding of the baby carrier, because they tell you to do that with babies, even though Miles has been holding his head up on his own since day one—my determined little Aries ram.

Before trekking the three blocks to my friend Melanie's,

where we are spending the night while she's away, I think, *I should go back upstairs to do one last sweep of the apartment. Just in case we have forgotten something.* With Miles strapped to my front, I step up the long flight of stairs outside our apartment, the same flight of stairs I walked barefoot up and down, up and down, in pain five months ago during my labor. I skim the apartment. I check the bedroom: nothing. The living room: only the stack of books the landlord said he'll bring to the library for us. The bathroom: empty and clean. I close the kitchen window, saying my last goodbyes to the place where I home birthed my baby boy.

I decide to fill my water bottle before leaving, and when I open the freezer to get some ice, I see it.

Oh damn!

There on the top rack, next to the ice cubes, is the metal mixing bowl covered with plastic wrap. Inside the metal bowl is Miles's frozen placenta.

Oh damn.

So much for planting the placenta under a maple tree. So much for sending it off with the midwife who knows a guy who pulverizes placentas in the dehydrator and turns them into capsules with other immune-boosting herbs to take if we are feeling under the weather. So much for boiling it into a stew and eating it like I had read some cultures do to fend off postpartum depression.

No, we haven't done any of the above. We haven't done a thing with Miles's placenta. There, under the Saran Wrap, the red slop of a placenta, frozen to the metal mixing bowl—the only thing we forgot. And here I am, alone, with a baby and our placenta and only a couple more hours of daylight before leaving our three years in California.

What the hell am I going to do with a frozen placenta?

I walk down the stairs and set the bowl on top of the stroller. I look down the block, mapping my walk to Melanie's. It is hard to see past the shadows made by the robust rose of Sharon that hangs off the neighbor's gate, and I am blinded by the sun's rays ricocheting off the metal bowl.

I've got to get to Melanie's apartment before it melts. One hand desperately trying to balance the metal mixing bowl, the other pushing the stroller, I clumsily walk down the street. Every crack and bump in the sidewalk is a threat. The liquifying placenta is sloshing side to side inside the metal bowl.

At her apartment, while Miles fusses on the couch, surrounded by pillows so he won't fall off now that he is teaching himself to roll over, I look at the photographs, postcards, and drawings tacked with black, circular magnets on her refrigerator door. I am so full of unknowns, so unsure of what our last-minute choice to move to Martha's Vineyard will bring us. There is one drawing that catches my attention. It is of a bird with its wings spread. Above the bird is the sun, and inside the sun, the word "FLY." Below the bird, at the bottom of the page, is a quote by Joseph Campbell, written in purple pen: "We must be willing to get rid of the life we've planned, so as to have the life that is waiting for us."

I open the freezer. I move Melanie's ground buffalo meat onto the box of popsicles and slide the bags of coffee beans to the back of the freezer, behind the ice trays. I place the metal mixing bowl in the space I've carved out. On top of the plastic wrap I put a yellow Post-it with a note written in red Sharpie that reads "Do not eat!!!"

Martha

There's a saying: "You don't choose Martha's Vineyard; Martha's Vineyard chooses you." They say her magnetic force is so strong that when she wants you here, under her red clay cliffs and lapping Atlantic Ocean, she'll pull you here no matter what. That your life before, all that you once knew, will feel like a distant dream once she gets her island claws in you.

We were pulled to her, and Martha does not disappoint. Martha gives us friends with acoustic guitars, cedar-wooded trails to get lost on, lobster rolls on Friday nights, and beach plum jelly. She gives Miles sandy dunes to roll down in summer and perfect-sized hills to sled on in winter. She gives us a new kitty named Shadow, with gray-and-black fur, a lush patch of white that covers the left side of her face, and an extra toe on each paw.

Martha even holds on when I am not in the mood, when I am at my wits' end with insular life. This happens when you live on a floating patch of land in the middle of the ocean, where everyone not only knows who you are but knows the car you drive—even more so when you are a wash-ashore. Especially in the off-season, when the population whittles down from 140,000 to 12,000, and you feel a bit claustrophobic. And when you are a New Yorker and used to a certain amount of anonymity, and especially at Cronig's grocery store, where you run into all the people, and all you want to do is check the things off your list and run home.

A Smoke and a Song

It's then that Martha digs in. She'll have you bump into that one person you've been avoiding, who says something like, "We missed you the other night at the potluck," reminding you that you are living in a community of people who not only notice you but who care about you. People who want you around. People who listen and let you become the person you have always meant to become but couldn't before, because in every other place you felt unseen, unheard, and underappreciated.

How lucky to have ended up here. And so last minute! Nestled in Martha's arms, we have received one blessing after the next. In her embrace, she gifts the graces, with courteous goodwill and generosity. She gives, and I learn to let myself receive.

Rob left his acting career and personal trainer dreams in California and took up gardening. He found us a place and a job all rolled into one—a little two-bedroom apartment, on the second floor of the 1970s shingled Cape at Heather Gardens, a local nursery. Rob waters plants and sows seeds in the greenhouse with Mike and Kerry, the couple that lives downstairs. We even have a pool in our backyard where Juniper and Miles swim. The local yoga studio is just half a mile down the road.

I found a circle of new moms to bond with as soon as we moved here, other women with baby boys the same age as Miles—soul-sister women, women I like, apart from the babies.

We met at story hour at the West Tisbury Library when our boys were just six months old, and we formed a little co-op. Two of us watched all four babies while the other two got two hours off, twice weekly. Two hours was just enough time to get a breather and be a person, a human again, not a mom, for 120 minutes, before our breasts leaked through the nursing pads and bra, the two wet circles staining our shirts, signaling pick-up time. Like Cinderella's slipper that no longer fit after midnight, two hours was about all my body could take without Miles. And in the worst-case scenario, we agreed, if one of us was running late, we could always breastfeed each other's babies, if we had to.

I used my baby-free time to take a yoga class, run, or do some form of exercise, and usually with Maddy. I loved being active postpregnancy, to feel parts of myself that mom life didn't give space for. And my prepregnancy body was starting to reveal itself under the extra, pillowy layers of motherhood. I could breathe when I buttoned my jeans again. And I liked that feeling.

It happened on one of those days, when my mommy friends Signe and Lexi had Miles from ten to noon. I missed the ten o'clock yoga class, so Maddy and I went Rollerblading in the state forest instead. Spring had sprung, and the forsythia was everywhere, casting a yellow glow on both sides of the narrow concrete path. I was freewheeling, literally, the breeze behind me, assisting my strokes. I loved mommy-ing; I did. But I missed feeling useful in a bigger way, using my smarts for more than sorting goldfish and cutting grapes into sandwich-sized baggies.

I said, "I am ready to work again, but what will I do?"

"Do what you love," Maddy shouted, her strokes faster than mine; she was way ahead of me on the path. She jumped and flipped around to face me, skating backward. "It's your chance to start over!" She flipped again, and with those long legs of hers, she took off.

I skated as hard as I could to keep up with her. I yelled out, "Maybe I'll make yoga my thing?" My prenatal yoga classes in California had such an impact on my life. "Maybe I can be a Rocky for other women!"

That night I did some research. No one else on the island was teaching prenatal yoga, so there was a need to fill—check. I found a training program in Harwich, on Cape Cod, just a few towns from Provincetown, that happened to be the next month. I signed up.

I got certified a month after Miles's first birthday and started teaching right away. The local midwife put my flyer in the pregnancy packets and invited me to teach breath work to couples at the birthing classes at the hospital. I rented the studio down the

road on Wednesday evenings from six to seven for my class—
Miles's witching hour. I left Rob to deal with bedtime one night
a week.

Right away, I had ten mommies registered. Sharing yoga
came easily; I was a natural from the start. Guiding others to
connect to their bodies and babies perfectly aligned with all that
was important to me then—pregnancy and motherhood, exercise, camaraderie, a space to read aloud my favorite poems and
inspirational quotes, and the opportunity to empower women
during this special time in life. I rolled it all together, and all to
a great playlist, of course. Thievery Corporation for our warm-
ups, Mozart for visualization practices, with an occasional Led
Zeppelin or De La Soul track to ramp up the mood during our
warrior series and squats.

I added to my repertoire as I was called to offer more. Teach
first, feel it out, then get proper training. When asked to be at some
of my students' births, I got certified to be a labor doula. After my
first round of mommies had their babies, they requested baby-and-
mommy yoga classes. When those babies were placed in day care,
the moms wanted a class without the babies. Of course, I said yes.
I followed the flow of demand. I had a built-in clientele. Women
will always get pregnant. Women will always birth babies. Babies
will always grow up. Touch them at this significant moment in
their lives, and these women will bond with you forever.

Now, three years in, I teach prenatal, baby-and-mommy, vin-
yasa yoga, and I created a hybrid yoga-and-fitness class that I call
Fusion, for all the exercisers who don't think they like yoga but
are willing to try if it makes them sweat. People say they love my
kick-ass sequences and music mixes. And I get to walk around in
yoga leggings all day. This me on Martha fits just right. Not too
loose, like in California. Not too tight, like in New York.

Another gift that Martha gives is quiet winters. The island gets
cold and so empty that you can drive across from the North to

South Shore and only pass a couple of cars along the way, and no one seems to hold it against you if you close shop and take off for a couple of months. If somehow you have scraped enough savings during the busy summer season to hit the slopes or sail the Caribbean, well, that's what you do.

Lucky for us, we have free places to stay in warmer climes. We spend the winters in Ojai, living in my father-in-law's old RV, or in Mexico, where my aunt Gretchen built a house, or in the Bahamas, at the Sivananda Ashram. All our winter trips revolve around yoga. Miles has grown into quite the little yogi too. He comes to classes, situated between me and Rob, where he plays with his set of mala beads or rolls around. He hums the Sanskrit chants, which he learned by osmosis when he played by my feet while I scrubbed burnt stew off the bottom of commune-sized pots at the ashram—karma yoga, in exchange for tent space to live, while Rob did a yoga-teacher training last winter.

After teaching yoga at various gyms, I am offered my own yoga niche inside a local dance studio. For a very reasonable rent, I am given the space in the mornings to hold as many classes as I can fit in before the dancers get out of school and I pick up Miles from preschool. When it comes time to make a website, I know I need to choose a meaningful name for my business. I think about all that has happened in our lives since we left California in 2002, and how we almost did not live here, and I almost would not have been a yoga teacher. I remember the moment I put Miles's placenta in Melanie's freezer. I remember the Joseph Campbell quote under the drawing that caught my attention of the bird and the word "FLY."

Fly—slang for "just right," a term we used in the city back in the day for when things seemed to click. "Yeah," we used to say. "That's fly."

F for Freedom, *L* for Life, and *Y* for Yoga. *That acronym is fly*, I think to myself.

I name my business FLY, or more specifically, FLY Yoga.

A Smoke and a Song

I store a little box filled with votives, incense, and a selection of yoga and poetry books in the corner of the room at the studio. When it is my time, I go there early to set the mood. It's no Sivananda Ashram, but I know how to create a soothing yoga vibe. Before each class, I walk around cleansing the studio with sage. I dim the overheads, light votives around the space, and make a temporary altar with printed quotes on pretty pictures and other things I love: a postcard of Ixchel that I have held onto since my Mexico days, rocks collected from my favorite beaches, smoky quartz crystals given to me by students that have been "charged" by the full moon every month, a photo of Miles. Once the room feels ready with intention, I open a book to find a poem or quote that offers some overarching context to use as my dharma talk, or lesson for the day. Everyday experiences have become fodder for yoga sharing. I can barely have a conversation without making some metaphor connecting to a yoga pose.

I open every class with "Namaste. The light and the dark in me bows to the light and the dark in you."

After class, there are usually two or three students waiting to talk with me, wanting to share some revelation they had during practice, to tell me something that is going on in their life, or to thank me.

I'm finding meaning in being a person with whom people find safety, someone they can talk to, a person who can hold the space. It's organic for me; I've had a lifetime of practice. I take on this role liberally and, admittedly, a bit too seriously. I'm a no-frills yoga sharer. I am not one of those yoga teachers who speaks with a wispy, creepy "yoga voice." I do not sugarcoat when I teach. I speak with authority and conviction. I urge my students to go "there," and I do so with a stern and supportive tone. And for some reason, which I do not question, people listen to me. I

[152]

am surprised at how willing my students are to do what I say, without any resistance.

I notice that yogis have a habit of putting their yoga teachers up on a pedestal, as if we are their priest, mother, lover, and therapist all at once. Perhaps it comes with the territory, being that yoga is part of a guru lineage. I am no guru, I know that, but when my students come to me, I mentor, I offer advice, and I stay after class longer than necessary. I tell myself I am being of service to them; however, I know it feeds the part of me that needs to be needed. I'm aware of it, I try to steer from it, but it is seductive. I walk away from every class with the perfectly sweet serotonin buzz we get when we help others, high on the dopamine rush we get when praised for how good we are at it.

Yoga fills our home too. It is our new glue. Rob and I down dog together, and Miles climbs on our backs. We put little altars on our windowsills with smoking sage and seashells. We are closer than we have been in twelve years together. Two yogis and their yoga-baby.

Rob has been talking about teaching ever since he got certified, but hasn't yet. I think it's a great idea. I coach him. I show him clever ways to offer hands-on assists in the poses, how to create the perfect arc in sequencing, and how to pace by counting beats in the song. I give him my journals of class themes and stick-figure drawings of the poses.

"Do it!" I say. "We can be *that* family. With *that* life. A sweet little yoga family of three."

"Slow down, girl," Rob says as he polishes his golf clubs. "Bobby got to move at his own pace."

The Layers

I have read this poem a thousand times—in yoga classes while students rest in Savasana, during my women's new-moon circles. I even have a line from the poem tattooed on my right foot. While reading, I know exactly where to pause, how to pace, and when to ponder. I recite it with expression, tone, and cadence. Sharing the poem, I feel worldly, willful, and wise. "It's like this poem was written for me," everyone says at the poem's end.

But today, "The Layers" gets the best of me.

I'm fidgeting, pushing down a cry with deep-nostril breathing.

I can practically see his small-framed silhouette standing up at the microphone. His shoulders twitching toward his ears with each syllable, elbows bent, and leaning on the podium, with paper in hand.

But he is not up on the stage. He is gone. My beloved Grandpa Stanley has passed, just months before his 101st birthday, and we are all in Provincetown to celebrate him. The auditorium of the Provincetown Fine Arts Work Center is filled with a parade of people. Former students, fans, just about all the literary types who are still alive are here. We sit with my mom, my sisters, my aunt and cousins, and niece and nephew in the second row, Rob to my right, Miles to my left. Miles is drinking apple juice from a highball glass poured for him at the bar. There are no sippy cups at this event. He spills some on his shorts. "Hold it with two hands!" I whisper.

If she were here today, Grandma Elise would be standing in the back at the bar, flirting with the bartender. She would say something like, "Such fuss! He was just a man. You should see his boxers by the bed!" as she grazed the bartender's arm with her fool's gold–adorned fingers. But she is not here, either. Grandma broke her hip two years ago when she slipped on her bathroom rug and spent weeks in the hospital declining. She stopped talking, refused solids, and lay limp, only moving to swat away the nurse's hands when she came to check her stats. She only exercised her voice to yell when my mother visited. "Why is *she* here? Somebody get her out!"

We all agreed it was best to bring her to Twelfth Street for whatever time was left. A hospital was no place for a woman like her. Surely, she would want to be surrounded by art, books, and picture frames. One morning, about a month after they returned her home, while Grandpa Stanley was in his study writing his last book, Grandma Elise died in bed.

I often imagine her last moments, in their dimly lit room in her silk nightgown, next to Grandpa Stanley's stack of *New Yorkers*, listening to his typewriter clacking down the hall. I imagine her leaning over her marble-topped nightstand, fondling for her silver handheld mirror and ivory hairbrush, smoothing down her white bob, and clipping her bangs with a barrette. Surely, she smeared on one last coat of Revlon #710, despite being completely blind at the time.

Grandma hated getting old; she used to joke with me about it often. She'd say, "If I ever get too decrepit to put on my lipstick, darling, please take me out back and shoot me."

What was she thinking as she drifted off into the mist of the afterlife? Did she know she was dying? Was she afraid? Regretful? Did she wish she had been kinder, more affectionate to my mother? Probably not. My guess is that as she faded away, as she left her body at the bottom of her very last exhale, her soul flew three blocks to her studio to put on *Porgy and Bess* and sing at the top of her lungs while she painted and smoked one last cigarette.

A Smoke and a Song

Grandpa Stanley almost died, too, that year, a couple of months before Grandma Elise did. For weeks he lay in a cot, which Mom and my aunt Gretchen rolled out to the living room so all his admirers could come by and say their final words to him. He was barely breathing, ready to go. Then, like a miracle, Gretchen found him typing in his study in the middle of the night. Just like that, he lived two more years.

Whatever he saw and experienced during those days in and out ignited more living in him, and he spent the next year and a half on his last book, *The Wild Braid*, with his assistant and coauthor, Genine Lentine. The two sat together daily, first during one last summer with his beloved garden in Provincetown, followed by his finale in New York.

The Wild Braid was a farewell song. A compilation with poems, Marnie Crawford Samuelson's artistic photographs of Stanley, his musings on poetry and gardening, memories of his childhood, and the messages that came to him from the gods when he almost left the earth plane. However far-fetched it seemed, it didn't surprise any of us that he was given the gift of near death and then rebirth before he died. If there was anyone on the planet, my grandpa Stanley was the one man who could piece the language together to help the rest of us grasp what may be on the other side waiting for us when it is our turn.

Of all people, *the* poet Mary Oliver is at the celebration. She walks in, moving as if she is Jesus parting the seas, wearing a white-on-white pantsuit and amber-tinted sunglasses. After Stanley, Mary Oliver is my second favorite poet. I read her poems at the end of yoga classes too.

Mary was a student of Grandpa and has a house in Provincetown too. She and he spent quite a lot of time together, pondering perfectly arranged prose on the bench in his garden, by the row of peonies that bloomed in the early June sun or walking the bay during low tide in the fog. She even wrote a poem entitled "Stanley Kunitz."

"She's so radical," I whisper to Rob, starstruck.

She saunters to our row, holding a drink in her hand, and says to my entire family, "What a loss! I raise my glass to the poet I loved and adored." She raises her glass, and so do we.

One by one, the poets Grandpa Stanley mentored, mostly women, the Big Hairs as they were nicknamed by Grandma, are called up to the podium. Each share stories of how Stanley's kindness rubbed off on their art and their lives. A tall woman with frizzy locks reads a passage from Bill Moyers's book *Fooling with Words*, in which Moyers interviewed Stanley on his ninety-first birthday.

"His early poems were layered in metaphors," the woman says as she flings a strand of hair from her face. "Of the toil of a young man's yearning for his father."

I have heard only a little about my great-grandfather. Solomon Kunitz, a Russian Lithuanian Jewish dressmaker, drank a bottle of carbolic acid on a bench in Elm Park, in public, in the middle of Worcester, Massachusetts, six weeks before Grandpa Stanley was born. After the suicide, my great-grandmother Yetta removed any trace of Solomon's existence from their home, leaving Stanley and his two sisters, Sarah and Sophia, to walk through life with a silence, as if their father never happened.

The suicide later became the inspiration behind much of Grandpa Stanley's poetry. And it's probably why he was so kind to my mother after she tried to take her life, and kind to us for being fatherless. In "The Portrait," he wrote of the time his mother slapped him, after he found a photo of Solomon in the attic and brought it into the kitchen to ask her about the "long-lipped stranger" in the photograph. "In my sixty-fourth year," Grandpa Stanley wrote, "I can feel my cheek still burning."

For the next hour, we hear tales of Stanley the poet's career.

A Smoke and a Song

He spent decades teaching English at various colleges: Bennington, Yale, Brandeis, Columbia. He accomplished his goal to teach at Harvard, where he graduated summa cum laude, even though he was told by the Harvard headmaster that Ivy League students wouldn't want to get lectured to by a Jew. He won a Pulitzer for his book *Selected Poems 1928–1958* and the National Book Award for his collection *Next to Last Things*. He was the poet laureate of the United States twice, first in the midseventies and again during Bill Clinton's presidency.

The tales are accompanied by a slideshow—large projections of his poems, photos of him holding rusty shears in his garden, and black and whites of him as a young man. These are photos I know well, photos that hung on their hallway wall.

Rob leans over and whispers in my ear, "The man had mojo. He'd make any twenty-first-century hipster envious!"

His list of achievements is impressive. But to me he was not just the poet, he was the man who helped me write my college essay and walked me down the aisle. He cared about my heart and gave me wise words of advice. He was the closest thing I had to a father.

I have this memory. I was a tiny thing. Grandpa and I were down at the bay. He rolled up his pants to the knees and flung me on his shoulders to wade the high tide. We were on a sea-glass-collecting mission. He told me that if I half closed my eyes, the sparkles of sea glass underwater would brighten, especially from up high. We spent hours at the water that day, collecting remnants of bottles thrown out to sea.

"There's one!" I would point, and Grandpa would bend down, carefully balancing us both so we didn't fall in, and pick up each piece, marvel at it, and then drop it in the empty jam-sized mason jar that earlier held his martini inside the breast pocket of his blazer.

That night, he emptied the jar and pushed our treasures into a pile in the middle of the table. We stayed up way past my bedtime making mosaics down in Grandma Elise's studio. Grandpa laid our sea glass out on small blocks of wood, patterned like a poem.

"Aqua blue," he said. "Like the summer sky."

"Smoky clear to remind you on bad days that the sun will still shine through."

"Green like the plants, my dear, for you as you continue to grow."

Last summer, I took Miles here to see his great-grandfather. I wanted to make sure the two had a moment together, at the Provincetown house, even if Miles was too young to later remember. The three of us sat in the corner living room overlooking his garden, mostly in silence in an early-evening light, while the sun crossed past the bay toward the ocean side, readying itself for sunset. Miles, usually bouncy and busy like a jumping bean, was still on Grandpa's skinny lap, running his tiny fingers through his great-grandpa's sideburns. Grandpa Stanley cupped his fingers around Miles's ears. Every now and again, one of his shoulders would twitch, and when it did, Miles would nod and bury his head into Grandpa's frail but huge-hearted chest. As I watched the two, I felt the undeniable bond between them, protected and loved within the space they shared. They were communicating in some nonverbal language understood only by them, as if the two were conspiring something secret on my behalf. At some point, Miles said out loud in his squeaky three-year-old voice, "Don't go."

Grandpa opened his wide, graying brown eyes and kissed the top of my son's head and said, "Blessed one. We can't always have the poet. But we can always have the poem."

Rob squeezes my hand. Under my composed exterior, sweat slides down my cleavage, pooling in my bra. There is a scratchy nest of memories and tears in my throat. Miles climbs on my lap. I play with his blond curls as I look through the huge glass doors that separate the auditorium from the coastal landscape and quaint cottages on side streets. I see a mama osprey tending to her babies on the top of a flagpole. She turns in our direction, but then she takes off, flies over the bay, and disappears. *Is that you, Grandpa? Are you the force under the osprey's wings?*

The clouds, some puffy whites and others graying from the storm that is on its way, hurry in the sky. *Is that your voice I hear in the wind?*

Petals from the wisteria are littering the grass. *Is it you, in the trunk of the tree? Are you proud of who I've grown to be? Can you feel how you've infused me?*

Just then a crack of thunder explodes. Everyone in the auditorium starts to clap and cheer, "Hear! Hear!"

Miles gets startled and jumps off my lap. He stomps my foot, hard. I bend down to rub it, and through my two sandal straps, I see the line from the poem tattooed on my foot. I look up, and projected on the screen is "The Layers."

> I have walked through many lives,
> some of them my own,
> and I am not who I was,
> though some principle of being
> abides, from which I struggle
> not to stray.
> When I look behind,
> as I am compelled to look
> before I can gather strength
> to proceed on my journey,
> I see the milestones dwindling
> toward the horizon
> and the slow fires trailing
> from the abandoned camp-sites,
> over which scavenger angels
> wheel on heavy wings.
> Oh, I have made myself a tribe

The Layers

out of my true affections,
and my tribe is scattered!
How shall the heart be reconciled
to its feast of losses?
In a rising wind
the manic dust of my friends,
those who fell along the way,
bitterly stings my face.
Yet I turn, I turn,
exulting somewhat,
with my will intact to go
wherever I need to go,
and every stone on the road
precious to me.
In my darkest night,
when the moon was covered
and I roamed through wreckage,
a nimbus-clouded voice
directed me:
"Live in the layers,
not on the litter."
Though I lack the art
to decipher it,
no doubt the next chapter
in my book of transformations
is already written.
I am not done with my changes.
—Stanley Kunitz, 1905–2006

We can't always have the poet. But we can always have the poem.

Yellow House

With the money I inherit from my grandparents, we have just enough to put a deposit down and buy our first home on Martha's Vineyard. It's an 1870s yellow clapboard farmhouse that has been abandoned for many years, forgotten about. Rumor has it the house was the first bank on the island and later a law office, and used to sit in the center of downtown Vineyard Haven where the ferry comes in. In 1970 the house was moved to Andrews Road, a side street in a lower-income neighborhood near town that local folks call Bargain Alley.

The house has great bones, but everything is needed to fatten it up with love: new windows, new walls, fresh coats of paint. It is fitting for the mix of antiques and midcentury pieces we got from my grandparents' apartment. There are old oak floors, thickly plastered low ceilings, and a brick Rumford fireplace that stands center in the living room. Every feature speaks old-world New England, reminding me of their Commercial Street home in Provincetown, which, thankfully, Mom and Gretchen have decided to keep.

We fill the kitchen cabinets with my grandparents' red-stained glasses, handblown, and the elaborately glazed platters that once carried Grandpa Stanley's famous orange-cranberry sauce to our Thanksgiving table or Grandma's potato chip–crusted apple pie topped with a scoop of vanilla ice cream—just the right amount of salty to the sweet. I unpack the long-humidified crate with Grandma's paintings and curate the living room. The fireplace mantel is the right spot for *Tiger, Tiger*, the painting that used to hang in our kids' room in Brooklyn, named after William Blake's poem. I use one of their pale blue tea saucers to hold the burning sage needed to cleanse the corners of the rooms. Rob says, "In spring, I'll work on a garden."

But the heart of the renovation project is the downstairs bathroom. The floors under the claw-foot tub are blackened with mold and warped from over a hundred years of dripping pipes and wet feet. It looks as if the entire tub will fall through the floor if we dare fill it for a bath. Wallpaper is peeling off the wall. The small pedestal sink is falling off its hinges. Rob detaches the sink and takes it to the dump. I remove the wallpaper. We replace it with wainscoting and add two fresh coats of paint to the walls, the same cobalt blue as Frida Kahlo's home in Coyocan. Plank by plank, Rob starts on the floor that is rotted under the tub. I rent a sander and get to work on the parts that are still intact.

It takes me, Rob, Maddy, and Philippe to carry in Grandma's marble sink that has been sitting in storage since the studio was sold after she died. It must weigh hundreds of pounds. We carefully fasten the sink on top of her black rod iron Singer sewing machine base. I dress the sink with a little dish I got from the studio and place three rose-oil, pearl-shaped soaps on it. To the left of the sink, I add the old shaving kit with the small round mirror on the long stem. I loop one of her pink floral-print hand towels through the ring next to the sink and hang three of her mythical-creature drawings in gold frames in a triptych on the wall. In the corner, I set the rococo-era chair, with a fleur-de-lis design etched in the wooden frame and a lumpy seat that you can feel the springs through. The chair once belonged to E. E. Cummings, Grandma's friend and favorite poet, who left it to her when he died.

Our bathroom is like a living shrine, an ode to people gone but not lost. It's always a talking point while we host Christmas Eve potlucks with our circle of friends, while the kids chase each other around the fireplace. Inevitably, conversation turns toward the bathroom and to my grandparents, and sometimes I read aloud one of Grandpa Stanley's poems to our friends.

I spend some of my most memorable moments in the yellow house in the downstairs bathroom, hours on E. E. Cummings's chair. The acoustics are perfect for singing with Miles as he plays with his plastic superheroes in the tub. Every bath, Shadow the cat walks the rim of the tub to be closer to Miles, slips, and falls in. Every time, Miles says, "Silly Shadow girl!" While pooping, Miles leans forward to stack his hands on the marble sink and rests his chin on his knuckles, so he doesn't fall into the toilet, being that his tiny bum is smaller than the ring. "Tell me a tory, Mama," he says while he labors over his push. I tell him of my years living in Mexico and about my favorite day ever—the day he was born. I tell him about how my friend Melanie buried his placenta by shack number ninety-nine, deep in the sand on Venice Beach, in the middle of the night so no one would see.

What I do not tell Miles during tubby time is that when you decorate your new home with your dead grandparents' belongings, your grandmother's ghost might latch onto the furniture and hijack the energy of your house. I do not tell him about the subtle residue, unseen to the eye but felt deep in the pit of the belly and in the groin, of buried ancestors and their stories that seeps into the sink water and into the pores of your skin when you wash your face. I do not tell him that, whether you want it or not, you might inherit the mantras of the dead along with the dishes.

"Most days it'll be just you and you, darling," the rose soaps whisper.

Stick-to-Me Kid

Miles is a stick-to-me kid. If he isn't riding piggyback or piggy front, his favored modes of transport, he hitches a ride on my leg, his two little feet stamped on one of mine, arms tightly around my waist. He lives up to his nickname, Monkey, although Baby Kangaroo may have been better apt for him. He is the kind of son who tucks his head into my crotch in public places. At parties, he nestles on my lap instead of climbing trees in the dark with the other littles. He twirls my skirt through his fingers, or cups my face and kisses me, child blocking me from any adulting whatsoever.

Sleep training is a bust. Miles begs for stories while Rob or I swap nights lying with him on his single mattress on the floor, covered in stuffed animals, extra pillows, and Shadow the cat. We summon fantastical tales of him and friends on adventures of lost treasures and rides on Batmobiles. As we close out one story, he pleads for another. When he finally gets tired enough to close his eyes, he throws his hand behind his back and gestures for me to pat his bum. I count in my head, *One, two, three . . .* all the way to a hundred until I feel his body surrender and get heavy with sleep. I carefully lift my hand away from his tiny behind, and tiptoe out of the room. On my second or third silent step, he inevitably pops his adorable blond head up from the pillow.

"Butt, Mama, pat my butt."

I climb back into bed to restart the count.

On date nights, he bawls as the babysitter does her best to

distract him from our exit. Those nights are pointless. Before we even get our cocktails, the cell phone rings and Rob calls the waiter over.

"Can you pack up our meal to go and bring us the check, please?"

I'll admit, sometimes I feel a bit claustrophobic. Sometimes I just want to hide and give myself a minute. It is always in those moments that Miles clings harder, as if some inherited sixth sense kicks in and he fears that if I go, I might find another life where I can roam freely without a monkey on my back and possibly never return. I would return, of course, but I must admit I fantasize the same story a few times.

It is Miles's first day of kindergarten, an apprehensive morning on all our parts. Will his teacher let him stand by her legs during recess, or will he be thrown out to the pack of five-year-old wolves to fend for himself? I stress the drop-off and map out my strategy. I plan to do as his teacher suggests in her welcome letter: "Bring them in, give them a hug, and promptly leave. It'll be easier for them once you're gone."

I promised Miles a bagel with lots of cream cheese in exchange for trying on kindergarten, so we go to Mocha Mott's, the local coffee shop, before school. There, I run into Patrie. She is a friend of Maddy's and someone I chat with here and there but do not really know. Patrie has a soft face, long, curly black hair, and darker toned skin like me. I have an affinity for women like Patrie, especially on this island. Martha's Vineyard is dominated by dirty blondes, WASPs, and hard-edged Puritan Bay Staters. There is an innate trust that comes along with being an anomaly, as if we belong to a secret I-see-you, I-know-you, how-ya-doing-here club, and I feel this way with Patrie.

She says hi and bends down to Miles's eye level.

"Hi, Miles." She looks up at me and says, "You seem worried, Mama. Is everything okay?"

In that higher-than-necessary, positive-parenting pitch that is supposed to make the children feel like everything is wonderful but really says *Help!* I say, "Miles starts kindergarten today!"

"How exciting!" She speaks directly to Miles. "Lucky guy."

I lean in closer and whisper in her ear, "I feel like our world is ending."

She takes the collar of my jean jacket into her hands and wraps it closer around my neck and smiles.

"May I offer you advice?" she asks, which I find considerate, coming from someone in the I-see-you club.

I nod.

"Always let him be the first to walk away. When he goes, stay facing him. He'll turn around to see you; they all do. They peek over their shoulder two or three times to see if you are still there or not. What he sees will shape him for life."

I never do thank Patrie, nor do I say that her advice was pure gold, the best parenting suggestion I have ever been given! But her suggestion polishes my mothering from that day forward. I may not ever be the chocolate chip cookie–baking type of Mom. You couldn't pay me to chaperone school trips, nor will I do fundraisers, or hand stitch Halloween costumes—like my mom friends do—but I will never turn my back on my son.

I used to hate the feeling of someone needing me. I used to equate neediness with being weak. But not with Miles. He teaches me that being needy is not only a mark of strength, but that it is triumphant. I admire his ability to ask for what he wants and demand he get it. I could never do that at his age. Honestly, I still can't. So what if I am the last mom to leave the classroom? That has got to be better than my lineage, where daughters could easily recall the patterns on the back of their mother's jackets but could never quite picture the lapels.

Papa Is for Having Fun

I proudly maintain my role by being the grounding Mama Bear of our home. I keep Miles on his sleep schedule. I help him with homework. I get him to birthday parties on time. *But Papa?* Papa is for having fun.

As many children do, Miles goes through a real daddy phase. At about age seven or eight, it is all Papa this and Papa that, and Rob rises to the occasion. He is the ultimate dad, loving, affectionate, and encouraging. He gives Miles his own shaving kit without the blade so the two of them can pretend to shave together. They go on beach hikes and woods excursions. Rob rakes leaves in a pile for Miles, his buddies, and Shadow to jump into and hide under.

One mild summer day, the three of us are in the backyard. Rob is showing Miles how to swing the bat as I watch from the hammock. The sun is coming through the leaves of the black oaks, casting shadows on the lawn with one sunny patch where they stand, like a spotlight.

Maybe it is the way Rob squats down on the deep green grass and positions Miles's hands around the bat. Maybe it is the low tone in his voice while he gives direction, with patience and kindness. "Step your right foot back, my boy. Watch the ball coming, and then slice it straight across the air." Maybe it is the way Miles tilts his head up to look and listen to his father with wide eyes and curiosity. Whatever it is, I am overcome with a wave of heavy, as if someone has just plunked a stone on my belly and it sinks me and the hammock to the ground.

Papa Is for Having Fun

Sometimes we don't know what we've missed until it is shown to us through our children. For the first time, I feel the true weight of not having my father.

The feeling lasts for months. While Rob kisses Miles's forehead when buckling him into the back seat of the car. While Rob carefully splits peas and pizza to opposite sides of the plate. While they wrestle and our entire yellow house fills with laughter. I grieve my dad. I am finally grieving him. Not his death—I am okay with that piece. But I am grieving his absence in my life. What would life have been like had he stayed, or at least visited or called us sometimes? Who would I be if I had a father to love me and teach me about life?

The tricky thing about grief is that grief does not let you grieve for one thing at a time. It's like anything and everything you've ever had to grieve for in your whole life tries to pull you underwater all at once. Like the chained anchor thrown to sea from the boat, with its iron spikes and hooks that drag and stick in the murky muck, we get tangled in the seagrass and the bottom feeders of grief.

As I grieve my fatherless childhood, I grieve other losses—my Grandpa Stanley, my cat Marley in Mexico, my life in sunny California. I grieve for my mother's teenage years since she's too busy to grieve for herself. I grieve for my grandmother's paintings, which are suffocating in bubble wrap in the basement of our Provincetown family home. I grieve for Joaquin. I wonder what happened to him, and the baby girl we never had. Does he, too, regret walking down the dusty path to the doctor's house in Merida on my twentieth birthday?

Some days, I imagine all the invisible chords still energetically tied between mothers and the babies we've let go of, and the fathers who we would have parented with. The image is busy and familiar like a Norman Rockwell painting, but somber—men and women going about their days, on different parts of the planet, each on their own patch of land. They fold laundry and give presentations in a meeting room, write poetry at a desk, or push shopping carts, posturing normal life. Each one holds up a mask on a popsicle stick in front of their faces, with painted ear-to-ear smiles on the front. But if you look from a side view, you can see their honest faces behind the masks—strained, wrinkled with regret, flushed with longing. Everyone looks older than their age. Around their hearts are ropes made of steel, the kind of cables that hold bridges, lifting from their chests, toward the top of the painting where the separate steel ropes tie around the would-have-been mother and would-have-been father. Both are forever attached to one little soul floating, like a helium balloon, toward a gray sky.

I welcome the grief. I go toward it. There is something familiar, refreshing even, in mourning, in allowing the melancholy to deepen me. It is a visit from an old self, the me-who-kneeled-in-my-mother's-plants self, the me-in-my-mother's-worried-womb self, perhaps even a past-life self that lives in bones and marrow. It is cleansing, purifying, a returning home to an ancient thread. It is my grief, yes, and it belongs to all the fatherless great-grandmothers of time, sewn with needle and thread through generations. As if a call from the wailing women of Jeremiah, or the Hindu Dharma Shastras, I celebrate the tears as ceremony.

But my grief bothers Rob. He's not a grief kind of man. He barely allowed himself time to mourn his mother's death when she passed a few years ago. It's odd, because he's a Cancer, a water sign, and a big feeler. But then again, he's a Californian, a surfer. He gets overwhelmed, so he opts for gliding on the surface. He paddles and takes the waves with no interest in scuba diving or deep-sea fishing.

"Try not to be so heavy all the time," Rob says.

"Deep does not always mean heavy," I say.

"Why always so dark?" he says.

"Why always so light?" I say.

I don't force it. I do not want to snuff out Rob's Papa glory with my grief. So I grieve alone. I wake up in the wee hours of the morning for daily grief rituals. I wander through woods, with my boots in hand, inhaling cool moss, exhaling my feet to the earth. I hug a tree and sit with the ants. I visit the ocean; I feel spirits in the wind whipping, my hair slapping my face. I match my breath to the ebb and flow of the waves. I take out pen and paper and write bad poetry and lyrics of songs I'll never sing. I find solace on my yoga mat.

Even more than it already has, my yoga practice becomes a life jacket, my Styrofoam bubble. I light some sage, put on a Krishna Das song, and roll around into shapes in the smoky room. I move a muscle and I nose-dive the emotional waves. My mat becomes a place to languish in my losses. It's a place to inhale and exhale, and be me. A place for me to feel, instead of judging, numbing, or bypassing feeling. A place to cry. An invitation to work out my stuff, or perhaps, work my stuff "in."

Lifetimes, lived and lost, are squeezed into yoga shapes. Forward bends release the secret sadness I have held for decades, and with that comes the opening for self-nurturing. Backbends, uplifting and empowering as they are, bring up my fear of vulnerability and my fear of showing my weakness. Inversions help me to see things from a new perspective, even in the difficult patches. With each pose, I oscillate through different moods. If I keep breathing through them, I feel okay. It is as if there is some magic ingredient that they mix in with the PVC my mat is made of that allows my time on it to be so different from how we are expected to behave during the rest of life.

As I say to my students, "We don't do yoga; yoga does us."

My yoga asks nothing more of me than that I practice. My practice does not negate my feelings, nor does it require me to move on or let them go. My practice becomes the tender touch of the mother, the protective and patient father, the husband who will sit and feel with me. Emotions, which once felt firm and fixed, transmute into motion. Feelings are just energy, and energy wants to move. Body and breath alchemize rejection to protection with this practice. Abandonment becomes a knowing that I want to cultivate self-love with this practice. Resentment shifts to motivation with this practice. Use the grief as fuel. We've got to feel it to heal it.

As the many yoga teachings suggest, "Practice, practice, practice, and the rest shall come."

As I touch my own grief, I am gifted the sensitivity to feel others in a renewed way. It is not thought; it is visceral. Tiny hairs on my skin become antennas that sense vibrations that read wordless stories written in the physiques of my yoga students. I intuit burdens in rounded shoulders, shame in hallowed stomachs, fear in tight hip flexors. I open the barn doors of my heart. I open my hands and close my eyes, and I can feel the souls of the humans in the room. I teach from that feeling.

"Allow your ribs to rest into your upper back instead of pushing them forward like a gymnast. Keep some of you for yourself. You don't have to give it all away. You were not born to mend everyone else's life."

"Breathe beyond the borders of skin; let your spirit fill the entire room. The days of playing it small are over."

"Use your fingers to peel apart the shoulder blades. Widen the upper back and let your heart open to that which is behind you. Lean into the past. Let it inform your way forward. You are the loving. The love. And the loved."

We teach what we need to learn.

On My Back

Mom is renovating the loft again. She calls my sisters and me and says, "You have two days to get your shit out."

I zip to the city and back overnight and get my shit out.

Back on the island, I am unpacking the car in the driveway. As I lean in to take out my wedding dress, of all things, the hatchback of our wagon lands on my back with a slam. I feel a crunch in my low spine, and I scream. Rob runs out to help me.

"I can't move," I say, breathless. "I'm stuck."

He lifts the hatch and gives me a hand. When I try to stand up, a burning, electric zing shoots from my right hip, down the outside of my leg, and to my right pinky toe. I can barely walk to the house without collapsing.

I try everything, for months: chiropractors and acupuncture; craniosacral, restorative yoga; special creams and potions; clean diets. I try binge-watching stand-up comedy, in hopes that the laughter medicine will help. But nothing helps. The pain in my back won't quit. Some days, I just lie on my yoga mat and cry. Miles lies next to me, Shadow by his side, and builds with his Lego bricks.

"I'm so sorry I can't jump on the trampoline with you," I say.

He kisses me and says, "It's okay, Mama. We can play this way."

On the days when the pain is too unbearable to even crawl on my knees, Rob carries me from room to room.

Each day becomes harder than the last. I'm neck deep, buried in the quicksand of wallowing, angry at my own body, at God, or whoever is in charge, feeling sorry for myself. *What did I ever do to deserve this?* I am humiliated by my failing body. I try the "fake it till I make it" approach. I grin and bear it, hidden in a back brace for my ninety-minute classes. After, I impatiently wait for the last student to leave so I may loosen the noose around my waist, and cry. I try to rally so we can have a normal life again, but I am just in too much agony.

After nearly a year of chronic pain, I finally get an MRI. I have a herniated disc in my spine, between lumbar vertebrae four and five. The herniation causes the jellylike substance of the disc between the vertebrae to squirt out and push on my sciatic nerve. The doctors suggest a steroid shot, and if that doesn't work, surgery.

Steroid shot? Surgery? Oh hell no! I can fix this myself! I'm a yoga teacher!

I have relied on my body for my career, my identity, and my self-worth. I have made a name for myself as Sherry the Yogini, the one who solves problems with yoga poses and yoga anecdotes. I am the one who can do all the fancy postures without even warming up. But I can't seem to fix my back. I can't even do any yoga poses. Even lying down hurts too much.

I am stubbornly attempting to heal myself on my own with no luck. Rob tries to convince me to listen to the doctors and get the steroid shot. I object to the help. I feel as if I'm in some spiritual-awakening process, and this pain is par for the course. Maybe there's something here for me to learn. This pain cannot be in vain.

One night, in bed with Miles, and not really expecting an answer, I ask a question out loud.

"What if I can never walk without pain again? What will I do?"

Miles puts his head on my shoulder, reaches his arm up the side of my face, and rubs my earlobe. He says, so sweetly in his crackling nighttime voice, "Then you'll live in a wheelchair, Mama."

Miles is right—as I've done before and I've got to do now, I must accept my fate and grow from it. Since sitting is the only position that does not hurt, I take it as a sign. If I'm going to be sitting, I may as well sit right. *Get to the real yoga. The yoga you've avoided. Sit your ass down, Sherry. Meditate.*

Sitting still and meditating does not come easily. There is static, too many interferences. I'm met with laziness and the spinning hamster wheel of mental restlessness at the same time. There is pain in my body, feelings of separateness, stubborn stuck-ness, gooey muck-ness, frazzled fear, old stories dragging me by rope and horse. All that—in the first minute.

But I have learned from my posture practice over these years, and I know that when we stay in a pose for longer than we want to and breathe, a shift happens. The practice asks that we lean in deeper to our edge, reach a tiny bit further, beyond our perceived stopping points. So I stay and say, *Show me the way.* I breathe and ask, *What is this injury trying to teach me?*

I try on many different meditation techniques—staring at a candle in one pointed focus, counting beads on my malas, reciting mantra, mirror gazing. I sit. I tune into sounds in the room and outside. I pay attention to smells, the taste in my mouth, and the sensation of clothing on skin. I see speckles of light, shape, and texture behind my eyelids. From there, I track physical sensation in my body, noticing what places are calling my attention and other parts of my body that I don't even feel are there. I notice how my temperature changes as I body scan. I witness my thoughts and feelings like passing clouds.

Like the painted, wooden Russian dolls that I played with as a kid, I open myself to find another and another. Like the line in my grandpa's poem that is tattooed on my foot, I "live in the layers." I stay right where I am, until mind dust settles, under the radio static of thoughts and feelings. I ride the magic carpet of breath, past the physical sheaths of skin, bone, muscle, and organ. I find myself inside channels of subtle, vast matter. I become the music of the flute. I become the colors of the rainbow. Old knots loosen.

It is here, ass on cushion, cushion on floorboards, earth under floor, strapped in a back brace, literally getting on my own nerves, that the real yoga does me. Or better said, it undoes me. Here, there is no pain, no body, even. Separate, polarized parts recalibrate and harmonize together as one. Right and wrong, yes and no, body and mind merge. They pulse and pendulate like contemporary dancers on a stage. Like snakes winding up Ixchel's staff. Like the yin-yang tattoo on my shoulder, a perfectly balanced circle of dark and light. I am not injured Sherry, nor the mother, the wife, the yoga teacher, the daughter, or the sister. I am not my back pain. I am a knowing, glowing nothingness.

Meditation gifts me crisp clarity—an acute awareness about myself that is so obvious, it is almost funny. When I exit the meditation and return to my room and reconvene with logic, I get "hits" about my nature that up until now I have ignored.

I begin to see my back injury as a metaphor of how I have been living my life. Be the strong one, the rock, the tree trunk for others to climb to get to the fresh air from the top limb. Without a father to keep the peace, keep Mom stable, or keep my sisters in check, I took on the role as the man of the house. I was both buoyed and burdened by it. It earned me affection, attention, and reassurance, yes, but not without a cost. And now it is easy to see that I have re-created the family dynamic in many of my other relationships since. As wife, friend, and yoga teacher, being the person for everyone else to lean on keeps me in the center of all my circles. It is the very foundation on which I have built all my houses, especially my yellow house. My subconscious motto: *If everyone needs me, then no one will leave me.*

The Sanskrit word *kavaca* means a cover, like the orange peel, bark on a tree, or a tortoise's shell. Protective gear, grown organically based on the environment we are born into. Coverings to help us survive. Being strong has been my *kavaca*, but it has kept me wound around solitude, always feeling as if something is missing. That which helped me survive as a kid is no longer helping me thrive as an adult. Not anymore.

Habits are formed by repetition. Nerves that fire together, wire together. They create neural pathways, like tire tracks on a muddy road. Grooves that get so ingrained in our internal systems, we return to them over and over by default. In the yoga science, these deep grooves are called samskaras. It sounds like "some scars," and that is exactly what it feels like. Samskaras are the subconscious ruts formed from our life experiences that hook us in habit and cloud our true sense of self. I have made the mistake of misinterpreting my hard shell as my nature, or aspects of my personality, and assumed they are fixed and unchangeable.

When I rehash the scene of the day that I reached into my car to get my wedding dress, of all things, and the hatchback slammed on my back, I see so much more than my spine being herniated in that moment. That hatchback cracked my *kavaca* and severed my subconscious, self-protective habits along with my spinal disc. Now I cannot hold anyone up—not even myself. Now I can't help but wonder, does anyone have my back?

I decide to get a steroid shot, and after eighteen months of pain, I finally feel some relief. There remains a dull ache, but the acute nerve pain is gone. Three months later, I get a second shot. I move with caution, I am careful, but I can move again. I begin my rehab slowly with light stretches, core-stabilizing movements, and twice-daily meditation. Little by little, I return to peace in my body, but I am changed.

My back brace helps me to create the boundary I have been unable to create for myself. I am more conscious of what I allow into my space and what I keep out. Now I ask Rob to take over the bill paying. Now when Mom calls me for support, I suggest she talk to her therapist, not me. Now I wear my back brace over my clothes as I teach, for everyone to see. I take myself off the able-bodied yoga teacher pedestal, and I sit my ass down on the floor on a striped blanket and use nothing but words and feeling to guide the class.

My role as a yoga teacher is not to be everyone's friend or savior; it is to cultivate a sacred, brave space for others to undo, to put down their armor, to shed the layers of protection they, too, have used to survive. I talk my students through meditations, visualization practices, and slow, deliberate, tiny micro movements. We spend five to seven minutes in each pose, slowing our roll way down so that we can unwind and relax, and see ourselves underneath the habits we have formed. Sometimes, I have them sit back-to-back and just breathe together for the entire practice. Other classes, we push the yoga props out of the way and clear the floor. I put on Bob Marley, African drumming, or house music so they can have a dance party. Many classes, we lie over bolsters in restorative poses and chant om.

As I and my teaching style change, so do the people who come to practice with me. I no longer have full classes. Many of my former students have moved on to practice with other ass-kicking teachers, and I am okay with it. My teaching style cannot be for everyone. There are others who can instruct the party-trick poses. I want to teach to the soul.

I tally the gifts from my injury, illuminated by nearly a decade of yoga practice and teaching, and I am inspired to write again. I want to put language and theory to my experiences. I want to be versed in the traditional teachings, understand the philosophy from a contextual place of where and when they were realized and translate those to modern life. I reread the sacred scriptures—the *Yoga Sutras of Patanjali*, the *Bhagavad Gita*, and the *Upanishads*. I learn more of the Sanskrit chants and teach myself to play the harmonium.

On My Back

I take out manuals from my various yoga trainings, highlight what I loved about them, and take note of what I think is missing. I fill in the gaps. I ask my teachers if I can assist their trainings to observe how to train teachers from the insider's view. I note what they each do beautifully and where there are weak spots. I map what I will do differently.

I spend the next six months writing the curriculum for FLY Yoga School, a two-hundred-hour training program. It's three hundred pages of anatomy, energy-body science, philosophy, posture breakdown, teaching techniques, business strategies, mantras, meditations, breath work techniques, self-study exercises. I turn in the curriculum to Yoga Alliance, and the curriculum is approved.

In the spring of 2011, along with thirteen beautiful souls willing to take the ride with me, I graduate my first batch of yoga teachers. We did the training on a private property gifted by one of my clients—ninety acres of secluded woods, with its own private beach, where we not only practiced yoga but lived and ate together. For the graduation ceremony, I make all the students T-shirts that say "Original Gangsters of FLY Yoga School."

Home after the ceremony, exhausted from pouring my entire being into the yoga teacher training for ten days straight, I can't wait to climb into bed with Miles for a storybook, tickle, and a snuggle, something I desperately missed during these ten-hour days of training. I look to the bookshelf for my and Miles's favorite early childhood nighttime read, Margaret Wise Brown's *Big Red Barn*. "Mom, come!" Miles calls to me from his bedroom. As I pull the book out, my old Frida Kahlo biography gets pulled with it and falls to the floor. One of the pages I had tucked inside falls out, floats in midair like a falling feather, and softly lands on the oak plank next to my foot. I pick up the page and read the question I had written to myself some twenty-four years earlier: "When do we get to be the person we are inside, outside in the world?" I smile.

A Smoke and a Song

It may have taken me a quarter-century, but I figured out how to take my pain and make something beautiful from it. Sometimes, something beautiful comes in the disguise of a most unexpected thing. My art form was found in the slam of the hatchback. Sometimes, something beautiful demands we break the old us, to become the person we are meant to be.

Relationship Status:
It's Complicated

She's the whirling dervish, the woman who absorbs all the oxygen in the room. People admire her for her youthfulness, her love for learning and adventure, for all her rings and bracelets, wild style, and white locks. She's the first one to arrive to the wedding and the last one off the dance floor, the one kicking up into handstands in yoga classes. Whenever her people want or need her, be it a word of advice or just a call to say hi, she picks up on the first ring and stays on the line for as long as they need her to stay. I hear she really is a great therapist. She's also the most generous grandmother.

I appreciate her spunk—of course I do. I have compassion for her; I always have. I know she's covering up loneliness by being such a big presence. I know she's doing the best she can in the ways she knows how. She survived a terribly lonely childhood and traumatic teen years. She was left alone to raise three girls, and single mothering ain't no picnic—everyone knows that. Now that I am a mother, I can understand. Mothering is like this. We throw a hook and line into the deep ocean of loving and see what bites. We cannot predict what the outcome of our casting will be. All we can do is reel it in and see what is on the end of the hook and release the rest.

But I can't keep pretending that we are better than we are, not to her or anyone else, not anymore. She means well, that I do know, but she can't help herself. She's gooey, porous, unaware of where she ends and I begin. We are not the same person, some dynamic duo, a mother and daughter who bond over yoga and writing and cups of coffee.

And yet, we are.

Our relationship status: *It's complicated.*

When I try, when I open a door to real connecting about wanting a real relationship, when I beg, "Please, Mom, just listen," she is Ms. Floodgates. I give an inch. She takes a marathon of miles, gaslighting every conversation to deny my feelings and make it about her. Her life. Her needs. Her schedule. Her, her, *her.* So I stay on the surface. I feel guilty for my short sentences. I really don't want to cut her off and shut her out, but she doesn't leave me with any other choice. I give myself permission to clearly divide the placental membrane that separates us now. It is me who gets to choose the space between us.

Yet I yearn for a relationship that feels like it looks. I crave leaning into her. I want to share stories, and songs, and love each other openly. I need my mother, especially being a mother. I need an elder to offer me sage advice, especially since Grandma and Grandpa have passed, more so with all this spiritual awakening that is happening inside me. And even more so with the doubt of where to place it in real time—in real life. But with us, it always ends up the other way around. Sherry counsels Babette. We just can't seem to break the pattern.

My therapist suggests asking my mother if she'd be willing to try therapy with me. "Maybe she'll surprise you?" she says. "Maybe you're the one keeping the relationship the same?"

She's right. I am forty-one years old, way too old to have these lingering issues with my mother. As Lisa would say, "Get ovah it. She's never gonna change. Move on, already."

When I ask Mom, she is delighted. My mother wants nothing more than to be close with me; I know this for a fact. She always has. She just doesn't know how to meet me where I am.

Relationship Status: It's Complicated

We plan for me to go to New York for a long weekend so we can have some sessions with Carl, her therapist of two decades.

The three sessions are helpful, but not groundbreaking. Carl is a decent therapist, but I don't think he's great. He's skilled at open-ended questioning, gesturing further inquiry by tilting his chin up and saying things like, "Let's explore that." But he's clearly taking her side. He doesn't seem to understand why it creates a divide between me, Maddy, and Lisa that she says one thing to one of us and another thing to the others. And that then she lies when we confront her about it. Or that she kept her ex-boyfriend in Cuba—who she was supporting financially for nearly a decade!—a secret from us.

Under Carl's one-sided supervision, Mom and I hash out some issues, rewind a couple of old-story tapes, have a few cries, and hug it out. In the end, not much is resolved. Carl suggests a plan for moving forward. Mom promises to be a better listener and to be more transparent. I promise to try to see her as my ally and not my enemy.

The night before leaving the city, after we dine on sushi and a bottle of cab, she goes to watch the ten o'clock news, and I go into her office to call Rob and check in on his and Miles's day. Sitting on top of her printer, I see an ivory card stock with the words "Certificate of Completion" on it. I pick it up to look closer. It has her full name, and underneath that is "OM Yoga School." The certificate is sealed by the stamp of a gold om symbol.

You've got to be kidding me!

I look at it again. I text a picture of it to Maddy. "Mad, what's this about?"

"You didn't know?" she texts back. "Mom has been in yoga-teacher training for over a year."

How dare she do a yoga-teacher training! What, is she now going to teach yoga? At seventy-four years old? How dare she hide it from me! Especially after our sessions with Carl!

A Smoke and a Song

I almost storm into Mom's room for an explanation but stop myself. Instead, I just turn the certificate facedown on the desk.

I'm angry. But if I'm being honest with myself, under the anger is hurt.

How could Mom spend a full year in someone else's yoga-teacher training and not mine?

Hands

I am sitting on a blanket in a candlelit studio in Venice, California, with about forty other yoga teachers, training. My hands are resting on my inner knees, palms up. I am distracted and achy from the travel out west and the late-night catching up with Melanie, who I'm staying with while I'm here for a long-weekend Somatic Healing and Integration Immersion, the final session of an advanced holistic-yoga studies training.

The training is taught by my favorite teacher. He's an austere yogi, dressed in all white except for the sandalwood mala beads around his neck and wrists, who speaks with a warm, honey-toned voice. He is telling us a story about monkey traps in India made from a hollowed-out coconut shell that is chained to a stake. Inside the coconut, the hunters put cooked rice. The scent of the rice lures the hungry monkey, and he sticks his hand through a small hole cut into the coconut.

"The monkey's hand fits through the hole when it's open, but when he grabs the rice, his clenched fist can't back out," my teacher says. "He pulls and pulls but is not able to escape."

I feel my fingers swell. With each inhale my hands get larger, colder, and more tingly, and with each exhale, they freeze into ice sculptures on my lap. I fight the urge to shake off my hands to stop the sensation. I have been practicing long enough not to run from the things that find me while I am meditating. I breathe. I track the sensations I feel in my furled hands. All fourteen phalanges hinge at the little joints, locking down arteries and veins.

A Smoke and a Song

There is zero blood flow to my fingers. My fingertips are numb. I cannot move my hands, not even if I wanted to.

I hear my teacher continue to tell us about the monkey.

"All the monkey needs to do is let go of the rice, and he'll be able to run away. But he clings to the rice, and thus, he clings to his death."

I am breathing—present to both the story about monkeys clutching and my frozen, knotted hands.

"We are not unlike the monkey," he says. "Attached to our desire and our fear. Clinging to our lives."

A cold, liquid sensation travels from my hands up my arms to my throat and pours down my spinal line. As it passes by lumbar spine, I feel a zing where I herniated my disc.

"The mystical teachings tell us, the more we grasp, the closer we are to our death," my teacher says, as the cold spreads through my pelvic bowl and slinks through the creases of my hip sockets.

"There are hundreds of channels of energy that travel from the heart chakra to the hands and the hands to the heart chakra, the home of unconditional love," he says. "Those channels gather in the center of our palms. When the heart is open, a two-way river of pure-love consciousness, represented by a glowing emerald light, is expressed through our fingers and palms. Thus, we say the term 'healing hands.'"

The lower half of my body starts to throb. I keep breathing. He keeps talking.

"The hands render the map of our heart space, both through pressure points that correlate with our heart organ, and through the causal, or spiritual, heart center. When the heart chakra is blocked, hardened by protections, deficient of love, and longing, it manifests in grasping and the need to control. We become the monkey, and our yearning for unconditional love, the rice."

My knees start to flap up and down uncontrollably. I attempt to push my legs firmer into the floor with my hands, but my

Hands

hands are in lockdown on my wrists, and I cannot move my arms. Everything hurts.

"Release what grips you," the teacher says.

I feel a bowling ball of pressure on my tailbone.

"Let go of what you cling to. Let it all go," he says. There it is again, that stupid phrase. The most overused expression in my line of work and my biggest pet peeve. *Wouldn't we let go if we knew how to?* "All you need is already in the palm of your hands," he says.

I have a memory. I am young, maybe twelve. I am in my bed at the loft. I am banging on the wall between my room and Lisa's. My hands are larger than the rest of me, and they are frozen. I am frenzied, calling out to her, "Lisa! Help!"

Oh no, not the hands.

It has been decades since I remembered the reoccurring nightmare I had as a kid. In the nightmare, my hands would grow into these thick, heavy, cold, larger-than-life masses. I'd wake up in my dazed half-dream, half-wakened state and hold out my rope-skinny arms and see my fingers as grotesque ice blocks right before my eyes. I'd crawl off my mattress, and clumsily climb down from my loft bed, almost falling, in a panic, my feet practically missing the rungs of the ladder, hands numb. It was impossible to get a grasp on the rails. I'd feel my way, with my snowball, monster hands, to Lisa's room. Back then, Lisa would be up, high and still moist from dancing at the Funhouse, the club she used to go to.

"My hands, my hands; look!" I'd scream.

Unable to see the beasts that hung on my wrists, she'd say, "Calm down, Baby Bug Out. You're having a bad dream. Just relax."

She'd pull me under her covers and do her best to slowly open my fisted fingers and warm my hands in hers. I'd flop my exhausted arms over her side and spoon her, nestling my face into her hardened, Aqua Net hair. She smelled like a cross between stale cigarettes and rose oil.

A Smoke and a Song

The weight of the bowling ball now fills my entire pelvis, and there is so much pressure in my body, I feel I might implode.

"Open your hands, unclutch," the teacher says.

After Lisa was sent away and her bedroom was empty, the hands nightmare got worse.

"You are not your pain," my teacher says. "You are not that which hurts your heart. You are love."

I open my eyes for the first time since I sat down. I look around the room to see all these serene people sitting, hands open on their laps.

I have to get out of this room.

I hobble to the bathroom. I lock myself in one of the stalls and sit on the closed lid of the toilet. My breath is shallow, my hands, icicles. Whatever is weighing on my pelvic floor wants to come out. It feels real—something solid, dark, and not mine, like some evil energetic entity has crawled up inside me. I feel like I am being possessed, in some exorcism, my body ambushed by this intense sensation of needing to bear down and push.

I have no other choice. I contract every fibrous muscle in my core and force the weight I feel in my pelvis downward, just as I did when I birthed Miles. This pressure gets tighter and more painful. My pelvis might splinter into a million bone bits if I don't do this, so I push.

As I'm pushing, I remember.

We were playing, I thought. He tickled me. I laughed, at first. But when he pinned me down, the empty in his eyes said, *I'm not playing anymore.* I tried to kick him off, but he was dead-man heavy, buried-under-sand-at-the-beach heavy. He grabbed the back of my head. His hands were fire hot, branding me. I tried to turn my face, but I couldn't. He put his lips to mine. He pushed his tongue past my teeth. His breath tasted like bloody steak. His mustache was scratchy.

Hands

"You've been wanting that, haven't you?" he whispered, unlatching his lips.

I had been wanting a first kiss, that was true. But not from my mother's boyfriend Len.

Len jumped to his side of the bed, sat back against a stack of pillows, and pretended he was watching TV, just in time for Mom to come back from the bathroom. I smelled her perfume, Clinique Aromatics Elixir, and I knew she was there. I knew she saw what he did. But she didn't say anything. I lay there, staring up at the ceiling, like a wooden plank, my toes curling, arms stiff by my sides, hands locked in two compact, frozen fists. The spirals on our tin-tiled ceiling detached and dropped on me like snow.

I remember Mom climbing over me to get into the bed. She lay down between me and Len, her back turned to me. Len was talking, but I could not make out the words, only echoes. Mom and I were inches apart but separated by an entire Arctic Ocean— Mom and Len on their own boat, and I was on a patch of iceberg, alone. I could still feel Len's handprints hot and throbbing on my skull. Even worse was the throbbing in my ears from my mother's silence. I split in two. Half of me remained on the bed, cold as ice, stunned silent. The other half had disappeared out the window, toward the skyscrapers.

I keep pushing. I remember more.

He lurked in the bathroom while I was in the shower. I knew it was Len. This was not the first time this happened. I pulled the shower curtain closer to the wall and stood in the middle of the tub with my arms wrapped around my body, shivering. He drew open the curtain. His shirt was off, and he was unbuttoning his jeans. I jerked back and bonked my head on the wall of shower tile. "Ouch!"

"Quiet," he whispered. "Stand still. I just need a minute."

I closed my eyes. I squeezed toward my insides to make myself smaller. I hummed in my head. I heard his zipper, his heavy breathing, a quiet moan, the door open and close.

A Smoke and a Song

I did not tell Mom about the showers. Instead, I stopped taking showers at night. I stopped making Mom her coffee. I stayed out late into the night and started misbehaving with my friends. I did not tell my sisters, either. I knew if Lisa found out, she would have escaped the group home just so she could kill him, or even worse, murder my mother. I did not want to be the reason why my sister was put in handcuffs, not again.

I remember that one day, Len never came back to the loft, and I never asked if he was coming back. I knew the answer when I saw Mom throw his mustache clippers in the black bathroom trash bin. I suppose I followed her lead. I took Len, the kiss, and the showers and buried them in the bottom of the black trash bin of my memory.

I have no idea how long I am in that yoga studio bathroom stall pushing, but I do know that the memory that was in my body for thirty years is now out. My legs are quaking. I press my bare feet onto the brown-tiled bathroom floor to ground myself. I look around the stall to get my bearings. I see a circular, metallic lock on the door, a toilet paper roll, and the plastic tampon bin attached to the beige stall wall. I hold out my hands in front of me. My fingers are limp. I wrap my arms around my shoulders, giving myself a hug. I breathe into my upper back, using my fingers to peel apart my shoulder blades and fan my back ribs, to make more space for each inhale.

You are okay. I am okay. It's over.

I walk out of the bathroom, feeling ten pounds lighter. Even my yoga leggings feel loose on me now.

During the anatomy lesson I learn about neuroception, our internal surveillance system, or our "automatic threat detector." Through touch receptors on the skin, a two-way communication system of body-to-brain and brain-to-body helps us to sense if we are safe or in danger. If a threat is present, or perceived to be,

Hands

the sympathetic response kicks in, known as fight-or-flight, and our body releases cortisol—the stress hormone. Cortisol redirects blood flow away from our extremities toward the torso, where it increases heart rate and pumps blood to the muscles needed to fight or escape the danger. In the hands alone, there are seventeen thousand of these touch receptors.

A common side effect of a person with high levels of cortisol, one who has experienced prolonged levels of stress, one who suffers from post-traumatic stress disorder, is cold hands and nightmares.

Cosmic Knowledge

I'm back in Mexico with Don Miguel, only I'm forty-two, not twenty-two. And it's a different Don Miguel, not my Don Miguel from San Juan Chamula. This one is my yoga teacher's teacher, also Mayan, from Merida, of all places. I have been invited to come study shamanism with him, although he looks more like a professor than a shaman. He's about my age, dressed in khakis with a striped button-down, balding with a bushy unibrow and John Lennon glasses. We are on day four of a five-day excursion doing Don Miguel's Mastering the Winds initiation. Today at Uxmal, an ancient archeological site known as "the city of the kindness of the moon," we are standing in the courtyard of the Nunnery Quadrangle in a circle.

"Uxmal," Don Miguel begins, "was the feminine university for priestesses, where Mayan women received both human and cosmic knowledge."

He walks around, passes each of us a card, and says, "*In lak'ech.*" (I am you.) We say back, "*A'la k'en.*" (And you are another me.) A few students are drumming. I'm participating but also rolling my internal third eye. I love these types of rituals; I can drop in easily, but it feels a little ridiculous to be standing in this ancient site doing a ceremony with a bunch of privileged American women, especially with all these tourists staring at us. I am one of these women, I know, but somehow, I convince myself that I am different from them. *I lived in Mexico. I speak the language. I've done ceremonies, way before they were trending.*

Cosmic Knowledge

On each card is a drawing of a Mayan symbol that is, as told to us by Don Miguel, "to be our guide for this ceremony." On the other side is a translation in English. He says, "Ask for support on a problem."

I don't have anything much to ask about. Things are okay right now. Miles has adjusted to his new junior high school and even has his first girlfriend. I'm about to begin my third round of teacher training, and with seventeen students this time. Rob has finally found his thing with Broga, the name he coined and trade-marked for his yoga-for-men program. Although I am not a fan of commodifying yoga, I am glad he's found some fire to go after a career, and even more relieved he found a business partner in his endeavors, so I don't have to help him organize his teaching schedule anymore. And despite my resistance to adding more to my plate, Rob and I recently purchased a nine-hundred-square-foot condo in the commercial zone of Vineyard Haven where we will co-home Broga and FLY Yoga School. Renovations are underway. We'll be able to open Yoga Haven before the busy summer season.

I hold my card, close my eyes, and internally say, *Show me what I am here to learn.*

I look at my card. The image on my card is my girl. Ixchel! The flip side of the card reads, "Seven generations forward and back."

I feel a little woozy. Dehydrated, possibly. Probably. Heat in the Yucatan is something fierce. Don Miguel comes over and instructs me to hold out my card so he can see.

"Ixchel," he says. "The most powerful mother of all."

He instructs me to look up. Up above me is a ceiba tree. Between the limbs, I see the piercing high-noon sun and some puffy white clouds rolling by in the sky.

"Ceiba tree is the bridge between woman and the under-world, and woman and the sky. Between the past and future."

The tree above me starts to rattle. The clouds, the branches, and patches of sky form into strange patterns. Don Miguel is still talking, but I can only make out a few phrases of what he is saying. I close my eyes.

"Seven generations . . . destiny . . . great-grandmother, grandmother, mother . . . you must . . . child, grandchild, great-grandchild . . . axis."

When I open my eyes again, I'm flat on the ground. There are specks of light between me and everything else. The red flowers from the tree look like blood drops hanging from the branches.

Don Miguel helps me sit up. I blink my eyes. The temple etchings ricochet off the stone and hop across the quadrangle. My ears are ringing. I must have fainted. I brush off the dust on my bare shoulders and arms. He asks one of the women to pass him her shawl and drapes the pale pink, silk wrap over my shoulders. He sits on the dirt in front of me and gestures for the others to go away. He waits until they have disappeared into the doorway of the stone temple across the quad before asking, "The mothers of your lineage suffered, no?"

"Yes," I say.

"And they have hurt each other and the children because of their suffering."

"Yes. A lot of mother-daughter suffering in my family."

"Heal your wounds, then you heal their wounds. Three generations back. Three generations forward."

I ask him to explain. He pushes his glasses higher on the bridge of his nose with one finger.

"Each of us has the power to cut the chords of karma," he says. "You must transmute the family pain through love. Then you will transform into the woman you are meant to be."

"I am trying," I say.

"Just because you can do many things well does not mean you should," he says. "It weakens you. When you do too much, you leak your power to do the real healing. Pick three things. Devote all your energy to them. What is not meant for you will fall away." He makes a karate-chop motion with his hands. "You are a mother, so raising your child and caring for your family is number one," he says.

"Yes, always. Miles is always number one."

"And you are a teacher of teachers. That is number two."

I nod.

"And you are a daughter, yes, still? Your mother is alive?"

"Yes."

"That is number three." He releases my hands.

"This one is hard for me," I say. "It's complicated."

"My child, all our relations mirror that which we have with the mother," Don Miguel says. "You must access unconditional love and forgiveness for your mother. Her way comes from your grandmother, and hers from the great-grandmother. Each generation has passed the pain to the next. They may not have known better than to do so. But you do."

"I try," I say. "I do try."

"We do not complain of too much sunshine"—he points up to the sky—"nor do we anger at storms. We adjust to nature's temperature. Love your mother like you love Mother Nature—with all her seasons."

"But how?"

"We break the family patterns without breaking the family connection."

"It's not easy."

"No one said it is supposed to be easy," he says. "Heal the mother wound. Back and forward." He stands up and then helps me to stand too.

"But how?" I find myself asking him again.

"See her *with* love, not *for* love."

"With love, not for love?" *Hmmm . . .*

We walk toward the others in our group. He puts a hand on the back of my heart and says, "We inherit the wounds, yes, but we equally inherit the wisdom. Your destiny depends on which one of these two you choose to live by."

Hoʻoponopono

"I'm sorry. Please forgive me. Thank you. I love you. I'm sorry. Please forgive me. Thank you. I love you. I'm sorry. Please forgive me. Thank you. I love you."

I commit to repeating this mantra forty times a day, for forty days straight, just as one of my teachers suggests I do. I write it with Sharpie on all the mirrors in our yellow home, so that I read it while washing my face or brushing my teeth. I pencil it onto a yellow Post-it that I stick to the glass of water I leave by Miles's bedside table, because he needs it too. I teach it to my students.

Hoʻoponopono, the ancient Hawaiian forgiveness prayer, means "to make things right." The first part of the prayer, "I'm sorry," is based on the idea that we must first accept responsibility for our own healing by forgiving ourselves for anything that happened to us and for any subconscious, self-sabotaging habits that have been developed as a result. We may not be at fault for them, the prayer suggests, but we are accountable for our healing them. We apologize to our body first, then our minds, and then our spirits for any harmful choices we've made toward ourselves. The second part, "Please forgive me," is to remove harm we've done to others, so that we may receive redemption and repentance. "Thank you," cultivates infinite possibility for new beginnings with the healing power of gratitude. "'I love you,'" my teacher says, "always accelerates the healing process."

Hoʻoponopono was made popular by Dr. Ihaleakala Hew Len, a psychologist who was tasked to counsel incurable patients in a criminally insane ward at the Hawaii State Hospital in the 1980s. Dr. Hew Len never practiced talk therapy with his patients. Instead, he would read through their files and then chant ho'opo-nopono to himself. Studies report that within months most of the patients were taken off medication, and within a year those that were shackled were allowed to walk freely. Without ever see-ing his patients face-to-face, Dr. Hew Len healed the entire ward by meditating on the mantra. Over the course of four years, all the patients were released back into society. Without patients to cure, the hospital closed its doors in 1987.

I am chanting this prayer in hopes to heal my past, in hopes that it may trickle down and improve my relations. I can't seem to figure out why I put so many barriers between me and the people who try to love me the most. I swung to the other side of the pendulum after my back injury. I'm what you call overly "boundaried" now. Especially with my husband.

I knew opening a studio together was probably not the best thing for our marriage, but I didn't listen to my gut. And the studio is now a nine-hundred-square-foot wedge between us, carving a divide.

Rob's Broga business has taken flight in new directions. He's off island most of the week, guest teaching around the country and doing press interviews and photo shoots. Although I have wanted something like this our entire marriage—Rob fulfilled, passionate about his career, making a name for himself and mak-ing money—now I'm not so sure. I'm overwhelmed with having to run all the things alone. I feel used. I carried him for years. I showed him how to teach. Now I feel disposable.

When I went to my teacher for guidance, I said, "I'd expect my marriage to get better with my spiritual practice, but every-thing seems to be getting worse."

"Just chant."

That's all he said.

I'm sorry. Please forgive me. Thank you. I love you.

A Smoke and a Song

I don't want to admit I'm losing my attraction to him ever since he started using my coconut-vanilla body lotion, nor that I am agitated when we are together and lonely when we aren't, not to others or to myself. We are the perfect yogi couple, a sweet family of three; we have a great life. Why can't I just be satisfied with what is?

I push my doubt away. It bounces back to bite me. This is what psychologists call retroflection: that which is not expressed on the outside turns against itself. When I am with Rob, I become someone I don't like. I'm hard on him, and I'm hard on myself for it.

When I call my teacher on day thirty-nine to tell him it's not working, that I feel worse, he says, "Do another forty days. And another forty if you need after that. Keep chanting."

I restart the count.

If Dr. Hew Len could heal an entire ward of criminally ill patients with the prayer, who is to say I can't help my marriage by chanting?

"I'm sorry. Please forgive me. Thank you. I love you."

Mosaic

I am rushing through the kitchen like a train off its rail. It is already after eight, and I am late getting Miles to school. I grab the straps of my bag off the kitchen island and scream, "Monkey, let's go!" As I throw my bag over my shoulder, I feel it snag, drag, and pull something heavy with it. I spin around, throw my hands out to catch it, but it falls to the floor just short of my fingers.

Smash! Pieces splinter in all directions as it hits the unforgiving oak planks.

Fuck! Not the bowl! Not the bowl!

Not the exquisite, white, porcelain Tuscan salad bowl given to us at our wedding! The last wedding gift I own is gone. All the wedding gifts are gone. The kitchenware, the sheets and pillows, and the small bookcase handcrafted by Grandpa have been broken, left behind, or lost during our moves from East Coast to West and West Coast back to the East. The Turkish rug has been donated to the thrift, the bread maker regifted to a friend. The photo collages are with Rob, in his new place. The inevitable wear and tear of fourteen years of marriage . . . all gone.

I look down and see white pieces of ceramic, showing their sandy brown clay behind the glaze, splintered all over my recently mopped oak floor. A large chunk is tipped on its side by my left foot. The rest are in puzzle-shaped shards, scattered under the dishwasher, below the dining room table, with one lonely sliver next to the woodstove. And dust—too much dust, everywhere.

A Smoke and a Song

Of all things, the bowl. *It figures.*

How symbolic. Our container, broken in pieces.

I look at the bowl and say, "I'm sorry. Please forgive me. Thank you. I love you."

I burst into tears.

"What was that?" Miles has come downstairs. "Mom, are you okay?"

"I'm fine, sweetie," I say. "I just dropped something."

But I am far from fine. I barely slept last night. It was another hard night. Even with the three melatonin gummies, I stayed up all night. I have had so many sleepless nights these past few months—grieving the past, doubting my present, worrying about the future. It is hard sleeping alone after almost twenty years of sharing a bed.

Last night, Miles was upset during dinner. He was frowning and picking at his food, barely eating more than a few bites of his chicken and peas.

"What's up?" I asked him.

"Nothing," he said, in that pre-teen grunt I get from my son these days.

After dinner, he went straight upstairs to his room. He slammed his door, which he never does, and stayed in there for the night, instead of binge-watching *The Office* in the living room with me, as we have been doing lately. I went upstairs to say good night to him before bed, and when I leaned down to kiss his forehead, he shrugged to the side and pulled away from me. In the blue glare of his iPad, I saw his eyes were bloodshot and his cheeks flushed. He had been crying.

"Aw, sweetie," I said and sat down on the side of the bed.

"Why won't you let Dad sleep home?" he demanded. "You're so mean. He wants to come home, you know?"

I felt a lump in my throat as big as the Croton Dam—a forest full of sticks and leaves and mud stacked by the beaver, lodged in the base of my Adam's apple. I didn't answer him truthfully.

I didn't say, "Because the things that made you fall in love with somebody are the exact damn things that later you can't stand about them."

I didn't say, "What is not meant for you eventually falls away."

I didn't say, "Because Dad is acting like a man-child, and what example would that set for your future?"

No, I didn't say any of that. I had to uphold dignity. He is his father, after all. So instead I just said, "I love you, Monkey. I know this is hard. Things will be okay. Try to sleep. Tomorrow is a school day."

But things are far from okay. And my son deserves to know the real deal. His whole life is about to change. Soon he will be moving from house to house every other week. There will be no more family tickle time, no more winters in California or Mexico, no more movie nights with buttered popcorn on the couch. Our sweet little family of three is dissolving. And I am evolving, birthing a new me.

It happened one morning, three months ago. Just a regular moment on a regular day. As Rob and I were brushing our teeth next to each other over the marble sink, I looked up and saw him. There it was, right before my eyes, reflected in the mirror—my husband was gone. *Poof.* He was standing next to me, yes, but he was gone. And even more frightening was, although he was looking at me, I could see in his eyes that he no longer saw me—the real me, the woman I have matured to be.

"I think we should try therapy," I said.

He paused, bent down, spit out the frothy toothpaste, wiped his face with a towel, and replied, "Honestly, I'm just not up for it."

"You're not up for it?" I repeated, making sure I heard him right.

"Yeah. No. I'm just not up for doing the work."

He said he felt okay with the way things were, that he didn't see the problem. "We're fine. I love you; it'll all figure itself out."

A Smoke and a Song

I didn't feel fine. I felt flattened by our nonconnection. We were paper-plate cutouts of the couple we once were. In the way that metal corrodes under the elements, rust had formed in our marriage—in places it wasn't meant to form. Our playful humor tarnished by sarcastic stabs. Date nights hardened into stubborn silence across two-tops. Our passion has been severed by separate blankets on separate sides of the bed. Our life on a silver platter is oxidized, junkyard loot. The fool's gold pin I wore as we said our vows has lost its luster.

And it did not all just figure itself out. I figured it out! The propane payments, Miles's baseball schedule, holiday dinners. I updated the website for our studio, and I took on extra private yoga sessions when our mortgage was due. He traveled. He surfed the Internet. He got to coast. I was tired of being the man of the house—and Rob refused to man up. The more alone I felt, the louder I yelled. The louder I yelled, the more avoidant Rob became. The more avoidant he became, the more alone I felt. And so, we spun, around and around, on the same old cruel carousel.

"But don't you want something different?" I pressed. "Something more real? A relationship with purpose and plot twists? Don't you see we are disappearing?"

He looked at me blankly and said, "Not really."

I leaned closer to the mirror, twisted off the cap to my mascara, applied one full sweep of black liquid to my lashes, and said the words I had been holding back, the words I knew deep down were my truth. "I think we should separate."

I am squatting down, looking at all the broken pieces of the bowl in the morning sunlight that splashes from the bay window. I can't help but think about how this bowl was once just a clump of clay, living on a hillside or at the bottom of a pond somewhere in Italy. And how the clay was sold to the potter who formed it into a bowl under his hands at the wheel. I picture the clay hardening under thick layers of white glaze while burning in the fire of the kiln before being perched on the drying rack with the other bowls. I imagine it being boxed and shipped overseas and put for sale on a shelf in a store somewhere in New York City. Until one day, it was bought and wrapped in yellow paper with a white ribbon, dressed with a handwritten note that said, "Cheers to a long life of love!" and put on the gift table at our wedding, on the lawn at my mother's house in the Berkshires, on that sunny mid-September day in 1998.

The bowl lived with us for fourteen years. It was family. I can't even count how many salads it carried to potluck dinners. Or pieces of fruit it's held on display on our kitchen island in the summer. Or times it's been rinsed by hand because it took up too much space in the dishwasher.

Now today, the bowl and my marriage and I are in pieces on the kitchen floor. I put my bag down, pick up the pieces, and put them inside the half bowl that is still intact. I throw that lot in the trash. I look down to the top of the garbage pile. The broken pieces are too beautiful to throw away. I won't throw them away. I can't throw him away, not entirely. He was my best friend. And he is Miles's dad. And the bowl is all I have left from the wedding.

To know love is to know that it is fragile. Real things break. That's how we know they are real.

I lean down and take the bigger pieces out of the trash and place them on the island. I sweep up the rest of the shards and leave them in the dustpan on the floor.

"We have to go; we're late," I say to Miles, who has been helping to clean up the pieces.

I will deal with the rest of the wreckage later.

In the evening, after Miles has gone to bed, I sift through the broken bowl pieces on the island—finger-sized triangles and zigzags, and one even looks like a pointy heart. I hold it up to the light. I see sparkles, the tiny crystals in the dry clay. I go to the trunk where I keep art supplies. I take out glue, a small canvas, and a gold marker. I spread out the broken bowl bits onto the canvas, arrange them in different configurations, filling in some of the gaps with golden curves and swirls and the ceramic crumbles and dust I collect from the dustpan.

I design a six-petaled rosette. It is one of my favorite shapes. I memorized this shape while studying the mandalas of sacred geometry. The six-petaled rosette symbolizes the ongoing, never-to-be-broken connection between all things. I stay up all night, gluing, arranging pieces, crying, drawing, sprinkling dust in the cracks, remembering, and gluing some more. It is cathartic.

In the morning, I leave the mosaic on the kitchen island with a note for Miles that reads:

My sweet boy,
Even when broken, all the pieces are all still here.
The clay is still clay, whether it is a bowl or a mosaic.
You, me, and Dad will always be family.
We've only just changed our shape.
—Love, Mom

Give It to the Water

"Let's divorce with love and integrity," I say to Rob. "We'll do it for Miles and in honor of the years we shared."

"Let's do that," Rob says. "That sounds like a good idea."

"We are two yogis," I say. "We have the tools."

But from what I see, Rob must have lost his tool belt. At pickup or drop-offs with Miles, or when we swap time at our yoga studio, which we technically still co-own, I barely recognize the person he has become. He looks the same, but he has changed. When we talk, I can't find him. What happened to the do-good father I was married to?

I hoped that asking him to leave would put a spark under his ass to try harder to fix us, but it backfired. And now there is no turning around. He has been flailing, like a turtle on its back. He promised he'd help with mortgage while we figure out the financial piece of our divorce but forgets to pay it. I ask him to take his boxes of things from the attic, but he doesn't. He schedules trips on the weeks he is supposed to be with Miles. And the rumors. Martha's Vineyard is a very small rock. His alone time is now wedged with welcomed independence, right swipes on his Tinder app, women and self-worth he never was able to find during his years with me. I see the texts, which come in on Miles's iPad. His list of hookups grows by the weekend. And I know these women. These are *my* women—students of mine, one of my clients, even one of my yoga teacher friends who teaches at the studio!

I pretend I don't see the texts and that it doesn't bother me when someone stops me to tell me they've seen Rob on dates with these women. I'm *extra* nice to him. But I'm twisted up inside. Life has turned Shakespearean. I have become both the author and the antagonist in my own tragicomedy. Nobody told me that the dynamic you have in marriage only seems to amplify in separation. It is as if we are playing some twenty-year Monopoly game and I have given him a life supply of get-out-of-jail-free cards. *And why not collect two hundred dollars while you're at it?*

I wish there were some magic stop-loving key that I could slide into a lock and twist. But long-term love boomerangs. Some days I feel lifetimes away from loving Rob. Others, love hooks back, hurls me to the dirt, and tramples me whole.

I still love him. I just can't stand him anymore.

Not every love story is meant to be a life story.

Maybe love and hate are just different sides of the same coin. Both carry the same weight. Both keep us attached to the person we are loving or trying to hate. The opposite of love is not hate. The opposite of love is forgetting.

I wish I could forget him, but I can't. He was my best friend, and he's Miles's dad. He's Miles's dad.

My friend Kim suggests I take some time off from teaching. "You give so much support to others during their difficult life transformations," she says as we walk through the tall beach grass on the pathway to Lucy Vincent Beach. "How about you give some back to yourself? Feel the loss," she says. "Give it to the water."

I try on Kim's advice. I cancel my classes, and while Miles is in school or asleep, I spend the month of December in the tub. I fill Grandma's marble sink with candles and turn out the lights, bathing by the flicker of fire or the moonlight that shines in from the window above the tub. I place my laptop on the rococo chair and play sad songs. The voices come through the laptop speakers like angels coaxing my humiliation.

During those long in-between spaces of separation and single mothering, I soak. My bones loosen and become floaty, like all the buoys bobbing on the Vineyard Haven Harbor. Tears, spit, and fears drip into the suds of the bathwater.

My time in water is more shamanic than any ceremony or meditation, more healing than any yoga position I make on my mat. That bathroom becomes my medicine woman. It takes one month of sobbing and soaking, shaking and pruning, to wring out nineteen years of Rob from my skin.

It is a Tuesday morning, early January. I am getting ready for class. I am excited to see my students and get to the studio again. The music is blaring India Arie's song "Strength Courage & Wisdom." Something has started to lift. I am feeling a little more like myself, and the yellow house is feeling more like a home again—a place for Miles and me. All to ourselves, a sweet family of two.

I notice a strong whiff of roses. I tilt my head down to see Grandma's face appear in the mirror, like a hologram mask over my own. I look like one of the weird creatures in her paintings, haunting and marvelous. One part, still married me, the other, someone wiser, older, and more defined. My face is thinner. My jawline protrudes. There are at least a dozen new crow's feet from all the crying carved into the sides of my eyes. I hear her voice, as I often do when I'm in this bathroom.

"Darling, can you see now how light always shines more brilliantly through the dark cracks and hard edges?"

Beautiful Juxtaposition

"Spell your name again for me, ma'am."

"S-i-d-o-t-i," I say slowly. "Sidoti."

The Emirates Airline agent stares at her computer screen, her perfectly frosty-pink fingernails making little tacks on the keyboard. She looks up at me with her perfectly matching frosty-pink lips and says, "I'm sorry. We don't have you on this flight."

"Of course I am on the flight. I booked my ticket months ago!" I plead. "Please look again."

She looks again. "I'm sorry, Miss Sid-oooo-ti, we do not have you on this flight."

I take out my phone to search for my confirmation. It is not in my inbox, the trash, or the spam. The confirmation has evaporated off my phone. And the agent has no record of me on the flight. It's as if I don't even exist.

I am getting used to this feeling, being lost in existence—the feeling of being somewhere and not anywhere at the same time. The feeling of no longer being who I was but not yet becoming the person I will be. Ever since my separation two years ago and especially since the divorce last March, I have been seeking my place underneath the story I am living. Am I the strong earth mama who seems to have it all figured out, or the single mother fumbling without a road map? Am I the self-realized and self-actualized yogini who can remain best friends with my ex-husband, or the abandoned girl stuck inside a metal box that was never even locked?

Beautiful Juxtaposition

Apparently, I am the chick without a confirmation for this flight.

I beg the attendant to put me on the flight. "I'll pay whatever price."

But the flight is full, and there are no seats for me to purchase. She hands back my passport and visa.

My travel companions, a group of lifelong friends from the suburbs of Boston, all who have taken my yoga-teacher training on Martha's Vineyard, have already checked in. I see them standing in a small circle by a Starbucks kiosk. They have been planning this trip for over a year and have every detail arranged. They invited me to come along as part friend, part teacher, and I jumped at the opportunity. I have been dying to go for over a decade. Plus, a trip abroad, to anywhere off the island, is exactly what I need. All I was responsible for was my flight, the flight I am about to miss.

I walk over to explain the situation to my travel mates. They make calls to their husbands to see who can call a guy who knows a guy and get me on this flight.

"We won't leave without you," they say.

"Go. Go on. I'll find you girls there. I'll book the flight out tomorrow. It's just a day." I stand, brave faced, watching my friends walk through the crowded security gate.

Months ago, when I was doing research for the trip, I emailed one of my teachers to tell her our plans. I asked her for recommendations on where to go and what to see while there. She wrote back, "When Mother calls you to her, she'll shake you up to make sure you are ready for whatever you need to discover. My advice? Close the books. Burn them if you must. Roll up your mat. Take the beads off your neck. Disrobe. Have faith. There is no such thing as either/or inside the mother. Everything is both/and."

She was not kidding. I haven't even gotten out of Logan Airport, and I am already being tested by India—shaken and stirred.

A Smoke and a Song

I spend the next twenty hours alone in an airport Ramada with a bourbon on the rocks, watching bad TV, and sleeping off the wait. Then another full day of travel—Boston to London, London to Delhi, Delhi to Varanasi.

I am in a bare and musty hotel room in Varanasi, with a bed, a toilet, and a shower, which is all I care about. My body feels more like a bag of bones than a human body. I can't wait to shower and rest. There is a knock on the door. I open it. Gita, the local woman my friends found online to lead us on this long-awaited pilgrimage to experience the birthplace of yoga firsthand, says, "We must meet the boat captain in ten minutes at the riverbank."

We are going to the evening ritual, called *arti*, where hundreds of people gather for prayer every night on the banks of the river Ganges. I throw on my long emerald prairie dress and purple shawl and follow my friends downstairs. Outside the hotel, I scan the humid panorama with my overtraveled, overtired, and overwhelmed eyes. I see ancient, stone-fort-looking buildings, most of which have been converted into hotels with neon signs flashing from their rooftops and slanted stone paths bleeding into the river. Piles of garbage line the banks and float in the brown, murky water. Cows and donkeys walk about through the crowds of people. Hundreds of small boats float on firelit water.

We climb into the rowboat waiting for us, assisted by the captain, who can't be more than fourteen years old. The boat rocks side to side. It is a tiny, rickety wooden thing with chipped paint and rotten planks around the rim that you can see water through. The rowboat does not look like anything that can hold our young captain and Gita, let alone a handful of zestful xenophiles.

I sit down on the bench next to the captain, next to an altar tied to the helm adorned with candles, herbs, and God statues. In a cardboard box plunked in the middle row, there are a bunch of paper bags. The captain instructs me to pass them out. Inside each bag is a handful of marigold heads, a short white candlestick, and a paper plate. Gita explains the flowers are to be offered into the water while we row down the river. "The mari-golds are an offering to the life-giving waters, which sustain us." We are told to set the candles on the paper plate, light them, and carefully place the plate with candle on the water in front of the crematorium. "For the soul's transition in the afterlife."

We glide down the shoreline, which feels more like a pagan amusement park than a river. The other women ooh and ahh and toss flowers into the water. They laugh. They take selfies. They seem to have acclimated to this Wild Wild East, this oth-erworldly world, by this point. I, on the other hand, feel as if I am tripping, or dreaming, or in the scene of a Tim Burton movie. All I can do is sit silent and breathe it all in.

People are plunging, playing, and praying. Women are dressed in bright-colored saris, washing in the river, their jewelry reflecting reds and yellows from the fire flames that burn on the bank. Men with shaved heads and men with dreadlocks row the boats. Children are splashing. Firecrackers smack sound waves. Smoke is clouding the purple-and-blackened sky. It burns my eyes and my lungs.

We arrive at a central hub, where two banners with Hindu deities painted on them hang as high as a small skyscraper. I rec-ognize them both. There is Ganesh, the half-man, half-elephant god. He is the remover of obstacles, considered the gatekeeper of new beginnings. I got him tattooed on my left forearm, after Rob and I separated. A "special" young man drew it for me, and at the time, it felt like the right thing to do. On the second banner is Gopala-Krishna, the baby cow herder whose devotion represents doing our duty with unconditional love and without attachment to the outcomes of our efforts. Gopala-Krishna is my favorite. Years ago, in another life it seems, at the Sivananda Ashram in the Bahamas, when Miles was a tiny toddler and Rob was doing his yoga-teacher training, Miles was given Gopala-Krishna as his spiritual name by the Vedic priest.

I close my eyes and picture my twelve-year-old son—round

cheeks and curly blond locks and enormous, compassionate brown eyes that seem to take up the top third of his face. I get a pang of mother's remorse. I am so far away, in another space and time. A month will be the longest I have ever been away from him.

Under the banners, the devotees are chanting over static loudspeakers: "*Om gam ganapataye namaha. Om gam ganapataye namaha.*" (Salutations to the Lord, the remover of obstacles.) Babies are crying. Dogs are barking. Sensory overload. Too many feels. I am not used to feeling with all my senses at the same exact time. It is all too much. So I do what I have learned from my teachers. I close my eyes. I focus on the pit of my belly. I feel the skin of my ass press on the wooden bench seat beneath me, and the bench seat resting on the floor of the boat, and the sway of the boat atop the water. *Ground. Center. Breathe.*

Centering oneself is not a luxury in India. It is not a nice idea to do in a perfectly candlelit yoga studio with a pleasant view before we start to move through the poses. *Close the books. Burn them if you must. Roll up your mat.* Here, centering is a necessity. It is survival.

We drop anchor in front of the open-air crematorium and light our candles. Gita talks; we listen.

"Country people come from all parts, traveling with the dead on their backs or strapped on the roof of rickshaws to be cremated at this holy site. We believe that those cremated here help their loved ones burn the karmas from this life and gain higher caste for reincarnation."

There are seven or eight small bonfires on the side of the riverbank, stacks of wood piled twenty feet high, buckets of burning sage and ashes spilling into the water. Loved ones are stoking the flames of their dead relatives. I smell the herbs burning with the dead bodies and think, *These are real human beings burning. This should be terrifying.* But it isn't. It is the most beautiful juxtaposition. Life and death side by side, immersed, as one. Jarring, yes. Disturbing, yes. Life giving, also yes. It *is* both/and.

Beautiful Juxtaposition

I lay my chin in my hands and breathe with my whole being. I feel skinless and raw, with smelly feet and tangled hair. I try to cover the Ganesh tattoo on my forearm with my sleeve, embarrassed that I was so disillusioned not long ago to think I had earned and deserved to be inked with something that is so sacred to the people here.

I picture my quaint island town back home—perfectly landscaped gardens with stone wall borders and neatly mowed lawns. Inside, fabulously outfitted humans are wrought with depression and self-hate. Injecting ourselves with Botox and suffering boot camps—how ridiculous that we spend our life running from death back home, as if it'll keep us alive longer. Avoiding the fact that we are all going to die anyway, someday. Even our yoga practice is sold to us as a fountain of youth.

Is beauty found in the plumpness of our lips, or the sweetness of the words that exit them when we speak with kindness? Is strength found in the toned muscles of our legs, or how they kneel in reverence in prayer? Why would we want to smooth out the wrinkles around our eyes when they witness all this humanity?

In Varanasi, devotion to the dead is not a cute thing to do at the end of a class, a way to tie up the practice with a pretty bow, that little quip about honoring our ancestors and placing our hands at our hearts, namaste. In Varanasi, death and life are the same. The living dedicate their evenings to the dead. The dead help the alive thrive. Devoting life to death is survival.

Gita says, "Now throw something into the fire. Something you are ready to burn from your karma. Only when obliterated do we find what is indestructible inside."

I pick up a burning votive and place it in my open palm. I hold the votive up in the air, squint my eyes, gazing toward the smoke-filled riverbank. I bring the flame to my brow and say, "I throw away every boulder in my path. All of them, especially the ones I create myself—my tiny woe-is-me story, my disappointments, my resentment and humiliation. All my yearning for control, and the wounding. Take them from me!"

The skin on my forehead is hot. I am burning in my own inner crematorium.

Day two, we go to a Kali temple that offers free dinner to hundreds of sadhus every night. Sadhus are spiritual wanderers, karma yogis, who have given up ascetic pleasures. They are men and women who live on the fringes of society and spend their days praying to the divine to acquire the mystical powers needed for righting the wrongs of the world, relying on the bits of food and shelter that are given to them in the temples. Back home we'd call them homeless or mentally ill.

The Kali temple is humble: an empty hall, no windows, a small prayer space with a statue of the Goddess Kali, known as the dark goddess and the destroyer of ego. Kali is depicted naked with dark, blue-black skin; wild, long, black hair; and fiery eyes, and is wearing a garland of fifty skulls, denoting the fifty letters of the Sanskrit alphabet. Kali is fierce and loving at the same time, like Ixchel to the Mayans. Her job is to protect the planet from evil.

The story goes that young Kali would angrily stomp through the world to kill off demons who perpetuated greed, lust, and hatred. When she stomped and killed, every drop of demon blood that hit the ground would form a hundred new demons. The teaching being that rage—even with the right reason—will only manifest as more evil on the planet. As she saw this, instead of letting the demons' blood drop to the earth, she'd drink it. Kali used her body to transmute evil to greater good. Kali hangs on a tapestry in my yoga studio. I've always thought Kali looks a lot like my mother, Babette, and a little like me, I suppose.

"Make eye contact with sadhus in the temple, and you will receive the blessing," Gita says.

I see cleft lips and disfigured faces and a man with one eye missing. Normally, I might have looked away at such faces. But they are beautiful faces, exuding from the heart a certain sincerity, a Grandpa Stanley type of sincerity.

I have an opportunity to talk with a sadhu named Vishnu. I tell Vishnu that I teach yoga and ask him, "Is there any message that I can share with my students in the United States?"

He smiles, and his eyes brighten. "Teach people how to sit with themselves and be quiet."

"I try."

"When we find quiet inside and meditate on right action, we unify with the heart of all of humanity. We can emanate peace as we walk in this chaotic world."

I ask, "What is right action?"

He explains. "Right action means to do our duty, with right motive, the best we can, while maintaining an inner state of equanimity, as an offering to spirit."

"I see," I say.

"Your people of the material world hate so much," he says. "Why is this?"

I marinate with his question for a moment. I say, "We Americans are taught to make everything seem perfect on the outside instead of caring for the way we feel on the inside, and this creates a disparity that is unbearable to live and love with, so we turn to hate."

Vishnu takes my hand, places it on his heart, and laughs. "Divine being of spirit," he says. "Let's sit together and be quiet. For your people."

And we do. I sit in a crowded temple hall, eyes closed, beside a sadhu named Vishnu.

I see Miles in his room, on his bed. He has been struggling lately, cyberbullied by a boy in his class. He is too sensitive for this world. He cares too much about animals being mistreated, people living in war zones, teachers who never call on the shy kids at school. A mama pull takes over me. I am Kali. I want to drink the blood of evil for my boy. I want to swallow his pain whole. How can we do this to our children? Why do we teach them to strive for good grades and gold-star stickers and baseball trophies when they are suffering in their hearts?

In the Kali temple, sitting quiet is not just something we try on because our yoga teacher suggests it's a way to alleviate stress. Here, we meditate on right action to heal our children and correct the wrongs of the world. It is sustenance in the stomach of the sadhus. *Take the beads off your neck. Disrobe.* In the Kali temple, it is survival.

Day three, we go to *arti* from land. Before we cross a bridge, Gita tells us to remove our shoes.

"Say *swaha*. 'I surrender.' Then wait for the priest's blessing before you cross the bridge."

She points to a mountain of shoes of all sizes, colors, and shapes, sitting on top of one another or soaking in pools of dirty river water. I do not want to remove my shoes, because I have the om symbol tattooed on my foot. I had no idea, when I got it, that putting an om on my foot is a sign of disrespect. And I only brought one pair of shoes on this trip.

"There's no way I'll ever see these shoes again if I take them off my feet," I say, looking at the pile and then down at my dirty, gray canvas Toms flats.

"Trust," Gita says, "without attachment to the outcome."

I take off one shoe and look at the worn sole. And then the other. I think of my sisters and how I spent the first part of my life in their hand-me-down shoes. In Lisa's shoes, I learned to love when I could have raged, and yet I learned a hug is not a hug unless done with both arms. In Maddy's shoes, I learned that freedom comes from having discipline and form, and yet sometimes liberation is not giving a flying fuck about anyone else for a minute.

I have been walking in my own Toms shoes for years. I stepped out of my marriage wearing these shoes, dragged both feet heavily through a divorce in them, and marched into my midforties as a single mother in them. In these shoes, I relearned how to stand, and step, and walk forward in my life again.

I throw my Toms high in the air toward the pile. The pair divides, one shoe landing in a puddle on one side, the other lost in the mound.

"Swaha!" I wave to the pile. "See ya, wouldn't wanna be ya."

Practicing trust here is not an intention we write on a piece of paper and burn at a new-moon bonfire. Trusting to give it all away and having faith that we will get back what we need is a way of life. Throw your shoes on the shoe pile, have faith you will find them again. Here, trust is survival.

I get my blessing and merge into the crowd crossing the bridge. I dunk under, fully dressed. I could stay here forever. The water is silky, like my mother's sheets. The bottom is squishy, like the Buddha Hole.

I am crossing the bridge back to the city, my dress soaked and clinging to my body. If I reunite with my shoes, it will be a miracle. If I reunite with my shoes, I will take it as a sign to trust that spirit has my back. If I reunite with my shoes, I promise to see life with love, not *for* love.

I step off the bridge and look around for my shoes. There are too many people and too many shoes. I sit my ass down on the wet ground to scope out the landscape. I laser focus my point of view. Out of the corner of my eye, in a completely different area from where I had thrown them, I see my pair of Toms placed neatly on the outskirts of the shoe mountain. I get up and walk to my shoes. I look at them, pause, and exhale. I gaze straight ahead toward the horizon, where the paths that lead to the stone-fort-looking buildings bleed into the river. I take a big step forward, leaving my shoes on the ground where they are. I keep walking, barefoot through the streets of Varanasi.

THREE

Mad/Sad

Rob and I have divorced our way, even before Gwyneth Paltrow made "conscious uncoupling" a thing. We celebrate holidays together and sit next to each other at Miles's baseball games. Our hashtag: *#foreverfamily*.

With our parenting schedule of one week on, one week off, I scratch my itch to travel for work. I fly, as my business name suggests. In the off-season, when I'm not doing my training, when Rob has Miles, I take my yoga teaching on the road. I romp around the country, offering yoga workshops at my friends' or former students' studios, and before long, I'm leading retreats around the world—Greece, Guatemala, Cuba, and of course, Mexico.

On the weeks Miles is with me, he and I both unpack our suitcases and reacclimatize as mother and son. My fourteen-year-old is being the man of the house, which seems to give him the boost of confidence he needs to enter his early teens. The more I allow him to rise and own responsibility, the more it is helping him release from the awkward, reclusive, hide-in-his-room tween he was the past few years. He takes out the garbage, checks the basement for leaks after a downpour, and performs other chores that his father used to do. When I go grocery shopping, he hands me a twenty-dollar bill, earnings from his summer job docking boats at the harbor, and I take the twenty and deposit it into his college savings account.

I tried on dating after my divorce, but nothing seemed to

stick. I had a handful of one-off flings with men my age, but frankly, I couldn't be bothered. There's nothing worse than listening to a fifty-year-old man dredge on about banging nails or repairing roofs. I also tried giving it a shot with a way-too-young-for-me man for way too long of a stint. He love bombed, then ghosted, then zombied, then bombed and ghosted me again. It is a whole new dating world out there—it's like learning a new language. Who has time for that nonsense? I commit to six months of what the yogis call brahmacharya, or purposeful abstinence. I figure after being in relationships of one sort or another since the age of fifteen, maybe I could benefit from some conscious alone time—clear my energy field from men altogether for a bit, to purify. That way, I'll be ready for whatever love has to offer on the other side.

Six months of intentional single life later, I am lying on a nearly empty beach on the South Shore of the island. It is midsummer, and the waves are growling, leftovers from the storm that hit the Southern Carolinas earlier this week. I have my darkest sunglasses on, looking up at the late-afternoon sky. An airplane flies from the blue part of the sky into the rolling fog. I trace the thin line of white that follows it. Chemtrails—not great for the environment, but they sure make for a meditative skyscape.

I am a "tapestry thrown right on the sand" kind of girl. I warm sunny-side up, feeling the empty spaces between my low back and the ground, and I carve myself in, rocking side to side, shape-shifting the sand under the thin layer of fabric to fit my spinal curves. I attune to the rhythm of ocean's edge easily, especially in the afternoons, since it is my chill time of the day. I've made sure to set up my summer schedule to sandwich all my teaching in between 6:00 a.m. and noon. I earn my lazy afternoons. They are all mine. And today I am spending this one with a man named Jevon Rego.

Jevon props up to his elbows and looks at the water, squinting his bright green eyes that match today's ocean. A light five o'clock shadow trails out from his sandy brown-and-white goatee, and his face is smeared with a smile. I scan his shirtless torso, trying not to be too obvious about it. He's not too hairy, slender, in good shape, but not sculpted or tattooed, like my usual type. He lies down again, pulls his salmon-colored bathing suit from the bunch caught between his legs, and flips to his stomach. He is antsy. It is cute. *He's not a "tapestry on the sand" guy*, I think. *I should have grabbed a beach chair for him.*

He shifts again toward me and brushes a clump of sand off my left leg. Our first skin-to-skin contact. His hands are a bit rough, a casualty of being a painting contractor, but his touch is tender. His hands feel as if they have not touched a woman's leg in a while.

"You've been on my radar for months," he says.

He is unpacking the spread he brought for the date. Baby carrots, crackers, cheese, chicken salad sandwiches, cashews, and a little jar of local beach plum chutney, enough food for a small army.

"It was a lot of pressure to pack a picnic," he says.

He does not know if I am vegetarian, vegan, or gluten-free, so he just grabbed everything he could think of at the store.

"I scoped your Facebook profile for foodie clues," he admits. "But I got nothing."

It is endearing and considerate. I tell him I eat almost everything except nuts. I recently developed an allergy, while on an airplane to Guatemala. He quickly stuffs the cashews back into his cooler.

"It's nice to finally be able to spend time with you."

Jevon speaks louder than he needs to speak. But I like his voice, a tenor timbre. I especially like that he stops midsentence to smile.

"I was hoping you'd ask me out," I say. "I'm glad you found me again."

A Smoke and a Song

Jevon and I met on the ferry in March, a month into my no-men phase. I was on my way to Colorado to teach a weekend workshop. I bumped into my friend Lila, who used to live in Boulder, and I asked her for recommendations of places to go while I was there. She looked behind us and waved this guy over.

He's cute, I mouthed to Lila.

She winked and said, "I got you."

I shook my head.

He jumped up from where he was sitting with a gaggle of boys, dressed in a purple-and-black Vineyard colors windbreaker with "COACH" down the sleeve, and came to stand with us.

"Jevon's from Colorado," Lila said. "Jevon, Sherry's on her way to Boulder. Where should she go?"

He was friendly and talkative. He suggested a few hikes to go on that are within walking distance from downtown Boulder, a day trip to Nederland, lunch at The Buff. I thanked him, went to the concession stand to grab a beer for the boat ride, and that was that. But I'm not going to lie: I walked away wondering and wanting more.

"I wanted to ask you out sooner." He pauses to take a bite from his sandwich. "But I was taking time for myself after my last breakup. To get my head on right."

"I did that too," I say, but quickly remind myself, *Rule number one about first dates: never talk about your exes.* I change the subject. "What brought you to Martha's Vineyard from Colorado?"

"The usual story. I came here for 'one last summer' with a buddy from college and just never left. That was eons ago!"

I am surprised he and I have both lived here so long and have not crossed paths sooner. We talk about our children, how parenting is a game of roulette, and the challenge of coparenting postdivorce.

"Forget a 529 plan," he says. "Instead, I put a dollar a day into the therapy jar."

We both laugh. He tells me that his kids split the week. He has them Wednesdays through Saturdays and every other Sunday.

"It takes us all four days to get used to each other, just in time for them to pack up and go back to their mother's."

I know that drill, and it is hard. There is really nothing sadder than having your kids for only half their life.

"It's why I travel so much," I say. "My house feels too empty without my son home."

I picture fourteen-year-old Miles, walking away from our yellow house toward his dad's car every other Sunday, with an overstuffed backpack over his shoulder and the cord from his Xbox dragging on the grass behind his feet. I always feel like my heart is attached to the other end of that cord.

Jevon talks about coaching hockey for his eleven-year-old son Nick's team. *Ugh, hockey? Darn.* My least favorite sport. Everything about hockey is wrong: (a) It's cold. I hate the cold. (b) Fluorescent lighting; enough said. (c) It's loud, obnoxiously loud, and aggressive. But I like the way his lips lift and lean to the right when he talks about hockey, so I stay warm to the conversation. His son is a rising defenseman, and he expresses how proud this makes him. "But I try not to be one of *those* dads." he says, so he keeps his pride at bay.

He continues, "I am very close with my daughter, Alex." They fish together.

I take note that his daughter shares my middle name.

"But it's complicated, the daddy-daughter bond," he says, smiling again.

I take in the words "daddy-daughter bond." I feel a ping in my belly.

"She's studious and serious. She's been planning her acceptance speech to Harvard or Dartmouth since fifth grade."

His daughter and my son are the same age. Both are starting at the regional high school next month.

"I bet they know each other," we say at the same exact time.

A Smoke and a Song

"Jinx! You owe me a beer," I say playfully.

"How about a Coke?" he rebuts.

He says he had his last drink twenty-one years ago and is in "the program." I do not know much about AA, but I am pleased to hear he has discipline and a practice. Other guys I dated liked that I am a yogi. To them, it meant I could bend around them during sex. But none seemed to grasp the spiritual importance of my practice, nor the devotion I have in sharing it.

"Twenty-one years is impressive," I say.

He says he has taken some yoga classes. He started going a few months ago, after going through a rough patch and realizing he needed more calm in his life. He'd been a workaholic for decades. He's trying to downshift now, have more presence with the things that matter. He says he likes yoga "but I stick out like a two-by-four among the rows of women who bend like cooked spaghetti."

We compare some similarities between the steps and the yoga tenets, and how hand in hand they go. I like that he has all twelve steps memorized by heart. He takes my hand in his.

"I'm more curious about the philosophy than the poses," he says, so I talk through the *yamas*, or the "don'ts" of yoga, off the mat.

"The five *yamas*," I say, "keep us in check with how we are in the day-to-day stuff. As my teacher says, if you want to know how your yoga is doing, look at your relationships."

I pause and look out to the deep green ocean and align my breath to the rhythm of the waves, which are getting rougher by the hour.

"I'm not sure what that says about my yoga, given that I am divorced." He releases my hand from his and puts it on my back instead. I am conscious to keep it airy, light. I do not want to talk about Rob, nor do I want to sound like a teacher to him. I have other plans for us.

"Interesting," he says. "What are the five?"

"Oh, you know, the usual commandment-type things: non-harming, non-lying, non-stealing, not leaking one's energy, non-possessiveness."

"Reminds me of the fourth step—make a searching and fearless moral inventory of ourselves."

"Yes," I say. "You know how many yogis I know who are all love and light in class and then rude to the checkout person at the grocery store?" I scoop a cracker into the chutney and stuff the entire cracker into my mouth.

He chuckles, then admits it all sounds a little intimidating. "It can be too much to constantly live in check with yourself."

"The coolest thing is you don't have to do all of them to do them all. There's a saying—the way we do one thing is the way we do everything."

He looks confused.

"The idea is, if we practice any *yama* diligently, the others will happen organically."

"Interesting. Which one is your go-to?"

"Ahimsa, non-harming. It always goes back to that for me. I'm not very good at it . . . but I try."

"I guess that'd be the place to start. I've done a lot of damage in my past. I made some huge mistakes." He squints and looks down.

I am curious, but I don't ask for details. Best to leave that conversation for our second date. So instead, we talk about God. He believes in a higher power, but he is not, as he calls it, "a Big Book thumper" as some of his comrades in the program are.

"I'm spiritual but not religious," I say. "I believe spirit is within us, in our breath, and in the wind, the water, and the trees. I look to my body and nature to find God."

He raises an eyebrow when I say the word "body."

We both agree that our practices mean nothing without giving back to others. He volunteers for several town committees, he coaches, and he sponsors fresh recoverees. I tell him about my new outreach program teaching yoga and meditation at the

A Smoke and a Song

Dukes County House of Correction.

We sit side by side, staring out toward the fog, which has rolled in thick, blurring the horizon where sea and sky met just minutes ago. The day is too quickly inching toward evening.

"That reminds me," he says and looks at his watch. "It is after six. I have to be up island for the 7:00 p.m. meeting. I can't be late. I'm the coffee guy." He puts his hands up. "Have you ever seen a room full of dry drunks without their coffee?" He laughs at his own humor. "I should get going."

"Let's make that happen," I say. "We all need our coffee!" I stand, brush off the sand from my legs, stretch, and scoop up my tapestry and stuff it into my beach bag. I throw on my oversized sheer black cover-up and slide my bronze Havaianas flip-flops through my fingers.

He's still sitting. He puts the lids back on the containers and methodically wipes each jar down with a napkin, rolls the half-eaten sandwiches into the extra foil he brought from home, and then opens the cooler to rearrange the ice packs to place everything in its perfect spot inside. He stands, shakes his towel off to the side, to not get any sand in my direction, then folds his towel in fours, and stacks it on top of the cooler.

As I watch and wait for him to row up all his ducks, I can't help but think how it will be to navigate our different ways, like Felix and Oscar, the Odd Couple.

We make our way to the parking lot. He carries my beach bag over his shoulder and the cooler between both hands. He walks close, close enough that his upper arm rubs my shoulder. His hip knocks into my love handle with each stride. Each time our bodies touch, it feels electric—the yummy type of electric.

My guess is that he is in his late forties, given his years of sobriety and the laugh lines that trail above his jawline just under his goatee. But he has a youthful way about him. He walks with a light bounce, like a toddler almost, as if every other step is on his tippy toes.

"How old are you?" I ask.

"Forty-eight!" he says. "How did that happen?"

He's Maddy's age. 1968.

He stops walking to fix the bag on his shoulder and to get a better grip on the cooler. "But today," he says, "I feel like a teenager."

When we get to my car, he puts my bag in the back seat. He closes that door and opens the driver's door for me. I get in slowly, savoring the moment, wanting to stretch our first date for as long as I can. He closes the door after me. My window is open, as it usually is because we Islanders keep the windows down and our keys in the ignition when we go to the beach. He leans in, resting his folded arms on the sill. His frame fits perfectly in the window. He's not a big man but not small, either. He's just right.

"You are much more down-to-earth than I thought you'd be," he says.

"Thanks," I say and give him a quizzical look. "I think. What did you expect?"

"Well, you know. I thought you'd be more woo-woo. I thought you'd be talking about crystals and full moons."

I laugh. "Well, don't write that off yet; it's only our first date!"

"I thought you'd be harder to relate to. You have quite the reputation here."

"Oh." I suddenly feel overexposed, like a glass window, see-through. He stops talking. He plays with the beads on my wampum bracelet. I can tell he is carefully choosing what to say next.

"You are known as the spiritual teacher who calls her students out on their stuff."

I take a breath in. I've gotten used to being seen this way by others, and it's not entirely untrue. I do hold the people who practice with me accountable. I urge people to get to the root of their problems and get to healing.

I breathe out and say, "I love hard. I guess that can be taken in some type of way. I can be impatient watching people stay clogged in their everyday nonsense."

"I'm happy I get to know the person behind the name. She's Brooklyn. Tough on the outside, a softie at heart."

I feel seen. I say, "Now that part is true!"

He lifts his sunglasses. "I want to know more about you. The person you are in private. Tell me something that the others don't know."

It is a big question, the kind of inquiry I love but rarely get asked, and it is refreshing to be on the receiving end. I am usually the one asking questions like this. I have just met this man, but heart-mind tells me that if I can stay raw at this moment, things might turn around for me.

"One thing you should know about me . . ." *Yield. This is what vulnerability feels like. Slip into something more uncomfortable, Sherry.* "That is if I seem mad, I'm usually just sad."

He takes a minute with my response. I feel my body want to move into its familiar protective stance. I stretch my arms and press my elbows into my driver's seat, lift my chest and rib cage, open my mouth and eyes as wide as I can, then wrap my arms around my chest as I exhale and blink. After, I release my arms by my side and let my eyes and lips soften. He watches this repatterning-reflexes exercise I learned to interrupt my nervous system from switching into fight instinct but does not ask about it.

"So, if you seem mad, you're sad . . . hmmm." It's as if he is swirling fine wine around in his palette. "It's bound to happen."

"What is?"

"You know. Rough times. Arguments. When you seem mad, I'll remind myself that you're just sad. It'll be hard for me. I've been known to take things personally. But I'll try some ahamsa."

I smile. "Ahimsa."

He reaches in with his pointer and middle fingers to gently turn my chin toward him, and we kiss. It is a sweet kiss. Not too loose. Not too tight.

"We got this," he says and kisses me again.

Those three words sound good in his voice.

"We got this," I repeat. Those three words sound good in my voice too.

"Well?" he says. "Scram, Brooklyn."

It is, by far, the most romantic thing anyone has ever said to me. I am filled with hope.

The Lady Is Eighty

Although sisters, members of the same family who lived together, Lisa, Maddy, and I had such different childhoods, or at least each had our version of it. Our mother was certainly not the same mother to the three of us, and she never even seemed to try to hide that. When my sisters and I talk about our childhood, we remember similar facts and circumstances of stories, yet each of us carries our own individual chip on our shoulder because of the ways we played out our unique roles inside those stories.

The one thing we all remember the same is that birthdays were a big deal growing up. Three days a year, Mom would dole out love and attention, drop her schedule, and let us pick whatever activity our little hearts desired. And somehow, Mom miraculously found the money and time to make our wish come true.

Maddy, having a March birthday, had to do indoor things. She usually chose something like roller-skating at the Roxy with her posse, or Eighth Street to see *The Rocky Horror Picture Show* at the Playhouse, or to Macy's for a clothes-shopping spree. Lisa almost always chose to go to the season-opening Memorial Day DJ dance party in the amphitheater in Prospect Park.

For me, it was the theater. Mom and I would dress up fancy, and off to Broadway we'd go. Second grade it was *Annie*. Third grade it was *Grease*. Fourth it was *A Chorus Line*. After the show, we'd eat at Windows on the World, the swanky restaurant atop the Twin Towers and order Shirley Temples, and we'd pretend it was champagne. We'd look through the *Playbill* and decide which one of us was which character in the play. Pretending we were the cast was the after-show celebration.

Lisa, Maddy, and I decided we had to do something extra special this year. Mom is turning eighty, and now it's our time to treat her. While planning, the three of us got closer than we have been in years, perhaps ever. We spent months on the phone bonding over our children, laughing at stories, and doing what we do best—poking fun at our mother. We decided to divide and conquer. Each of us planned some part of the celebration, a whole weekend to honor Mom.

We kicked off The Lady Is Eighty celebrations with Lisa's plan last night: a show, not on Broadway, but on East Fifty-Sixth Street, at a club called Lips to see *Divas, Divas, Divas, the Drag and Dining Experience*. Mom sat under a spotlight on a stool on the stage with the Divas. She was adorned in a red wig and a penis headband, shouting, "Give it to me!" as she looped dollar bills over the G-string of a dancer named Queen Jesse Volt. Mom got the whole club clapping. The four of us drank a few too many vodka tonics and danced in the aisles with a dozen or so women who were at the table next to us having a bachelorette party. I had not seen my mother smile like that in years. Sweaty and so damn happy to "get our shit off" together again, we strolled down Fifth Avenue in the March chill, arms looped, dominating the sidewalk.

Maddy planned the big bash for tonight, Mom's actual birthday. She booked a funk band to play, friends of hers from back in the day. She hired a caterer and a bartender, who are due to set up around six in the evening. All Mom's people, from all her pockets of life, our friends, too, have RSVP'd and will come to boogie. Jevon, Philippe, and the kids are scheduled to arrive right before the party starts. We spent the slightly hungover Saturday morning rolling the dining table into Mom's office to make a dance floor in front of the elevator. Lisa decorated the loft in streamers, and Maddy pinned a giant red-and-gold THE LADY IS EIGHTY banner above the row of plants.

I am in the living room setting up for my part of Mom's celebration, the circle blessing. I put four pillows around the round glass coffee table. Atop it I have sage for energy cleansing, a couple of candles for mood, and rice paper cutouts with Grandma's colored pencils for the releasing ceremony. Next to it is the frame I hand painted as a gift from all of us.

Inside the frame are three of my favorite photographs. The top photo is of the four of us on our stoop in Brooklyn. Lisa is ten, standing on the top step. Her eyelids are brushed with bright sky-blue eyeshadow and thick black eyeliner. She's wearing a baby blue tank with beaded fringes that says, in iron-on, glossy letters, "Brooklyn Girls. Best in the World." She is leaning toward Maddy, her middle finger, crooked from the bike spokes at Dad's, up at the camera. Maddy is seven, in a Yankees cap, jean shorts, Dr. Scholl's shoes, and side ponytail. She is sticking her tongue out. I am five, wearing their hand-me-down, stained shirt with farm animals on it, bell-bottom red jeans, and knotted hair. I am holding my beloved stuffed animal, Lammy, sniffing her fur and sucking my thumb. Mom, with her wild salt-and-pepper curls, is on the bottom step, in one of her hand-crocheted bikini tops, a long paisley-patterned beige skirt, and brown high-heeled boots, smoking a cigarette.

The middle picture is just Mom—a close-up of her on the deck in the Berkshires, overlooking the running brook behind the house. I took it last fall, when Lisa, Mom, and I met there to pack up the country house. None of us wanted to sell, but we all agreed it was best. We knew we would need money for Mom's long-term care, which was not yet, thankfully, but coming down the pipe. Mom was no longer driving. We forced her car away from her after she took out the neighbor's mailbox and had a couple of additional fender benders, but not without a fight. "I will not let you girls bully me!" she argued, but eventually she gave in.

After the three of us cherry-picked a few pieces of furniture and the movers drove off, Mom said she wanted a moment alone before leaving. I watched her from the dining room French doors and took the photo. It was a tender moment, watching my mother say her goodbyes to the brook in amber afternoon light. I zoomed in on her tanned face, her white curls filling most of the frame, and captured the scene.

The bottom picture is from three summers ago. It is of Mom, Justin, Juniper, and Miles at the Provincetown Inn pool during their annual summer Gramma and Grandkiddos P-town week. The four of them are floating on rafts in a row in the chlorinated water, filled with buff, waxed men, drinking bright red virgin strawberry daiquiris with curly straws and slivers of pineapple propped on the rims of their clear plastic cups.

My sisters and Mom meet me in the living room at three. Although I lead circles all the time with my yoga students and girlfriends, I have never done anything spiritual with Lisa, or anything like this with all four of us together. This circle idea may be a shit show, I fear. For all I know, it will turn into a rage.

I start the circle by instructing us to hold hands. "May the circle be open and never broken," I say.

Lisa starts crying. I am relieved. The 80 percent Lisa is here.

Maddy laughs nervously, as she does when things get serious.

"Mom, today is your day," I say. "Please take what we say to heart. Try to listen, breathe, and absorb what we share. We are all here for you."

"Okay. Okay!" Mom says, agitated.

This is not a good way to start.

"Mom, we three are the only people in the world who know what your heartbeat sounds like from the inside," I say. "We are right here, right now, with you."

Mom's shoulders drop; her face softens. I lighten my tone. "You have been alive for eighty years, woman!"

"Old hag!" Lisa says, through her tears.

"You, Babette Becker, are one of a kind," I say. "When half of you was one in millions of sperm swimming toward that single egg, you didn't care that the odds were against you. And you've lived every day of your life with the same gusto."

"Seriously!" Maddy says.

We go around the circle sharing our wishes for our mother.

Lisa goes first. "I hope you can enjoy your grandkids, stop doing so much, and start being. I hope you eat a full meal. Like on a plate. And sitting down."

"All right! All right! Enough, Lisa!" Mom says.

Maddy's wish is that she calls us more, lets us help her now that she is getting "up there."

Lisa jokes, "More importantly, I hope you get laid again!"

We laugh, and Mom says, "Please, God, yes!"

I nod, close my eyes, and say, "I echo my sisters' wishes. I wish you peace. Peace in your body. Peace in your heart. Peace of mind and—"

Mom's been listening. She's trying, but she can't help it now. She interrupts me: "I'm fine! Don't put me underground yet! I still have plans!"

Lisa sighs, squeezes my hand, and bites her top lip. Maddy is about to say something, but I stop them. I suggest we all take a breath. We all breathe.

"This circle can have the power to make us better," I say. "Or it can make us bitter. I vote for better."

We all agree.

"Better," we say in unison, and the tone changes.

After the wishes, I instruct us to do the release part of the circle. "Let's each take a piece of rice paper and write down any resentments that we might still have toward Mom, ones we are ready to release. Then we will say them aloud as we burn them and throw them out the window."

One by one, my sisters and I go to the kitchen window. Lisa goes first. "I let go of you not lovin' me in the way *I* needed to be loved!" She lights the paper on fire, throws it out the window, and starts to cry. She goes back to the couch and gives Mom one of those warm, two-armed Lisa hugs.

Maddy is next. She walks to the window, her long legs taller than the sill, and says, "I let go of all the fighting, and, um, I guess the babying." She crumples her paper, then lights it, and throws it out the window.

My turn. I go to the kitchen window and look out to Fourteenth Street, to the new Urban Outfitters on the corner and a nail spa where Mom gets pedicures on Sixth Avenue. It's a clear March afternoon. The spike from One World Trade Center pierces the sky over the cityscape behind the Jefferson Library clock. I look to my mother, who is staring at me. She looks at me as if she knows my insides, as if she can read my thoughts. We lock eyes for a moment. Our chests rise and fall in synchronicity. I flick the lighter and hold flame to my rice paper. I close my eyes and go in. There are so many things I want to say. I could be at this window for hours. But instead, I say the only words that sum up what matters the most.

"I forgive you."

I toss it out the window. The rice paper looks like a little lantern floating above the open city sky.

The Real Revolution

I am woken by cold hands. It's happening again. And sometimes, when I lie staring at my ceiling in the middle of the night, feeling the weight of Rob's boxes, which are still stored in the attic, I get a whiff of my father's cigarette breath. I feel the throbbing of scar tissue lining my uterus, emotional residue from my botched abortion in Mexico. *Why didn't I just go back to the States for the procedure?*

Len looked like the actor Hal Linden from that show *Barney Miller*. My sisters were both shocked when I told them about the kiss and the showers. Maddy remembers him as a kind man who listened to classical music while he cooked beef and broccoli in our wok. "That makes me want to bash Mom," Lisa said.

I do not close my eyes when I lie awake at night, because when I do, I see Len. Then I see bald, big-nosed, boozy Sal, Teresa's father from the old neighborhood in Brooklyn, who tried to put his fingers inside me when I was still learning my ABCs. Then it's the jock at the high school rooftop party, neither whose face nor name I can remember. I had forgotten about it until now. I was practically blackout drunk; he turned me around, slid the crotch part of my underwear to my inner thigh, and did me doggy style.

The memories resurface and expand at night. They pendulate, twirl, and curl out of sequence. There is no time line with trauma, just a felt sense, as if they are happening in real time. I'm consumed by epinephrine, overpowered by adrenal overload, blood pressure spiking through the roof, with a cramping so deep in my middle back, it's as if my kidneys are on a washboard.

I, like most women by 2019, am triggered by all the #metoo posts. Triggered by Republicans attempting to overturn *Roe v. Wade*. Triggered by blatant white supremacy, anti-Semitism, homophobia, fatphobia, ableism, gun violence, and police brutality—all the moral sludge that seems to be oozing from America's psyche these days, thanks to our narcissistic, rapist, racist president. He's a crook, who gets away with groping women's vaginas without any repercussions whatsoever.

I am angry. Young Kali angry. Angry at patriarchy. At misogyny. Angry to learn that just about every woman I know has lived through sexual abuse. Tainted with shame and stolen innocence. I'm furious about the externalized and internalized hatred toward femininity, institutionalized systems of oppression, and colonization that takes home in our body and our minds. *Fuck ahimsa.* Angry is the only way right now. Some anger is righteous. Some anger is an act of self-love.

I am disgusted with yoga, too, at my community of "soul-seekers," the supposed woke ones, who in my opinion seem to prefer spiritually bypassing the dark for the light. Every day, a new story comes out: The fallen gurus who coerced their disciples to abandon their material selves for some promise of eternal bliss. Teachers who got blow jobs behind ashram temple altars, and later, preach nonattachment. I am disappointed at all my yogis who appropriate, manipulate, and sculpt the sacred teachings into sexy Cirque-du-Soleil Instagram posts. I'm embarrassed I teach yoga.

I share with Jevon the spiky bits that have bubbled up as of late—interior moods and attitudes, which before him, I have told only to the plants or twisted out in yoga poses alone. These lingering shame places. The unprotected, neglected little girl who resides inside. The young woman who tried to forget by smoking her grandmother's cigarettes, dieting, or kicking over garbage cans. The forty-nine-year-old woman who forces a run instead of taking a nap when she's tired.

Jevon, like most straight white men by 2019, has no idea how to help me. He tries. He wants to be patient, but instead he mansplains. All my attempts to self-soothe, resource my body, reorient to the present, or breathe in for three, out for six, are gone. And Jevon's dad jokes are making it worse. So, when I throw my notebook and it hits him on the side of his face, on the June night that the only thing that helps me is to rage like my birth sign, the bull, Jevon has just about all he can take.

"I love you," he says, "but I won't keep doing this."

Our therapist tells us to take two weeks apart to think about what we each want from the relationship and to come to our next appointment with a decision: stay together or call it quits.

In our next session, after I find out Jevon has reached out to an ex-girlfriend for moral support and I want to tear the hair off my head because my skull feels like it's on fire, Mr. Therapist says, "You cannot keep going to a Chinese restaurant, Sherry, and expect to get served pizza."

What a stupid thing to say.

"I'm done. I'm out." I grab my things and run toward the door.

What a stupid thing to do.

It is an awful summer apart from Jevon. For two months, I spin out. I stop practicing yoga, nor can I meditate; it only makes me feel more triggered. To make matters worse, I jump in the ring with another man, someone who I selfishly use to feel better because my ego and heart are bruised. It is wrong, I know. I am hurt. I hurt myself by walking away from Jevon. Jevon, the most steady, loving, and attentive man I know.

By September, I'm desperate; I want him back. I write Jevon a *War and Peace*–length apology letter and leave it on his dashboard when I see his truck in the high school parking lot at back-to-school night. Thankfully, Jevon is a man who knows what he wants, and lucky for me, it is me. Never tell an addict, and especially not a Capricorn addict, that he can't have what he wants. He will go after it with every bone in his body!

Jevon and I are back in therapy in mid-September—intense, soul-stripping, heart-shredding therapy, three-hour sessions three or four times a week. Not with the same guy we saw before, and not actually traditional therapy, but with my friend Kim, a relationship "heart whisperer." Her method is called "True-ing." She can hear what we are not saying behind what we say, especially when I am in reaction and fight-or-flight mode and Jevon tries to tame me. Kim's motto, which she has even made into a bumper sticker, is "The real revolution will be love." Kim says the more intense my rage, the more fear of loss lives under it. "The real love is not puppies and rainbows. Real love has us on raw knees."

For months, Kim has us put it *all* on the table for review. We dive into the deep end, incubated in a bubble. First thing on order: the betrayal, my summer fling. Jevon found out about the other guy from his daughter, of all people. Now she hates me. Add that to the list of repairing to do.

Next thing on the agenda: more trauma healing. With all his decades of sobriety he does understand that, even with all my decades of spiritual practice, I still have so much more healing to do. Kim sends us articles to read by the specialists: Gabor Maté, Resmaa Menakem, and Dr. Stephen Porges, to name a few. She has us watch YouTube videos on polyvagal theory, so that Jevon can better understand the physiological effects I have when I am in a "state of emergency." Kim has us explore our personal stories and puts them in relation to the global mess we are in. "We are all triggered these days. We cannot talk our way out of a trauma response," she says. "We are beasts of nature, and like all animals, we need to shake our traumatic imprints off the body."

During our sessions, Jevon and I scream and fight, then cling and claw our way back. When I want to run because I feel threatened by closeness and equally threatened by distance, Kim has us sit back-to-back and breathe or embrace and *literally* shake. If we forget and boil, she turns us face-to-face to eye gaze, or to hug until tears stream down our faces, and we remember again.

"Just like food, our life must be digested," Kim says.

Some experiences are sweet to the taste, full of healthy fats, proteins, minerals, and quality carbs—the joys, laughter, the celebrations. These are easy to chew, easy to metabolize. They give us energy. But we also have the heart shatters, the trespassing, the nights begging for mercy. These bites are too bitter or spicy to swirl on the tongue, so we swallow these memories whole. They take up residence in our cellular memory. The undigested residue of life gets lodged inside the body.

"Our task is to pull out the nutrients and release the waste," Kim says.

It is a damp New England autumn afternoon, the kind where the sky sinks below the horizon and merges inside the fallen leaves. Jevon and I have just left Kim's after a marathon session, and I am feeling loved like never before. I get in my car and follow Jevon in his truck down a long winding road, past a meadow. Like magic, a family of deer run across the road. The road ends by a patch of woods on the edge of the state forest. I park behind him and get out of the car.

He gets out of his truck, opens his arms out toward the meadow, and says, "Well, what do you think?"

"I love it," I say. "Where are we?"

He, with the widest shit-eating grin on his face, says, "It's called Butterfly Lane."

I scope the sprawling, rolling meadow. Goldenrod is everywhere.

"It's for sale," he says.

He walks in close and wraps his arm over my shoulders. "Let's do it."

"I want to keep growing with you," I say.

"Me too," he says.

The Real Revolution

I believe healing happens; of course I do. But I don't believe healing comes like a bolt of lightning from the gods or a miracle "Aha!" that is gifted after a rock bottom, at least not in my experience. It happens pebble by pebble, bit by bit, a slow and steady rubbing of coal into diamond, the collecting of shattered bowl bits into a new mosaic. Healing births only from whatever wisdom was gained from the healing that came before it.

It is not that Jevon and I heal our relationship with Kim's help, per se, although that is a welcome side effect. It is that he is willing to witness and hold my healing with me, in shared space, together. Yes, I will continue to break, get triggered, forget—this I know. But I will remember, and I *will* repair. And I do not have to do it alone anymore. I will do it with Jevon. The real revolution will be love.

I look to the field again, and then back to Jevon. I squat down, brace my hands on the earth. I get down on my knees and lift my face up to see his. I say, "Jevon Rego, will you marry me?"

"Of course I will, dummy," he says.

I Miss Hugs

Mom holds the phone out the window so that I can hear the pot banging, bell ringing, and whistling of New Yorkers from my porch on the Vineyard.

"I miss New York," I say.

"I miss hugs," she says.

I have made this our ritual, a nightly call while she makes herself dinner, another during the day so we can read aloud to each other short stories we are writing. We've been doing this for six months of the COVID-19 lockdown—six months by herself in the loft with no physical contact, except for snuggles with her cats, Hank and Sam. I worry for her. She does not do well with stillness.

"How is your heart today, Mother?" I ask.

"I'm fine."

Usually, she talks about her day: online concerts and yoga, FaceTiming her patients. Even in the middle of a pandemic, this woman finds things to do. It helps her. I suppose it helps me too.

But tonight, she sounds low, very low.

"I really did not think I'd be spending my glory days trapped inside."

Half a year gone to the global pandemic, and so much living lost: Miles's last semester of high school behind a computer, his baseball finale and his eighteenth birthday both canceled. We celebrated graduation from our cars, like a drive-in movie. My fiftieth came and went. So did Mom's eighty-third. But we are all staying healthy. There's that. And Mom, Maddy, Lisa, and I talk regularly now, which we've never done. There's that too.

And there is Butterfly, the three acres Jevon and I managed to purchase off profits from selling my yoga studio and the equity from our separate homes just weeks before the stay-at-home order. Just weeks before we all started wearing masks, washing our groceries, and walking six feet apart like zombies in an episode of *The Twilight Zone*. Timing was on our side, because now all the plots of land and all the houses have been purchased, sight unseen, from all the summer people who have escaped the city. Now property value on Martha's Vineyard has doubled.

"What do you think this virus wants from us?" Mom asks.

"I guess it wants us to slow down. Take inventory of what's important. Make the necessary changes."

Change has been the one constant with COVID—and slowing down, an understatement. My suitcases grow dusty in the closet. Zoom rooms are the only places I travel to now. I have pivoted, like the rest of the world, and moved the teacher training online, which worked, but was utterly exhausting. I am now taking some time off from teaching yoga. I need to reboot. I am listening to COVID. It says, "Back out and reload."

Now I shovel dirt, sift it, and pull out stones while Jevon clears brush with the Bobcat. Now he chops wood, and I carry buckets of water. I go on walks to the ocean's edge and throw shells in the water. Sometimes, I hug a tree. If he lets me, I hug Miles.

I hear Mom sigh into the phone. "I still have so much living to do."

"I know you do."

The loneliness is getting to her. The quiet is getting to her.

"I'm afraid I'll disappear," she says.

In my mind's eye, I see an image of my mother as a child, in her backyard by the rope swing, spinning in place. Whipping, turning, round and round like a dreidel, as children often do when they are overwhelmed and self-soothing, or like the Sufi spinners do as a moving meditation to remember God.

I've been doing this lately, picturing my mother as a child. I picture all adults as children these days. We are all a bunch of wounded toddlers dressed up as old people, yearning to be touched, craving living again, seeking reasons for our new reality.

"I'm afraid I'll run out of time," Mom says.

"This is just a tough day," I say. "Keep breathing. Move your body a little."

She's sinking, depressed. I wish I could go see her.

"I have an idea," I say. "Put your phone on speaker. Make yourself a cup of coffee. I'll do the same."

"Coffee," she says. "Good idea."

I hear her fiddle with the pots, the *tick tick* of her gas stove turning on, the fridge door open and close, the coffee grinder. A couple of minutes pass.

"I'm back," she says, taking a sip. "You there?"

"I'm here," I say. "Now go into your bedroom."

"Why?"

"Just do it."

I hear her footsteps as she walks down the hall of family photos, past the stinky kitty-litter nook, into her bedroom.

"I'm here," she says.

"Sit on your bed."

"Okay."

"Look up at Grandma's painting, *Toward the Void*."

"Okay, looking. What about it?"

"Do you remember what you said to me when you first hung the painting in front of your bed?"

"No."

"I asked why you would put that painting there, and do you know what you answered?"

"I don't . . ." She is quiet for a moment. "I can't remember."

I Miss Hugs

"You said it inspired you to get up every morning and prove that you belong."

I hear her laugh and swallow.

"Thank God for you!" she says.

I don't know if she's talking about me or the coffee, but either way, it works, so I let it be.

His Lamb

We are on the living room floor of our yellow farmhouse, sifting through the things I brought down from the attic. Shadow is climbing through everything, making a mess. A million memories scatter on the floor: Miles's artwork, of all mediums, in piles. Lego bricks in a plus-size storage bin. Puzzles with pieces missing. His notebooks from when I failed horribly at homeschooling him, during our winters in California.

"You were the worst teacher ever!" he says, laughing.

"You're right, I was," I say, remembering the time I set fire to the handouts his teacher gave him to light the wood-burning stove for the outside tub we had during the winters in Ojai. We soaked for hours that night, instead of doing his time line project. "I'm your mother; I'm not supposed to be your teacher."

He rolls his eyes. "Oh look," he says. "My learner's permit!"

We laugh at the photo of his shaved blond head on the faded card. His blond has since turned brown. Now he wears shoulder-length curls.

"Here it is," he says.

He's holding up the spare key to his black Volkswagen Bug that we couldn't find when we sold his first car. It was meant to be spending money for his supposed gap year abroad; now it's money burning a hole in his pocket.

My Generation Z boy, born into 9/11 and graduated COVID class of 2020, has gone and turned into a man, though his rite of passage into independence is on pause while he watches and waits with the rest of us. He doesn't seem to mind. He has thrived with COVID, as many introverts have. Quarantining is a relief to him. He's happy at home chilling with his girlfriend, gaming with friends, or making candles with me. He's always been this way. When he was little and adults would ask, "What do you want to be when you grow up?" Miles would answer, "I want to be an old man. A grandpa in a rocking chair. Then maybe adults will stop asking me what I want to be when I grow up." Ha! My sarcastic Monkey. I kept him at my hip for the first years of his life, and today he is moving out of the yellow house and into his own apartment. His plan is to work as much as he can at the harbor, help Jevon construct the house, and save money until the world opens again. "If it ever does," he'll say, shrugging.

I pass him the Glad bag of furry friends he told me to throw away in eighth grade, but I never did.

"I can't believe you kept these," he says, ripping open the bag.

I watch him reunite with his stuffed animals from early childhood—the teddy bear with only one eye, his favorite pillow ("Piwow," as he called it), and the white, fluffy lamb I put in his bassinet the day he was born. I pick up the lamb from the floor and bring it to my nose to smell her, just like I used to do as a child with my Lammy. This lamb does not smell like our brownstone in Brooklyn. This lamb is not scented like potted plants. This lamb does not carry the fragrance of the Greyhound bus or the cocktail of rose oil and cigarettes.

This lamb, his lamb, smells like musty attic, like the passing of time. She smells like the primal pull of mothering, like the nostalgia that hijacks my lungs these days and keeps my breath hostage, the kind that makes me want to hold my crotch with both hands. She has the scent of contractions or dried-up breast milk, the after-odor that lingers in the Diaper Genie. She smells like dusty baseball trophies tucked between stacks of Pokémon cards, or prepubescent socks on the floor.

I breathe her in again. She smells like a hint of Axe cologne.

A Smoke and a Song

I take out a Sharpie and write "To Keep" on a box. He picks up Shadow, stops me, and says, "Actually, Mom, I'm not taking any of this stuff."

"But what if you want these when you're older? Not even the lamb?"

"Nah, I'm good," he says. "Give them away."

I take one more whiff of his lamb. His lamb smells like goodbye.

Miles and Shadow go up to his room to get the remainder of his things together. I put water on in the kettle and prep for the rest of the packing. Tomorrow I, too, am moving out of the yellow house, the house I busted my ass to keep after the divorce, Miles's home. Tomorrow, I move to Jevon's where we'll live until Butterfly is ready.

Tomorrow, I am restarting. Empty slate. Empty nest. No home to maintain myself. I'm not even teaching yoga these days.

Who am I if not these Sherrys?

I sit on the smooth, warm caramel floors. I close my eyes and put one hand on my heart and the other on the wood. When we bought the house, the floors were warped and blackened with soot. Rob wanted to put in new floors, but I insisted we keep the old ones. I could tell underneath the years of wear and tear, they had potential. I spent days lifting the planks off their rusty nails, one at a time, vacuuming out the previous owners from under each floorboard, and then carefully setting them back into their original spot, before sanding and spreading three layers of polyurethane on them.

They are beautiful, just as I knew they would be. Sometimes we need to give what has been forgotten about a little extra love for a thing to reveal its magnificence again. Just like all the humans I know.

I look up on the wall to Miles's framed pencil drawing of the old lighthouse sitting proudly on the iconic clay cliffs. I trace the skilled pencil lines and the delicate shading that go from dark ocean to lighter by the shoreline. We used to call this part of the island Gay Head, but in 1997 Islanders voted to revert to its native name. Now it is Aquinnah, which means "land under the hill," given by the Wampanoags, the original people from this part of the Northeast. This drawing was made years ago; the lighthouse has since moved a couple hundred feet back, and the clay cliffs have collapsed into the Atlantic, beaten by the elements.

I miss those lost Sunday all-day beach days when we first moved to Martha. We families would meet up there with Frisbees and beers, and the kiddos swam naked. We'd burn driftwood and roast s'mores over the flames until our kids fell asleep with sticky fingers and sandy faces, or the cops would tell us to go home.

Sigh. Our sweet family of three. Even eight years after we separated. Even with my wonderful second-chance life with Jevon. Even with the beautiful new house we are building at Butterfly.

Rob and I probably could have tried a little harder and made our marriage work. We could have kept our family intact for Miles. We both know it. He and I talk about it sometimes, on those random moments when one of us is feeling nostalgic enough to call the other and speak it out loud.

"I'm sorry that I didn't fight for us," he always says.

"I'm sorry too," I say. "We could have done better."

"We were a great team while we lasted," he says.

"We were," I say. "Until we weren't."

I take the lighthouse drawing off the wall and cover it in bubble wrap. I think about how it happens to all of us. Erosion, that is. Floors. Marriages. Even our identities crumble eventually, like the clay cliffs of Aquinnah, into the lapping waves. Yet we stand, like the lighthouse that had to be moved back from the cliff—not where we were, but on new ground now. Perhaps less risky of a perch, a little farther from the edge. Determined to be who we have become from the choices we have made and, on the good days, illuminate a path for other weary travelers at sea.

A Smoke and a Song

Miles comes down with one bag and a box. "I'm going to get going now."

I look up to him, his six-foot frame towering above me, brick fireplace behind his face, and say, "You know you can save more money if you live with us?"

He puts down the box, throws his man arm around my shoulder, and says, "You know, Mom, I have to go."

I try not to smother mother. I wish I could summon some witchy wild-woman strength of every empty nest survivor and swallow their wisdom whole. I wish I could wrap both my arms and both my legs around his lanky frame and squeeze every muscle until there are no more squeezes left. I wish I could whisper, "Don't go."

But I do not.

I help him load his bag and box into the back of his Subaru. I give him a quick hug and a kiss on his cheek. I say, "I'm so excited for you, sweetie. I'm so proud of who you have grown to be. Call me when you get settled."

Mothers are made to let go. It's in our biology, our cells, our DNA. It is the job of our uterus to contract and expel, to push the baby out. To somehow, though seemingly impossibly, hold on for all the years, and then summon the will to let our babies go.

I watch him whip the corner, like a dare, until his car is no longer in view, leaving an aura of dust that lifts and suspends on a sunbeam streak between the long limbs of the black oaks that line our driveway. In my hand, his lamb.

Last Little Secret

I cling to my red zipper clutch that holds the purple pouch where I keep my last little secret. We are engaged now. We are moving in together. And now I have two choices. Share my secret. Or quit.

I haven't told Jevon that I sometimes smoke. I haven't told him that I love to watch the sunrise through the trees past the empty lot across from the backyard with my first cup of joe in one hand and a stog in the other. Bitter Café Bustelo hand poured through the filter, with a little milk and a little honey. Sweet tobacco, fresh from the pouch, hand rolled in the thin and crispy hemp paper, no filter.

How Jevon has never smelled it in my curly hair or on my breath, I do not know. Hasn't he noticed all the lighters I have in my house? It's not that he would judge me for it, I don't think. I just have not wanted to tell him I smoke. I haven't wanted to tell anyone that I smoke.

When I smoke, I pluck a book off my yoga-themed bookshelf and take it to my sit spot on the three wooden planks on an old milk crate I set up behind my shed—out of view, just in case Miles wakes up. I open to a random page, read an inspiration for the day, while I light the tip, taking a long, slow drag. I hold the smoke in my lungs, then I take another drag, before my first sip of coffee. Absolute perfection.

I cling to my secret like it's a flag of independence, raised only while alone, without witness. My "I survived and still thrive, you can't knock this girl down, I'm from Brooklyn" banner.

A Smoke and a Song

I order my tobacco online, and if I forget to do that before the pouch runs out, or the flakes get so dry they are not smokable, I put on sunglasses and tie my ever-recognizable hair under a cap, doing my best to disguise myself at the store. I'm afraid I'll get busted by one of my students, one of these times.

Ha! Imagine that: "Picture-of-Health Yoga Teacher Caught Buying Tobacco at Jim's Package Store!" headlining our small island rag.

Jevon should know that it was in a moment of despair when I picked up the habit again, before we met. It was March 14, 2014, when the judge stamped the divorce papers. After, Rob and I celebrated over a shot of tequila at the bar next to the courthouse. He hugged me goodbye and said, "I'll always love you; I will."

I was embarking on another yoga-teacher training the next day, and although I love what I do, teaching yoga teachers can sometimes suck the breath right out of me. How was I going to lead others through an intense, soul-healing journey for ten hours a day for ten days straight when I couldn't even manage to lift my head off the pillow, let alone get out of bed? I was a hot mess. And as we do when we are hot messes, we turn back to old lovers. And mine was cigarettes.

I drove from the courthouse to the store and bought a pouch of loose American Spirit. I put my feelings in rolling paper and buried them with an inhale. There is something about a drag of a cigarette that allows all the separate chaos of life to pull into one place—one manageable hit, straight to the source. In the yoga science, they say we process grief in the lungs.

Now, six years have gone by. Six years!

My Grandma Elise never told my Grandpa Stanley she smoked. Fifty-something years together, and she kept her secret to her death. I always wondered why she did not tell him. They were artists. Wasn't smoking a given?

Last Little Secret

They say that family karma hides in our DNA, that the cells of our body have the imprint of memories lived by generations before us: Moments that used to belong to a distant relative that hide in our organs and blood. Stories that may not be ours, but that we are destined to perpetuate if we don't do something to change it. Like an inherited Fibonacci spiral, the shape of the fiddlehead, the arrangement of leaves on a fern, the flowering of an artichoke. A shape that rolls in and out on itself over and over, ancestral energy re-creating itself from both sides of the veil.

This morning's read is *Yoga Sutras of Patanjali*, soft cover. I go to my spot and light up. Inhale. Exhale. Breath work. I do feel guilty for smoking; of course I do. How could I possibly smoke? I'm a yoga teacher! I give myself a pass. Smoking helps ground me. The indigenous use tobacco in ceremony. It is sacred. Even Don Miguel the shaman smoked during ritual.

But who am I kidding? I am no shaman. There are no sacrificial chickens, burning incense, or blue crosses in my backyard today.

I cling to each drag with a similar intensity that Meryl Streep's character held on to her two children. Quit or keep smoking? Which one will I sacrifice? Which one will I keep? A real *Sophie's Choice* moment.

I open the book, and with my eyes closed, I place my newly diamonded left ring finger on a random spot on the page. It lands on Sutra 16: "*Heyam duhkham anagatam.*" Translation: The suffering that is yet to come is avoidable. Future suffering can be prevented.

I swirl the teaching in my mouth, along with the tobacco smoke. One last drag. I tap the ember on the bench, rip open the remains, sprinkle the tobacco on the earth by my feet, and roll the rest of the paper into a ball. I throw the ball over my fence, to the neighbor's yard. Ritual.

A Smoke and a Song

Jevon honks. He's early, here to load the rest of my things in his truck. No time to brush my teeth. No time to wash my face. I dip out from behind the shed to make myself visible.

"Hi, honey!" I say, waving.

He's standing at the top of my stone-wall driveway, and for a moment I really see him, the man I will spend the rest of my life with. So damn handsome. We've each lived through divorce, coparenting, failure, repair. And here we are, daring again. There's no choice here to be made. We only lose what we cling to.

"I have something to tell you," I say, as I walk up the steps toward his truck, red clutch in hand. I open my palm and show him the tobacco. "Sometimes I smoke."

"I know, dummy," he says. "I can smell it in your hair."

Too Lazy for Both
Sex and Zen

I am perched in the doorway of Jevon's bathroom, naked, dripping wet, staring at the freshly made California King. I have committed to thirty days of morning meditation for the 2021 New Year, and I am on a good streak, day nine. Jevon wanted to make love this morning, but too lazy for both sex and Zen, I opted for Zen.

As I slather my body with rose oil and air dry to prepare for my sit, I think about how he and I used to meet on this bed to make love two or three times after our Kim sessions. Afterward, we'd both slide back into our workdays, flushed, sometimes with clothes on inside out, in an oxytocin coma. It feels eons away but was only a year and a half ago. It was while the kids were at school, when school was an actual building and not a computer screen.

These days, his bed, *our* bed, has become a place for watching *Breaking Bad* reruns, an occasional snuggle for a few minutes, and the on-and-off sleep patterns of middle age. Mostly, we lie on different sides of the bed. I am content on my side. The memory foam has graciously shape-shifted to the weight of my body, accommodating all the extra curves, which seem to be happening at a rapid pace since I stopped menstruating months ago—this time, permanently.

I call him my furnace. He runs on high, especially at night, when he finally checks the boxes on his never-ending get-'er-done list and falls flat out, often sitting up. How he can sleep completely vertical, I have no clue! There is no in-between for that man. It's all go or completely gone for him. And when gone, he cooks at an extra ten to fifteen degrees, like a semitruck after a long, steady, steep highway climb in need of coolant. My handsome, sleeping-and-waking, overheated, smoking hood.

I run cold—hands, toes, down-to-the-bone cold, shivering-even-in-the-summer cold. Even during menopause, between hot flashes—cold. He bought me one of those weighted blankets. He said, "Here, my love, to keep you warm," since he keeps the thermostat down to sixty-two degrees. Whoever invented that weighted blanket is a genius. It's the adult swaddle! Those flannel fifteen pounds help me not yearn for the days when Miles was a little monkey and slept on my chest.

Sometimes, I slide my left leg to his side and throw it over his body. He tries, sacrificing his needs for my wants for as long as he can, until a slick film of sweat exits the pores on his calf, and he can no longer take it. He pulls his leg away, kicks off the blanket, and sticks his leg into the open air.

"Sorry, love, I'm burning," he says.

"I know, honey, it's all good," I say.

Maybe it is a little nostalgic, the image of each of us on opposite sides of the bed, no longer needing to merge bodies on the daily as evidence that we do really belong together. But honestly, I am good with it. There is comfort, relief, in the mature stage of a relationship, where you accept a quieter version of love. There is the depth that comes with understanding that we are two separate people choosing to live our lives together, with little left to prove.

Jevon, being the generous man he is, hasn't forgotten that my love language is physical touch and still meets me in the ways I need to be met. Just days ago, he got out his industrial sander from the garage and sanded the bottom of my feet! I haven't had a pedicure since all the salons shut down. My heels were so calloused, they were like elephant hooves. So calloused that if I sliced off the bottom and slapped on a toe strap, they'd practically make a flip-flop! I sat outside on a deck chair with my foot on his lap as he sanded my feet to a smooth softness. If that is not love, I don't know what is.

I slip on my loose sweat shorts and a tight tank top, braless. Before sitting to meditate, I light one of the candles that sits on the pale blue dresser where I now keep my clothes. This dresser and I have a real love-hate relationship. Every time I try to close a drawer, I have to push the side of my hip into the big circular knobs. Every time, it sticks slanted to one side. I reopen and close it over and over before we find our groove, literally. It is almost as if the drawer and Jevon's kids are in cahoots to make sure I remember I am an outsider here, in their house. I swear the other day I heard the drawer say, "You might live here now, but you'll never fit in."

I made a deal with the dresser, and we agreed that if we are going to share space, we must find a common ground, an agreed-on purpose. So I place a few of my yoga things on top of the dresser: my vanilla votives, a wooden Ganesh statue, and a couple of little mirrors I have collected during travels. I light the candle and then open and close the drawer without a hitch, just to prove our agreement is working.

I sit down. I tuck a little pillow under my sit bones and cross my ankles into the upper corners of my inner thighs. Part of my knee rubs the scratchy carpet. I have always had an "ick" to man-ufactured, nonorganic materials. When I was a kid, Mom would have to cut the tags off my collars. Or God forbid my tights were askew—I'd never leave the house. She'd set me down on the kitchen floor to fix them, and say, "Sit still, Snaps. We can't be late for school another day for this shit!"

Carlos Nakai's *Canyon Trilogy* is playing on my phone, which is next to me. I focus on my breath. My inhale moves through my bones, as if they are bamboo, or Nakai's flute. Playing the music of contemplation.

I go in . . .

The phone rings. I forgot to turn off the ringer. I ignore it. It rings three more times in a row.

I finally look; it's Mom. It figures. She calls at the worst times. Why won't she just leave a message like you're supposed to?

I answer it. Without even a hello first, I say, "Mom, I am meditating; I can't talk now."

She's panting.

"Mom. What is it? Are you okay?"

"I'm dizzy. I fell in the elevator. I can't breathe."

"Hang up and call an ambulance!"

Tested

I drive around the West Village looking for a parking spot. Storefronts are boarded up. Bones of bikes with wheels and handlebars missing dangle off signposts. The sidewalks are riddled with humans who used to take shelter underground, but now that the city stopped running the subway at night, people have no other choice than to sleep on the streets.

The old neighborhood is looking a lot like it did in the eighties, except for the new outdoor restaurant shacks that are stacked side by side—mini curbside cafés made of plastic, plywood, or aluminum, with two-tops set six feet apart, each separated by plexiglass and heat lamps. A true sign of New York resilience.

It is my third time in New York City since January—not easy with COVID. I quarantine for ten days and get tested before I come, get tested when I go home, and quarantine again. A week-long visit becomes a three-and-a-half-week exit from my life, and life is full. The new house at Butterfly is ready; we plan to move in later this month. Miles is going to college in the fall, to the University of Massachusetts at Amherst. We are in the throes of financial aid forms, not to mention a wedding to plan for.

When we got her diagnosis three months ago, my sisters and I agreed to rotate being with Mom during her chemotherapy treatments, which are every three weeks. But to date, I am the only daughter who has made it during the chemo weeks.

Maddy tried last month. She went to the city but had a panic attack the night before Mom's appointment and left the loft in the middle of the night. She called me on her drive back to Martha's Vineyard and said, "I just can't do it." She could not support Mom's decision to go the medical route. She wants Mom to go holistic and try juicing instead. But Mom insists, "No juicing. I will continue chemotherapy, as long as I don't lose my hair!"

Lisa can't come. She's immunocompromised. It is too risky for her to leave her house. "Plus," she says. "even if I could, I wouldn't be able to stand it." The loft makes her sneeze, Mom makes her crazy, and "Manhattan is fucking *Dawn of the Dead* now."

I understand. I envy my sisters for knowing their boundaries and sticking to them. I am not so good at honoring mine. These days, it's not them. No one is pressuring me to be the dutiful daughter, not even Mom. But the old mantra is loud. *Someone has to be there for her.* She's my mother, after all, and she has late stage-three lung cancer. Of course I'm going to come for chemo.

I am comforted by the *rattle, rattle, clank!* the elevator makes as it lands on number eight. No matter how many houses I've lived in, in how many states, and in what country, this elevator always tells me I am home. I throw my bag and keys on the dining table. The keys slide across the table and bump into a stack of mail. The stereo is on, and it's loud—Thelonious Monk's *Straight, No Chaser.*

"Mom! I'm here."

Mom is asleep on the couch, arms folded on top of her puffed belly, her purple, swollen ankles crossed on top of the pillow. I tiptoe past her and the plants, to the kitchen. I look at the kitchen window. The windowsill and glass are filthy, full of construction dust. I find a paper towel and the Windex and start cleaning.

Mom jolts up. "Oh hi, Snaps!"

I go over to give her a hug.

"Hi, Mama. Sorry, I tried not to wake you."

"I'm happy you are here," she says. "Thank you for coming again."

"Of course."

Tested

I take off my shoes and coat and scooch in to lie next to her. "They've barely made a dent in the new high-rise," I say.

"Oy, what a goddamn mess," she says. "I haven't seen anyone working on it for weeks."

She fills me in on her day—FaceTiming her therapy patients, Zoom yoga class, and a guitar lesson. She might be dying, but she's back at life.

"Good for you! Fuck cancer!"

We high-five. Her breath is like an inside-out sneeze. When she swallows, she coughs.

"How is the cough?"

"Fine!"

She does not sound fine.

In the morning, I take her to Mount Sinai Hospital. I drop her at the door because I'm not allowed to go in with her—pandemic rules. Today, they are adding a new drug, Keytruda, to her infusion. Her oncologist says he is impressed with how she's handling the chemo and, although radiation is not an option because of how the cancer is presenting in the lungs and the lymph node in her chest, he thinks immunotherapy can help.

Mom swears she has barely noticed any side effects from the treatments. Leave it to her to be the only person on the planet not to be affected by chemotherapy. Either her oncologist is filling her IVs with sugar water, or she's hiding it. She talks about the treatment like she is prepping for a day at the spa.

"I can't wait to read a couple chapters of my new book," she says, before we part on the outside of hospital glass doors.

As she walks into the hospital alone, I notice all the long, white, curly strands of her hair on the back of her black wool coat.

I spend the first part of the day making lists of her accounts and passwords, sorting through insurance premiums, her medical proxy, her will and testament. The document is short and vague—no clear plan. Only a blurb that says: "At the request of Ms. Becker, and under all circumstances, it is to be noted that Ms. Becker's choice is to reside at her loft on Fifteenth Street, New York, New York, until deceased."

Nowhere in her will does it say that I am to inherit her record collection.

The latter half of the day I spend unpacking, plugging in, and setting up three Echo Dots—one in the living room, one in her bedroom, and one by the elevator door. If she's going to insist on living alone, we've got to have an emergency plan in case she falls again.

Before picking her up, I clear the dining table. I move the cats' water bowl to the floor, wipe the top, and place the platter of sushi from Whole Foods at the head of the table. I arrange the pink salmon slices with extra dabs of wasabi in a heart shape. I put the avocado rolls, slippery wet eel, and a pile of edamame in the middle. I rinse and dry two wineglasses and open a bottle of Malbec. I know both sushi and wine are on the "don't eat with treatment" list given by her oncologist, but I think, *Fuck it*. She deserves to enjoy her favorite meal.

After dinner and resting in her room, Mom comes out and plunks a cardboard moving box on the dining table. "Look!"

I sift through the box. Inside are some random school projects, my old jewelry box, and my lot of stuffed animal lambs.

"No way! My imposters!"

I pick up one of the lambs and bring her to my nose.

I was seven when I lost my beloved Lammy, the same day I lost my dad. Mom and I were on the train heading back to Brooklyn from the Port Authority. It was the part of the ride when the subway passed over the Manhattan Bridge, and it was dark out, already nighttime. My little legs were sore from walking the three miles to Kerhonkson that morning, and I was sleepy and cranky from crying through the entire night before, followed by the two-and-a-half-hour bus ride back to the city. I was resting my head on Mom's lap while she unknotted my hair with her fingers. I reached inside the front zipper pocket of my backpack, which I had lined with a cotton-ball bed and a washcloth blanket, so it would be extra cozy for my stuffed Lammy.

"Mom, Lammy's gone!"

We looked through my backpack. She was nowhere to be found. I cried the whole way home. Mom tried to soothe me, but I was inconsolable. When we got back to the brownstone, Mom called the station to see if the stuffed animal was turned into lost and found. No luck. For the next two days, she and I retraced our ride on the train, just in case Lammy was still there on the subway, a useless feat. I cried and begged Mom to find her, but Lammy was lost.

"I can't believe you have these," I say.

Mom is smiling. "I must have bought every stuffed animal lamb in New York City!"

For months, maybe longer, Mom would come home from work with a stuffed animal lamb. "He's too big," or "She's not the right color," or "This one is too scratchy!" I'd yell. "Not. My. Lammy!"

After one too many failed attempts, she finally sat me down and said, "You have to let Lammy go, Snaps. I know it's hard, but she's gone."

I put down the lamb in my hand and pick up a different one. "I put you through hell, didn't I?"

"You sure did," Mom says. "You are my stubborn one. You've always been hardheaded. My holder-on-er. From the day you were born. Your sisters came running out of the birth canal. You, on the other hand . . . I pushed for over three hours with you; the doctor almost resorted to forceps. You held on!"

Years ago, when I was studying to be a labor doula, I remember learning that the way we birth into the world is indicative of the way we deal with big transitions in life as grown-ups.

A Smoke and a Song

"It has made you loyal and loving," Mom says. "But it has also made you hard, and sometimes hard to be around."

"I think I've gotten better as I've gotten older, no? Haven't I?" I ask.

"Yes, you have. Life has sanded down your edges some. But I think you could still learn to ease up some, for yourself."

I nod.

"Your expectations are very high," she says. "You've always been this way, even as a kid. I used to tell you just to do your best. But that was never enough. You wanted to be *the* best. The best daughter. The best sister. The best granddaughter. The best student. The best friend to everyone. It is a lot of pressure to be the most important person in the room all the time."

"Yeah," I say. "I don't know where that came from. Losing my Lammy?"

"More likely it's from losing your father," she says. "There weren't enough stuffed lambs in the world to replace that loss. I knew that day when I picked you up that I'd never send you back to your father's. And then you lost your Lammy."

She continues, "I see you soften, Snaps; I do. With Miles, with your students. And especially since you met Jevon. My wish for you is that you can give yourself the same compassion you give to others."

Mom gets up to change the album. As she's looking through her records, I look at her. She's so tiny, her body riddled with cancer, her hair thinning. The thought of her suffering is unbearable. I always assumed my mom would live her vibrant life as usual and then drop dead during a yoga class or dancing at a concert. Not sick. Not slowly.

She chooses *Mirror Mirror*, Chick Corea's last release. Chick died a few months ago from cancer.

Mom lies on the couch, puts her feet up, and says, "I used to roll my eyes at your grandmother when she'd complain about getting old. But she was right. Old age can be cruel."

Tested

Her cat Sam hops up on her, walks a slow circle, and plunks down on her belly. "It's cat-petting time!"

I lie on the sofa across from them. Hank, her other cat, rubs against my sofa. I pet Hank.

It's probably not the best time to bring it up, but there's never going to be a good time. Lisa, Maddy, and I all agree. We need to talk about what we've all been avoiding talking about, and it's probably best if I am the one to bring it up. "Mom, we should talk about next steps," I say.

"Not now."

"I think we need to talk about it, Mom."

"The cats. I worry for them. What will happen to the cats?"

"Jevon and I will take the cats."

"I hate the thought of them being put in a shelter."

"Don't worry about the cats. Jevon and I will take them. You . . . We need to talk about you."

"Not now, Snaps. We'll talk about it when the time comes."

"Mom, the time has come."

"Leave it alone."

"Will you consider moving to Martha's Vineyard, or at least to Provincetown so you'll be closer?"

"Absolutely not. I want to stay in the loft. I don't want to talk about it anymore."

"Mom, you mean to tell me that you would rather be taken care of by a stranger, on your last days, alone, than to move in with one of us and be surrounded by your family?"

"Yes," she says, raising her voice and her hands. "That's exactly what I mean." Her bangles clank. Sam jumps off her lap. Mom coughs.

I want to say it is selfish of her not to talk to us about her end-of-life care. But I don't. I go to the kitchen and fill a glass of water. I look out the kitchen window, through the clear part of the glass that I rubbed out with Windex last night, through the unfinished steel skeleton of the abandoned construction project, and I see patches of night sky and the illuminated windows in rows up, down, and across the buildings of our West Village neighborhood. I think of all of us humans behind all these windows, doing our best to live and love, lean in and let go.

I walk to the living room and pass Mom the glass of water. She sits, takes a sip, and lies down again. I go to my sofa and lie down too.

We spend the rest of the evening listening to Chick Corea pound the piano with our eyes closed. We always close our eyes when we listen to music. It helps us to hear the music better.

Butterfly

I sit outside on the patio, under the kitchen window. It's early, before sunrise even, and the sky is still dark. The air today is both hot and moist, with a humble summer breeze that carries the bird's symphony as if we live in an amphitheater, surround sound. Not long ago this beautiful Amish post-and-beam house was just a dream sketched on paper in Jevon's handwriting, with the thirteen uppercase letters that read "BUTTERFLY FARM." I can hardly believe we have built ourselves a home from the ground up and that we are all moved in. A new day begins.

I stare at the large bluestone pieces of our patio, misshapen by the elements for thousands of years, set in place by a young landscaper named Jacob. I spent days directing Jacob to meticulously arrange and rearrange the pieces, so that it looks organic to the West Tisbury landscape, as if the patio just fell from the sky to the ground this way.

Past the stone-patio puzzle is a long, wide, thick slope of black topsoil that has been trucked in from an up-island property and smoothed over and over and over by Jevon in his Bobcat. Inside the topsoil, there must be a million seeds sown and germinating—lawn grass seeds, meadow grass seeds, sunflowers, butterfly weeds, wildflowers.

I impatiently check the soil for growth ten times a day, excited, animated, awaiting the moment these seeds push from their shells, root, ripen, and rise into tiny spikes, stems, or stalks above ground. When will they pop and become what they are meant to become? I fertilize. I nurture. I make a ceremony of watering. It takes over two hours to water everything. I drag around hoses connected to hoses—male heads fastened to female tails. I hum into the water as it sprays from the hose to the earth. I tiptoe around, encouraging the seeds: "Keep growing, little seeds, despite it all." It's my new yoga.

Soon the sun will rise across our neighbor's unmowed meadow, just above his vegetable garden with four locust posts and chicken wire fencing to keep the deer out. When we were clearing the land last year, when everything was still shut down, before we were all vaccinated and the foundation hadn't even been poured yet, the neighbor's goats, BlackBerry and Comet, would roam over to say hello. They are social creatures, the goats, especially these two. They were raised on Native Earth teaching farm, the farm that gives goat yoga classes to schoolkids.

What are the chances of that? A yogi buying property next to two yoga goats?

I took it as a sign that we *do* belong here, in this 7a frost bottom zone of Martha's Island, on this sacred patch of earth that was once stewarded by the Wampanoags for hundreds of years before we came along. Now we have a deed that spells our names on it—a fact I find challenging to contend with in my heart of hearts. Sometimes I swear I can smell ash and embers from ancient fires. Sometimes I feel a low *thump thump pow, thump thump pow* from the ancestor's drum, beating under my feet.

We planted forty-eight trees this year. I insisted, "Two for every tree we have to take down." Most of the old trees fell easily, barely making a sound. They were so rotten, hollowed in the middle, their bark held up by time and human absence and the ant colonies that took home inside the trunks. We gathered the fallen soldiers into a giant pile, where I tucked in satchels of dried sage and set off a raging bonfire—an offering of devotion to the dead, like *arti*. Where the trees once stood, we shoveled holes deep enough to stand in and filled the bottoms with compost made of ash, worms, wet black soil, and leaves. And then we planted the new trees: arborvitae, crab apples, weeping cherries, baby birch, lilacs, dogwoods, butterfly bushes, Japanese maple, and of course a juniper tree, for my niece and for Grandpa Stanley.

The other day, I collected sand from Lambert's Cove Beach and walked the perimeter of our property six times, as I was taught to do by Don Miguel, the second Don Miguel, in Uxmal. I sprinkled sand on the ground, asking for protection and abundance and boundless love from Yemaya, Ixchel, and Lakshmi, the goddesses of the ocean, fertility, and fortune. I tucked a dozen rose quartz crystals for unconditional love inside the crotches of the old black oaks and still-strong cedars along the trail in the woods that lead to the state forest, behind the basement walkout.

The basement will be the yoga room if I ever decide to do another training when COVID ends, or an apartment that we can offer to one of our kids if all three should want to live home for a stint. Summers, we may Airbnb it to make some cash. But really, the basement is meant to be a grandmother flat for Mom, soon, when she's too far gone to argue it anymore.

It's early, and everyone is still sleeping inside—all three kids, Jevon, and my mom. When the sun rises, after coffee and a shower, I will slip on my white strapless sundress. My hairdresser friend, Susan, will come at noon to do my hair and makeup. The chef will drop off the crudités platter, ice, and glass-bottled drinks.

At two, right when the sun passes behind the meadow and the fully leaved trees mark patches of shade in front of the farmer's porch, we will put on Chris Stapleton's "Joy of My Life" on the outside speaker. Miles will walk me, barefoot, our arms looped, off the porch to Jevon and the Japanese maple tree we picked to plant. Alex will FaceTime in Jevon's mother, Midge. The boys will shovel the dirt. Mom will pour in the water. Jevon and I will

A Smoke and a Song

sprinkle fertilizer. We will say our vows, and Jevon, our three kids, and I will become one—a sweet family of five.

But for now, I sit on the patio in the dark, breathing. New life is blooming. Loss is looming. And both gladness and grief grip at the gate.

Bermuda

"I'm not proud to admit it," I confess to Jevon.

I am wishing I felt different, but I have to say it out loud. I have to be honest with myself and with him, to be validated. He is my husband now. He earned my truth with the commitment he made to me two days ago when he said, "I do, I will, today and forever." He has proven that he can hold all my parts. The parts that are tough to admit out loud. Imprints and codes, gestated from an egg and implanted by sperm that lived in my mother and father and their parents before them, and the great-grand ones too. All those that have been passed to me, despite the forgiving, the regressing, and the guilt that later leads to renewed compassion, despite all the caring, despite all the *with* love, not *for* love, are still what make up my hard drive.

Jevon nods. He understands. He witnessed it this past week while she was with us. He finally got a taste of how she can be. Especially now, as she gets older and sicker, and more see-through.

Her hands are going numb; they hurt. My aunt Gretchen says it is a side effect from the chemo, and it's not an optimistic one. It is called peripheral neuropathy. It damages the nervous system, in the hands and feet. Typically, it comes on strong months after treatment. It can go away, but often does not. Usually it worsens, especially in the elderly.

Jevon gave Mom some of his CBD oil to help. She shrugged him off, threw her hands up, agitated, cold, snarky, and said,

"I'm fine!" and walked away while he was in the middle of his sentence.

"This is hard," I say, "watching her."

"I understand," he says.

We each have two tuna-sandwich slivers and two sugar cookies on small plates. I look out over the dramatic limestone cliff and the deep blue seas of Bermuda. We just made love, the kind we used to make, wobbly after a fight when we used to use sex to get back into alignment. Only today it was longer, and slower, with more soul now that we wear rings. Today was "we are on a honeymoon" lovemaking. Not twenty-something honeymooning sex, no; it was "we are in our fifties now" kind of lovemaking. The kind that makes you hungry and want to overeat tuna sandwiches and cookies and be lazy, "so lazy you are ready to nap on a fancy chaise lounge on the beach and confess a truth" kind of lovemaking.

On the chaise, under the umbrella that barely shades us from the microwave-hot sun, lulled by the waves, I sip on my Rum Swizzle and say, "I'm not proud to admit it"—another sip—"but I will be relieved when she passes."

"I understand," he says.

Borrowed Dust

Shadow, the once-feisty, ferocious fur being who used to climb trees, who disappeared into the woods for days at a time, who once dragged a dead raccoon onto our living room rug, is waning. She can barely walk some days. She takes three steps and falls into a puddle, then sleeps right there, in her favorite spot for hours, under Grandma's Singer sewing machine legs of the sink that we moved from the yellow house to Butterfly. Her breath is shallow and wheezing.

When we adopted Shadow almost nineteen years ago, the man at the shelter explained that she was a motherless cat, scrappy, sometimes aggressive, and fearful. "Don't be surprised if she escapes," he said. "Feral cats often do."

When we brought her home, she hid under the cabinets, way in the back by the wall, where she was too far for anyone to reach her. We put bowls of food on the floor, little fuzzy mouse toys, and cat treats. When she finally slinked her way out, she zipped past our feet and ran out the deck door. Miles cried, heartbroken, and we worried for her safety. Six long, tear-filled days later, there she was, meowing at the back porch.

For years, Shadow came and went as she liked. We joked that she must have had a double life; perhaps there was another family that fed her and called her by a different name, like Frisky or Flo. She always came back fatter than she left us.

At our house, she followed Miles from room to room. Nights, she slept in the middle of his stuffed animal pile, or crawled on his chest while he watched TV, to make muffins on his belly and nurse on his pj's. During tubby time, she'd walk the rim of the tub, inching closer to him, often falling into the bathwater.

When Miles first moved into his own apartment a year and a half ago, he had a bad bout of depression. He lay in bed for days at a time, distant, in a fog, unable to function. I tried to convince him to move into Jevon's with us, but he insisted on living alone. When it got so bad that he called me in the middle of the night, saying his thoughts were dark and that he was worried, I put Shadow in the car and drove the two of us to his apartment. When I went home later that night, after we spoke to his therapist and came up with a plan, I left Shadow with Miles. She did not run back to our house, as cats often do when they are moved to a new place. She stayed by his side and soothed him. She gave him reason to get up. She nursed him back to wholeness.

Now Miles is doing so well, thank God. He's living his second semester at college. He goes rock climbing with a group of guys from his dorm hall, goes to parties, and goes to the gym. And tomorrow is his twentieth birthday. Twenty years old! Jevon and I are going to Amherst for the night to celebrate with him. Rob is already there. We'll all have lunch together, maybe go up Mount Hitchcock, the hike I used to do when I was living in Amherst, at Hampshire College. Miles and Rob have a 4:00 p.m. appointment to get matching tattoos. After that, we all have tickets to go to the Amos Lee concert.

Shadow is not doing so well. When Miles was home for Christmas break, he and I picked a spot for her—between the maple tree we planted at our wedding last August and the weeping cherry by the driveway. Our plan is to put her into the earth, no box, and plant a bushel of *Nepeta cataria* in that spot, her favorite plant. It's the plant she loves to roll around in and then chew on the stems. Miles will paint her name on a rock, and we'll put it over her grave.

I told Jevon he better watch what we do for Shadow, because I want the same ritual for me when it is my turn, only with lavender instead of catnip.

He laughed and said, "I think that's illegal. You trying to get me arrested?"

I told him I've already done the research. All he needs to do is fill out a permit at town hall.

Mom made her arrangements, finally. She sent me the packet from Greenwich Village Funeral Home. I got it in the mail a couple of days ago. I haven't opened it yet. I find the manila envelope and sit on my yoga mat in the basement apartment, in the spot where I practice, in front of the three-paned window with the hanging fern and the clear quartz prism that makes rainbows on the walls of the room when the midmorning sunlight shines through it. I read through the packet. Inside, there's a receipt for the prepaid cremation. I call Mom.

"Don't you want to be buried in the plot in Provincetown next to Grandma and Grandpa?"

"Nope," Mom says. "Take me up to the roof of the loft. Have a party for me and then toss my ashes to New York City."

"I'll mix your ashes with some coffee grinds!"

"Ha! Perfect!" she says.

"And we'll eat candied skulls like the Mexican Day of the Dead!"

"Bustelo and sweet treats, por favor," she says.

"Thank you for doing this; I know it must be hard," I say. "And for sending it to me."

"You're welcome, Snaps. Share it with your sisters if you want."

"I will. But it may be null and void. Knowing you, you'll outlive us all."

She laughs. "Maybe I will!"

"Armageddon will hit. The only survivors will be the rats, the roaches, and Babette Becker."

She laughs hard. "Play a good song at my memorial!"

A Smoke and a Song

I say, "Of course! How about Aretha's 'Come Back Baby'?"

She says, "Or Davis's 'Flamenco Sketches'! Or how about Donna Summer's 'Hot Stuff.'" She's on a roll.

"We will get the boogie on for sure!" I say.

"Those are my favorite moments," she says. "Dancing with my daughters."

I picture the four of us, back in the day, dancing: Mom, with her eyes closed, chest and chin up, blowing smoke rings, singing at the top of her lungs. My sisters stomping their feet front and back. Bri, the fat cat, watching us from the dining room table.

"They are mine too," I say. "You did a fine job, Mom. You should be proud."

"I wish I was in a better place when you kids were younger," she says. "It was not easy, raising you three alone. I was in a panic most of the time. Some nights I would pace the streets for hours. I didn't want you girls to see me that way."

"Don't dwell," I say. "It was the eighties. Before cell phones and helicopter parenting. You unparented; it's all the rage now. You were ahead of the trend!"

"I wish I could have been more present," she says.

"You did the best you could, Mama. You did good. Look at us all now."

"Maybe my grandkids will want a little handful of me to keep. Before you throw me to the streets, let them take a pinch if they want."

"I will."

She sighs. "I love those kiddos to the moon and the stars."

"They adore you."

"And Miles turns twenty tomorrow! Wow."

"He's a full-blown man!" I say. "How did that happen?"

She sighs again. "I'm lucky I've lived long enough to see my grandkids into adulthood."

"They are the lucky ones," I say.

Justin, Juniper, and Miles do love their grandma. Last year, when she was first diagnosed, they pooled their own savings and sent her a beautiful bouquet of flowers and a gift certificate to her nail spa.

"Oh, I've been thinking . . . I want you to read the last stanza from Stanley's poem 'Passing Through' as you scatter me."

"Note taken," I say.

She pauses for a moment. I hear her take a sip and swallow. Coffee, I am assuming. "There is something I want to say to you."

"Yeah?" I hear her clear her throat and pause.

"I'm sorry about Len."

It is a huge moment for me.

"I'm sorry I did not protect you."

Her apology is everything I need. "It's okay, Mom, really."

"You know, when I was in the hospital, back as a teen, wanting to die after it happened to me, I used to believe I was not meant to be a person." She pauses. "I used to think I should have been music."

It is beautiful and divine, to imagine my mother as music.

"I don't want to be forgotten," she says.

"Impossible. Lady, you are unforgettable. You'll be inside me, in my morning coffee and in the trees. In the concrete. You'll be in the songs I listen to. Maybe you'll come back as a cat!"

"Cats *are* mystical creatures," she says.

"Yes, they are," I say. "Shadow is my spirit guide."

She asks how Shadow is doing.

"Hit and miss. Lethargic most of the day. But then, out of nowhere, she'll jump up and disappear outside. I think she goes across the meadow to visit the goats."

Mom says, "How cute!"

"She keeps on ticking, that cat," I say. "Every time I think she's ready to go, she surprises me and bounces back. She's holding on, that one."

"I can relate," Mom says. "Maybe she's waiting . . . to meet Hank and Sam?"

A Smoke and a Song

Maybe Shadow is waiting. Waiting for *me* to be ready.

"What a trip," she says, "to live all these years, just to die."

"What a trip," I say.

"A whole life. Boiled down to coffee, cats, and cancer," she says.

The two of us are silent for a while. I get up from my mat, take the fern off its hook, and bring it to the window ledge, phone on speaker, also in my hand. I set the phone down. I pick up the water pitcher and fill the rim of the pot. The water pools on the soil, bubbles, and then sinks into the dirt.

"Well, Snaps, I'm going to run now. It's cat-petting time! And I've got a busy day."

"Mom, thank you again. I love you."

We hang up.

I go upstairs, take Grandpa's book *Passing Through* off the shelf, and look for Shadow. She's under the sink, as usual. I lie down on the bathroom floor. I put my face close to her face. I brush her fur and rub her favorite spot behind her ears. She purrs. She's barely cognizant, eyes half open, glazed over. I flutter my eyelashes at her because Miles told me that this is cat speak for "I love you." Shadow looks at me and spreads her front paws open, revealing her sharp nails, then closes her eyes.

I roll onto my back and look up at the distressed-gold lotus light pendant on the ceiling. It's the one thing I took from the yoga studio before selling.

I teach my students that the way we leave a yoga posture is more important than the posture itself. The longer the hold, the more breaths we take in it, the more necessary it is to transition out of the pose slowly.

"Not unlike life," I say. "The more years in a career, a house, a relationship, the more care it deserves upon exit."

So that we don't hurt ourselves on the way out. So that we move into the next pose with full presence, clarity, and a clean slate. So as not to drag where we were into where we will be.

Borrowed Dust

"Pay attention and give your full devotion to leaving, before it becomes a memory," I say.

But when looking back, as I do often these days, it is easier to access the heroine who came to the other side from my experiences and flourished, but not as easy to recall my slow crossing of the bridge. It is easier to access the life lessons gained, but not the messy, slobbering, snot-filled tears while learning them. I'm able to picture the flashes, clips, and blips but can rarely recall the whole reel.

The smell of Grandma's wet paint.

Miles's warm newborn breath on my chest.

Rainwater seeping in on my feet through the holes in my shoes.

A smoke and a song.

Memory is not a time line of events. Memory lives in layers of gooey marrow, porous bone, slippery synovial fluid. It hides in soft connective tissue, in bunioned feet, inside the creases of our knees, and hair follicles. The mind often forgets. The body remembers.

Is freedom from suffering found in letting go, as the ancients, and my mother, insist? Or is it found by digging our heels deeper into the earth and remembering our humanness?

To remember.

To re-member.

To reunite the members.

To collect all the bits and pieces of our brokenness—like the picture frames Lisa flung off the wall when we were kids—into one whole again.

Yes, my childhood shoes had holes in them and the soles were worn out. But I would not be who I am today had I not walked all those years in my sisters' hand-me-down shoes. My shoes were holed, but I am not. I am not the sum of my brokenness. None of us are. We are all whole and holy. Whole and holy worn souls.

A Smoke and a Song

Shadow stands up and arches her back. I watch her slowly saunter over to the deck door, paws making little pitter-patter sounds on the wood floor. She meows. I stand up with the book and follow her. I open the door. It is warm, sunny—spring. The lawn is almost green again. The bright yellow forsythia has bloomed, and the cherry tree is just beginning to bud.

Shadow stops midway through the doorway. She stays for a long pause, half in, half out.

"Come on, girl," I say, nudging her with my foot.

She takes a baby step and stops again, in the threshold of the deck door.

"Go on, girl."

She stays by my feet.

I walk out the door, sit down on the deck steps, and sift the pages until I find the poem. Shadow follows me; she sits by my side. I look to the book. I read the last stanza of "Passing Through":

> Sometimes, you say, I wear
> an abstracted look that drives you
> up the wall, as though it signified
> distress or disaffection.
> Don't take it so to heart.
> Maybe I enjoy not-being as much
> as being who I am. Maybe
> it's time for me to practice
> growing old. The way I look
> at it, I'm passing through a phase:
> gradually I'm changing to a word.
> Whatever you choose to claim
> of me is always yours;
> nothing is truly mine
> except my name. I only
> borrowed this dust.

Borrowed Dust

We only borrow this dust, yes.

Shadow meows, and with a sudden burst, gallops off, down the three steps, onto the grass. She flops on her back. She's rolling side to side. I look at her. She really is the queen. Her fluffy fur that sheds over everything, the soft white patch over her left eye, her tail that always stands straight up like an antenna. I'm going to miss her terribly when she's gone.

It is time, I suppose, for me to practice the tender art of the exit, off the mat. Time to let go with faith and fearlessness, so that I don't drag where I was into where I will be. So that I go into the next with full presence and a clean slate. To devote my entire being to the bittersweetness of this moment, before it goes to memory.

Maybe the phrase "Let it go" got lost in translation. Maybe if we can just be still and *let*, then the *it* that needs to go, will go—when it's ready.

I say "Swaha!" *Let go.*

A monarch lands on the tip of Shadow's tail, which she whips in half figure eights. The butterfly latches on, taking a joyride before releasing, then hovers above her for a few beats, suspended, floating on the winds of after flap. The monarch takes off, dancing in the open spaces behind the lavender bush and the brown stems of last summer's daisies. Shadow stands up, stretches into her cat's version of downward dog, and then heads toward the meadow. Before disappearing into the tall grass, she turns back to me, to give me that look she gives me sometimes.

The look that says, "Keep growing, despite it all."

Acknowledgments

S tudent asks: "How can I know if my spiritual practice is working?"

Teacher answers: "Take a look at your relationships."

I could not be more humbly grateful to all those who have been part of helping me birth this book. Each one of my relations has been invaluable to my healing and the growth that has happened while on this "beast" of a book journey. To each of you, I owe the sun and the stars.

To Brooke Warner, Shannon Green, Julie Metz, and the entire family at She Writes Press, thank you for your vision to amplify women's voices and for giving me the "green light" to write and publish my book.

I bow deeply to all those who granted me creative permission to freely share my version of our stories. I equally honor and thank those who asked me not to.

I bow to my ancestors: Grandpa Stanley; Grandma Elise; Grandma Sherry; Grandpa Sam; my dad, Warren; and all those who came before them, now in the unseen world. Thank you for your guidance and protection.

Jevon, honey, I could never have written this book without your unwavering devotion to me, to us, to the kids, and to Butterfly Farm. Thank you for your willingness to do the deep dive together and for gifting me a second chance to build a life with you from the ground up.

A Smoke and a Song

To Miles, my son-shine, you have always been and will always be the inspiration behind everything good I do.

My sisters, Lisa and Madeleine—thank you for raising me and giving me ridiculous stories to write about. Thank you for helping me to remember. I am so grateful we three have each other, especially now.

To my nephew, Justin; my niece, Juniper; my stepchildren, Nicholas and Alexandra; and my mama-in-law, Midge. I could not imagine my story without you in it.

To Janna Hockenjos, I could never have pieced together the words or the pages without your skillful guidance, editorial attention, love for story, and heartfelt support.

To my dream team of first readers and blurb cheerleaders: Chelsea Handler, Anita Kopacz, Shalom Harlow, Jennifer Pasti-loff, Nancy Aronie, Kathy Elkind, Susan Madden-Cox, and Paul Samuel Dolman. Thank you for saying yes and gifting your time, your words, and all your encouragement.

Tabitha Bailey, Crystal Patriarche, and the publicity team at Booksparks, I am grateful for all the creative ways you hustle to get meaningful books into the world.

To my beloved Room 2: Susan, Conrad, Brigid, Lucia, and Michaela, and to Lara O'Brien, thank you for the safe container, listening, and for being my memoir's mirror.

To Kim Rome, my heart whisperer, thank you for holding space for me, and for the world, as you do. The real revolution is love!

To all the fierce women of my circles: Erica, Jenny, Andrea, Jill, Alexis, Signe, Beka, Jessica, Tuni, Jess, Barbara, Susan, Raquel, Michelle, Maylen, Leila, Gigi, Christina, Angie, Ona, Nonie, and Yvonna. Thank you for being chosen aunties for Miles, and soul sisters to me.

To all my students, all my teachers, and all the readers. I am you, and you are another me. As Ram Das said, "We are all just walking each other home."

Acknowledgments

Shadow, my cat, my spirit guide, thank you for holding on while I wrote this book.

I bow to Mother Earth and all the places on her that I have been so fortunate to call home—especially Manhattan, Mexico, and Martha's Vineyard.

And finally, with my hand on my heart, I give thanks and love to my first home—my mother, Babette—and to what will be my last home, my body. *I'm sorry, please forgive me, thank you, I love you.*

About the Author

Sherry Sidoti is an author and the founder and lead director of FLY Yoga School, a yoga teacher training program, and FLY Outreach, a not-for-profit that offers yoga and meditation for trauma recovery on Martha's Vineyard. A certified Labor Doula, Addiction Recovery Coach, and Somatic Attachment Therapy Program graduate, she leads spiritual courses, teacher training, and retreats globally. Her musings, infused by twenty years of practicing and teaching yoga, healing arts, and mysticism have been published by *The Martha's Vineyard Times, Heart & Soul Magazine, Elephant Journal,* and *Anthropology and Humanism Quarterly.* Her essay "Mosaic" is featured in the 2022 She Writes Anthology: *Art in the Time of Unbearable Crisis.* Sherry is most devoted to her greatest teacher, her son Miles, whose love, sensitivity, humor, and wisdom illuminate her path. *A Smoke and a Song* is Sherry's first book. She currently resides on Martha's Vineyard, Massachusetts.

SELECTED TITLES FROM SHE WRITES PRESS

She Writes Press is an independent publishing company founded to serve women writers everywhere. Visit us at www.shewritespress.com.p

Memories in Dragonflies: Simple Lessons for Mindful Dying by Lannette Cornell Bloom. $16.95, 978-1-63152-469-1. A daughter uncovers the hidden gifts of the dying process as she cares for her terminally ill mother in her final year—a journey that results in a spiritual awakening and an appreciation of the simple joys of life, even in death.

Life's Accessories: A Memoir (And Fashion Guide) by Rachel Levy Lesser. $16.95, 978-1-63152-622-0. Rachel Levy Lesser tells the story of her life in this collection—fourteen coming-of-age essays, each one tied to a unique fashion accessory, laced with humor and introspection about a girl-turned-woman trying to figure out friendship, love, a career path, parenthood, and, most poignantly, losing her mother to cancer at a young age.

Don't Leave Yet: How My Mother's Alzheimer's Opened My Heart by Constance Hanstedt. $16.95, 978-1-63152-952-8. The chronicle of Hanstedt's journey toward independence, self-assurance, and connectedness as she cares for her mother, who is rapidly losing her own identity to the early stage of Alzheimer's.

Bound: A Daughter, a Domme, and an End-of-Life Story by Elizabeth Anne Wood. $16.95, 978-1-63152-630-5. When Elizabeth Anne Wood's aging mother—a charming, needy, and passive-aggressive woman who has only recently discovered the domme within her—falls terminally ill, it is up to Wood to shepherd her through the bureaucracy and unintentional inhumanity of the healthcare system, as well as the complicated process of facing death when she has just begun to truly enjoy life.p

Finding Venerable Mother: A Daughter's Spiritual Quest to Thailand by Cindy Rasicot. $16.95, 978-1-63152-702-9. In midlife, Cindy travels halfway around the world to Thailand and unexpectedly discovers a Thai Buddhist nun who offers her the unconditional love and acceptance her own mother was never able to provide. This soulful and engaging memoir reminds readers that when we go forward with a truly open heart, faith, forgiveness, and love are all possible.

Her Beautiful Brain: A Memoir by Ann Hedreen. $16.95, 978-1-93831-492-6. The heartbreaking story of a daughter's experiences as her beautiful, brainy mother begins to lose her mind to an unforgiving disease: Alzheimer's.